DATE DUE

MR 03 '97		
MR 04 '97		
DE 12 '97		
DE 08 '97		
SE 27 '00		
SE 14 '00		

THEORY AND METHOD IN
ETHNOMUSICOLOGY

Bruno Nettl

THEORY AND METHOD IN
Ethnomusicology

The Free Press of Glencoe
Collier-Macmillan Limited, London

Autography by Kaumagraph Co.

For Becky

PREFACE

The field of ethnomusicology has undergone tremendous growth and expansion since World War II. Many American institutions of higher learning have begun to offer courses in this discipline and its various aspects and subdivisions. Many publications devoted entirely to ethnomusicology have appeared; most of these are devoted to the music of non-Western and folk cultures, individually or in groups, which is the basic subject matter of ethnomusicology, but there have been few attempts to bring together the methods which ethnomusicologists use and the theories on which their work has been based. There is a need, I believe, for the specialist in African music, in Finnish folk song, and in pre-Colombian instruments to have some common background of method and of theoretical orientation. The purpose of the present attempt is to show what ethnomusicologists try to do and what they are actually doing, and to provide some theoretical background for the beginning ethnomusicologist, whatever area of the world is to be his specialty. (As a result there is little information, except by way of illustration, about the music of non-Western and folk cultures *per se* in this book, or about the cultural context of this music.)

Several uses are envisioned for the volume at hand. It could serve as a basic text for a general course in ethnomusicology and its various aspects at the senior college and graduate level, and as a supplementary text for courses devoted to folk music, to the music of particular cultures or areas, to folklore, and to general musicology. It could be of use to majors in music, anthropology, sociology, folklore, and linguistics, and also to students with a minor interest in one of these fields. Also, it is designed to serve as a handbook for the scholar in a related discipline such as anthropology, folklore, sociology, linguistics, psychology, and, of course, general musicology who desires some acquaintance with the purposes, activities, methods, and theories of ethnomusicology without wishing to study the details of the musical cultures themselves. Folk singers and folk song enthusiasts as well as academic laymen with an interest in recent developments in the humanities will also find the subject relevant.

I have approached the task of presenting a compendium of theory and method as a historian who describes the works of past (sometimes very recent past) scholarship and as a teacher who wishes in a practical sense to help a student to learn about some of the activities involved in ethnomusicological study. The order of the book follows, very roughly, the order of events in ethnomusicological research. Sometimes, of course, it has not been possible to establish such a sequence; and surely it is unnecessary to point out that all research projects cannot follow the same outline and procedure. Nevertheless, after an introductory chapter on the nature and aims of the field, it seems logical first to acquaint the student with the bibliographic resources of ethnomusicology and with its most important scholars and publications. This is followed by Chapter 3, devoted to field work, in which a number of techniques and procedures are given in detail. Having collected and absorbed material in the field, the ethnomusicologist is faced with the problem of transcribing (Chapter 4) and with analyzing and describing first the style of individual compositions (Chapter 5) and then of groups or entire repertories of music (Chapter 6). The study of musical instruments, which is also discussed in Chapters 3 to 6, is given some special attention in Chapter 7, while the role which music plays in human culture —touched upon, of course, in the chapter on field work—is our final subject. It may seem that a concern with this large topic should come earlier in the work of the scholar, but a broad view of music as an aspect of behavior seems to me most appropriate after discussion of the more technical and specialized details of field work, transcription, and analysis. Thus Chapter 8 is concerned with some historical and geographic approaches to the study of music in culture at large, while Chapter 9 touches upon the role of music in the individual culture and in the life of the individual person, and upon the function of music in relation to some other forms of communication. In each chapter I have attempted to give some of the theories under which ethnomusicologists have operated, to survey the most important accomplishments relevant to the topic, and, where feasible, to propose some techniques and procedures which the student or novice may use. Suggested readings are listed in the chapter bibliographies and marked with asterisks. The Appendix lists some suggested projects to help the student or the layman in acquainting himself with some of these techniques in his home or school environment. These are, of course, not really ethnomusicological projects, but rather exercises preliminary to work in the discipline itself.

It has been necessary to discuss—sometimes critically—the works of many scholars, and it has also been necessary to omit mention of many works which might have been included. I will not attempt to justify inclusions and omissions here, but by way of apology I should like to say that as I worked on this project I became increasingly impressed by the tremendous variety of approaches and the large amount of theoretical writing which the field has produced. A true compendium of all theory and method in ethnomusicology would require a multivolume set. We have here attempted to provide only an introduction.

Many colleagues, ethnomusicologists and others, have, through their knowledge and wisdom imparted in conversation and discussion, helped in the writing of this book; I should like to express my thanks to them. I am especially indebted to Donald L. Leavitt (Library of Congress), to Roy T. Will (Boston University), and to my colleagues at Wayne State University, Professors Arnold Salop and Richard A. Waterman, for reading parts of the manuscript and for making pertinent comments and suggestions.

I am indebted also for permission to quote material which appeared in a number of publications. The List of Figures gives the sources of the illustrations, and I am grateful to the authors, editors, and publishers of these sources for allowing me to reprint them. I am also grateful to the following for permission to quote materials in the body of the text: to Dr. Joseph O. Brew, Director of the Peabody Museum, Harvard University, for permission to quote the questionnaire from David P. McAllester's *Enemy Way Music* (Chapter 3); to Roxane McCollester for permission to quote from her "Transcription Technique Used by Zygmunt Estreicher," in *Ethnomusicology* 4:130, 1960 (Chapter 4); to the editors of *Musical Quarterly* for permission to quote from Charles Seeger's "Prescriptive and Descriptive Music Writing," in *MQ* 44:184, 1958 (Chapter 4); to Anthony Baines, editor of the *Galpin Society Journal*, for permission to quote from "Classification of Musical Instruments" by Curt Sachs and E. M. von Hornbostel, translated by Anthony Baines and K. P. Wachsmann, *Galpin Society Journal* 14:21, 1961 (Chapter 7). Chapter 8 contains large sections, revised, which appeared previously in three papers of mine published in *American Anthropologist* (1958), *Southwestern Journal of Anthropology* (1960) and *Acta Musicologica* (1958); I am grateful to the editors of these three publications for permission to reprint portions of these articles. Finally, I wish to express my thanks to my wife for helping with much of the mechanical work involved in writing this book, and for keeping her patience while my typewriter clicked on inexorably through the peaceful early morning hours.

B.N.

Detroit, Michigan
May, 1963

CONTENTS

FIGURES

Chapter 1

WHAT IS ETHNOMUSICOLOGY?

DEFINING ETHNOMUSI-
cology is not an easy task, for there is a difference between what
those who call themselves ethnomusicologists have done and are
doing, and what they think they should be doing. For practical
purposes, it is simplest to say that ethnomusicologists in the
past have been students of the music outside Western civilization and, to a smaller extent, of European folk music. As such
they have worked in an area adjacent to musicology at large
and also to cultural anthropology. Musicology, defining itself as
the field which involves the scholarly and objective study of
music of all types and from all approaches, has actually given
the lion's share of its attention to the music of Western urban
civilization, the music of the European written tradition. And
while conventional musicologists have occasionally considered
also the music of other cultures, they have more frequently
withdrawn from this large area and relegated it to the ethnomusicologist, whom they have sometimes considered as just
another kind of musicological specialist, but at other times a
representative of a related but separate field from theirs. Anthropologists, especially those who concentrate on the study of culture, have claimed all of the world's cultures as their just
domain; but in fact they have spent by far most of their time
and the space in their publications on the cultures outside Western civilization. Thus ethnomusicologists, whatever their definition of themselves happens to be (and some of these definitions

1

are discussed below), have worked, on the one hand, as the special kind of musicologist who investigates exotic music and, on the other hand, as the special kind of anthropologist who investigates music rather than other aspects of human culture, again outside Western civilization.

Ethnomusicologists have contributed to these parent disciplines, and their work has been based largely on the methods developed in musicology and cultural anthropology. In spite of the relatively late recognition of the importance of ethnomusicological data by music historians, the role which ethnomusicology has played in musicology at large is considerable. Needless to say, the primary contribution involves the musicologist's desire to understand all music, i.e., all human music and even (if there is such a thing) musical phenomena in the animal world. Parenthetically, it is perhaps significant to find that the latter, although in no way a part of anthropology (which is by definition the study of man) has tacitly been included in the ethnomusicologist's sphere of interest, as if, perhaps, exotic cultures and non-human behavior shared common elements. The only really common element here is, of course, the strangeness in relation to Western civilization. As early as the late nineteenth century, musicologists recognized the need for having data on the music of other cultures available if they were to understand music as a universal phenomenon. Psychologists of music—and some of the early students of ethnic music were members of this group —have also felt the need for using material from other cultures to corroborate their findings.

But musicologists in the twentieth century have increasingly become specialists in Western music. Nineteenth-century musicologists were probably more interested in music as a universal phenomenon than their twentieth-century pupils, who have found it useful and necessary to concentrate on very specific aspects of the Western musical tradition. Ethnomusicology would appear to have less of a contribution to make to such specialized research, but it plays a role nevertheless. The relationship of Western music to that of its non-European neighbors

—to the music of the Near East, to the tradition of Hebrew music, to the music of India, etc.—and even more, the ties of Western cultivated or urban music to its unwritten counterpart, folk music, are at various periods in history quite intimate. The art music of Europe has always interchanged material with the folk tradition of its geographic environment, and influences on Europe from other continents have perhaps been stronger than is generally recognized. For the evaluation of these influences, for description of the musical styles and practices in which they originated, the methods of ethnomusicology are a necessary tool. To cite a widely used example, the study of the origins of European polyphony, which in the fine art tradition is assumed to date from the Middle Ages, involves non-Western musics which have polyphonic styles analogous or similar to those of medieval Europe. It involves also a knowledge of the musical styles which may have influenced Western Europe in the Middle Ages, and of the folk music (as it exists today, and as it may have existed then) which can be presumed to have been available for the exchange of musical ideas and materials. The examples which could be used to indicate the potential and past services of ethnomusicology to a study of the history of Western cultivated music are numerous; medieval polyphony is one of the outstanding ones. The data on non-Western and on folk styles must always be available for an intelligent interpretation of Western music history.

A similar case can be made for the need of musical information in anthropology. Music is one of the few universal cultural phenomena, for no people is known which does not have some kind of music. In spite of the great variety of musical styles the world over, there is enough homogeneity in musical behavior to make identification of music as such possible and simple. Thus, it is necessary for an anthropologist, if he is to be fully informed about a particular culture, to know also something about the musical behavior of the people. This is especially to be emphasized for those cultures—and there are many of them—in which music plays a role of great importance in cosmology, philosophy, and ceremonial life.

Music is sometimes used as corroborative evidence for particular theories in anthropology. The findings of E. M. von Hornbostel regarding the tuning of panpipes in Brazil—he thought the tuning to be identical with that used in parts of Oceania, presumably indicating prehistoric cultural contact between these areas—are a case in point. (This interpretation of Hornbostel's has, it should be noted, turned out to be controversial; but it is still a classic example of musical data in the service of ethnology.)

Studies in acculturation, that is, the result of intimate contact between neighboring cultures, have been pursued through music (see Wachsmann 1961;[1] Merriam 1955; and Chapter 8 of this book). Statistical measurement in cultural anthropology has been made with the use of musical phenomena, which lend themselves more easily to quantification than do some other aspects of culture, such as religion, social organization, etc. (See Merriam 1956.) And finally—perhaps this is another reason for the close association of music with statistics in cultural anthropology—there is the possibility of distinguishing between musical content and musical style, i.e., between specific compositions and the characteristics which they share with other pieces in their repertory (see Chapter 6). Ethnomusicological theory and research have been profoundly affected by this fact. It is possible for individual compositions, e.g., songs, to move from one culture to another and to change in the process, and it is also

1. Bibliographic references are given in the form of internal citations which refer to the chapter biblographies. A publication is cited by giving in parentheses the author's last name, the date of his publication, and, where applicable, the page number(s) preceded by a colon. For example, (Sachs 1962:56) refers to the publication listed under Sachs' name, dated 1962, in the chapter bibliography, and to p. 56 of that publication. In order to reduce repetition of names, I have used phrases such as "Sachs (1962:56) says . . ." to convey the same information. The chapter bibliographies also indicate suggested supplementary reading; the suggested items are marked with asterisks. Where relevant, the pages within a publication which contain the suggested readings are especially cited.

possible for stylistic features—types of form, scale, rhythm—to move from one culture to another and be superimposed on songs already in existence. This kind of distinction, which can be made more easily in music and the other arts than elsewhere in culture, makes musical data of special use in the interpretation of cultural phenomena by the anthropologist.

Thus we see that ethnomusicology is most closely allied to historical musicology and to cultural anthropology. And while the various ethnomusicologists differ greatly in their definitions of the field, and in their emphases, probably none would deny the importance of the two related areas in his work. The role of ethnomusicology in two other fields, which are in a sense part of anthropology—folklore and linguistics—should also be mentioned. Obviously, music in oral tradition (and this is the main raw material) is an important part of folklore, which involves those aspects of culture which live in the oral tradition, and especially those which involve artistic creativity. And since music is a form of communication related in some way to language, the field of ethnomusicology, which studies the world's music, can contribute to and draw on the field of linguistics, which studies the world's languages. Especially in studying the relationship of the words and music of songs are these two disciplines in close alliance.

The Scope of Ethnomusicology

For practical purposes, we may say that the ethnomusicologist deals mainly with three kinds of music. Most characteristic of the field and its history perhaps is the music of the nonliterate societies, those, that is, which have not developed a system of reading and writing of their own languages, and which, accordingly, have a relatively simple way of life. Sachs (1962) objects to this view—as do some other scholars—because he believes that presence or absence of literacy does not constitute such a major distinction between culture types. The peoples in the nonliterate category include the American Indians, the African Negroes, the Oceanians, the Australian aborigines, and many tribes throughout Asia. These cultures are frequently called "primitive," but the term is not really applicable because it implies that they are close to the early stages in man's history (which cannot be proved so far as culture is concerned) or exceedingly simple (which is not always correct, as some nonliterate cultures have a very complex social organization, complicated rituals, art, and indeed, musical styles and customs involving music). Moreover, members of nonliterate societies who have mastered a world language such as English (and these individuals are increasing in number) understandably do not relish being referred to as "primitives" in their readings. Thus the term "primitive" has been gradually disappearing from the literature of anthropology and ethnomusicology. The term "preliterate" has been used, but it has the disadvantage of implying an evolutionary, inevitable sequence leading to literacy. The term "tribal" is also found, but it is difficult to apply because it implies a particular kind of social and political structure which most, but not all, nonliterate cultures have. If a culture does not have a tribal organization, its music probably should still be included in the material under discussion, because it is, after all, distinguished by the lack of a written tradition. It is difficult to define "tribal" cultures. And thus the word "nonliterate," prosaic though it may seem compared with the shorter and more vivid-sounding terms as "tribal" and "primitive," seems the most descriptive one for the group of peoples with which ethnomusicology has been most closely associated.

A second category of music always included in the scope of ethnomusicology is that of the Asian and north African high cultures—China, Japan, Java, Bali, southwest Asia, India, Iran, and the Arabic-speaking countries. These are the cultures which have a cultivated music analogous in many ways to that of Western civilization, characterized by considerable complexity of style, by the development of a professional class of musicians, and of musical theory and notation. These cultures have for centuries had writings about music which have made possible a historical approach similar to that of the historian of Western music. Actually none of these nations makes use of a system of musical notation as complex and explicit as that of the West, and musical life, even in the urban areas, is largely in the realm of oral tradition where individuals learn music by hearing it and by being taught without the written notation. Thus it is often difficult to draw a sharp line between nonliterate musical cultures and oriental high cultures. Kunst calls the latter "traditional" (Kunst 1959:1), and the ethnomusicological literature, without committing itself too deeply to a classification, simply refers to this vast area of cultures as "oriental."

A third category—and this one is not accepted by all ethnomusicologists—is folk music, which may be defined as the music in oral tradition found in those areas which are dominated by high cultures. Thus not only Western civilization but also the Asian nations such as Japan, China, etc., have folk music, but of course that of the West has played a much greater role in research. Folk music is generally distinguished from the music of nonliterate societies by having near it a body of cultivated music with which it exchanges material and by which it is profoundly influenced. It is distinguished from the cultivated or urban or fine art music by its dependence on oral tradition rather than on written notation, and, in general, by its existence outside institutions such as church, school, or government. And it has become accepted as part of ethnomusicology by many scholars because its styles, though related to those of Western art music, are yet sufficiently different to allow it to be classed among the strange, exotic manifestations of music which form the core of ethnomusicology.

Some Approaches to Ethnomusicology

Like most young disciplines, ethnomusicology has engaged in a good deal of self-criticism and self-inspection. Since 1950,

a number of articles have been written about the problems of
defining the scope of ethnomusicology. While these give the
impression of controversy, the authors do not argue so much
about the outside limits of the field as about emphases within
the field; with few exceptions, they agree on the scope of ethnomusicology. Most of them are prepared to include all cultures
of the world, including Western civilization, but they recognize
the greater importance to themselves of non-Western and folk
music. Among the exceptions is Jaap Kunst (1959:1), who
stresses the role of oral tradition as a distinguishing feature.
Curt Sachs, in the subtitle of his general work on ethnomusicology (Sachs 1959), specifies that *Musik der Fremdkulturen*
(music of foreign cultures) is the material to be studied in what
he still calls *vergleichende Musikwissenschaft* (comparative musicology—the earlier term for ethnomusicology). The German
Marius Schneider (1957:1) specifies non-European music, and
emphasizes the importance, in defining the field, of comparative
work. Rhodes (1956) tends to support the same position.

Kolinski (1957:1-2), however, points out that it is not so
much the geographic area as the general approach which distinguishes our field. He believes that ethnomusicology has developed a point of view which results from the study of many
and diverse cultures, but which should be applied also to Western art music. The notion that the subject matter should be
limited geographically, i.e., include only the non-Western world,
has been the object of widespread objection and criticism. But
in spite of the acceptance by many scholars of the desirability
of including Western art music, it is taken for granted that only
in studying a culture foreign to himself can a scholar muster
sufficient objectivity. By studying his own culture, he may be
conditioned to too many prejudices and personal associations
to be properly objective—so many ethnomusicologists believe.
Thus one may envision Western music being investigated in
ethnomusicological fashion by African or Asian scholars, while
Westerners could continue to specialize in non-Western cultures.

Going even further in this direction, Merriam (1960) stresses the need for universal use of ethnomusicological methods. Indeed, Seeger ("Whither Ethnomusicology?", p. 101) believes that historians of Western art music have usurped the name "musicology," which should really be reserved for those now called ethnomusicologists; the mentioned historians would then be considered specialists within the broader field, coeval with, say, historians of Chinese music. While a case can be made for the justice of this proposal, there is not much point in urging its acceptance on the scholars involved. Finally, Chase (1958:7) defines ethnomusicology as the "musical study of contemporary man," including Western man; but he seems to omit from his definition the historical study of oriental cultivated music which is usually included, as well as the use of archeological evidence in nonliterate cultures.

In the matter of emphasis, most ethnomusicologists agree that the structure of music and its cultural context are equally to be studied, and that both must be known in order for an investigation to be really adequate. In the research done before 1930, analysis and description of the music itself outweighed the other approaches. Since 1950, on the other hand, the American ethnomusicologists coming from anthropology seem to have favored the study of musical culture over detailed work with the music itself. Merriam (1960:109-10) lists six main areas to which a student of one musical culture should give his attention, in addition to the music itself: 1) instruments; 2) words of songs; 3) native typology and classification of music; 4) role and status of musicians; 5) function of music in relation to other aspects of the culture; and 6) music as creative activity. Merriam also stresses the importance of field work, that is, of the need for the ethnomusicologist, in order to work effectively, to collect his raw material himself, and to observe it in its "live" state. Again, probably no one would deny the importance of field work. Before about 1940, however, it was taken for granted that some scholars would not or could not go into the field, and that they would do comparative work in the laboratory. It was also assumed that those who did field work would occasionally spend time at home working on music collected by others—general anthropologists perhaps—who could make recordings but could not analyze the music. These "armchair ethnomusicologists," according to Merriam (1960:113), are gradually decreasing in importance. Now, it may be argued that the basic field work can be replaced by the collecting and descriptive study on the part of native scholars in underdeveloped countries, for instance that the American field worker in the Congo can be replaced by the Congolese working in his own backwoods. Also, it may be said that an ethnomusicologist devoting himself entirely to a field study of one culture can hardly engage in comparative work. And if he is replaced by the native field worker, what will his function be? It may be argued that, in addition to field work, the armchair approach, broad and comparative, is a very essential contribution of ethnomusicology. According to Seeger ("Whither Ethnomusicology?", p. 104), "who will digest the results? It is the Hornbostels who will do so with great and lofty objectivity, and together the two techniques (field and comparative) will give us the music of mankind." On the other hand, few would seriously object to Merriam's statement that the primary understanding of music depends on an understanding of the people's culture (Merriam 1960:113).

Since 1953, a group of American ethnomusicologists has tried to achieve the kind of understanding envisioned by Merriam by immersing itself into foreign cultures as active musicians. The basic assumption of this group, whose leader is Mantle Hood, equates the musical style of a culture to some extent with a language, so that by long contact with a given musical culture, an ethnomusicologist can become the equivalent of a native musician. Just as it takes a great deal of learning and practice to learn a second language beyond one's native tongue, and thus to become bilingual, it requires time and frequent contact with another musical culture to become bi-musical (Hood 1960). Some ethnomusicologists have become as proficient as Siamese, Indian, and Japanese musicians, having studied with native masters. A member of such a group becomes a specialist on only one or two foreign musical cultures. This approach has been a great success, but it seems to exclude the possibility of the broad comparative approach, since a Westerner can no more become proficient in many musical cultures than he can learn to speak many languages perfectly. The concept of bi-musicality has also been used by ethnomusicologists in non-Western nations whose aim is not only the objective study of their music but the shaping of a musical culture in which Western and native elements are combined. This approach could perhaps be called "applied ethnomusicology," in a fashion analogous to "applied anthropology," whose function is to help non-Western groups through the process of acculturation with Western civilization. A much more comprehensive statement of Hood's position was published in 1963. (Hood 1963). Here Hood also surveys the history of ethnomusicology in America.

We see, then, that the field of ethnomusicology has a core of subject matter—the music of nonliterate cultures, the music of advanced oriental societies, and the folk music of Western and oriental civilizations—which is generally accepted as its field of competence, and that disagreements exist only in defining the outer limits of the field and in determining emphasis and approach. We can summarize the consensus in stating that ethnomusicology is, in fact as well as theory, the field which pursues knowledge of the world's music, with emphasis on that music outside the researcher's own culture, from a descriptive and comparative viewpoint. Field work and laboratory analysis, structure of music and cultural background, broad comparison and the narrower specialization associated with developing bi-musicality, synchronic and diachronic study—all are relevant and important. Needless to say, in all approaches, objectivity, avoidance of value judgments based on the investigator's own cultural background, and the acceptance of music as a part of culture are essential.

Finally, we may ask again whether ethnomusicologists should concern themselves with the music of the Western high culture; and if they did this, how they would be distinguished from the "ordinary" historians of Western music. My personal answer to the first question is a not-too-emphatic "yes." The second question will be answered, in part, in this book. In summary, this answer is that historians of Western music have concentrated on a few aspects of musical culture, and that they have sometimes taken things for granted which should not have been taken for granted. An ethnomusicological approach to Western music would take into account the role of music in culture, the problems of performance practice, those of descriptive versus prescriptive notation, the procedures and methods of describing music (which have barely been touched in Western music). The difficulties of studying foreign musical cultures have forced ethnomusicologists to develop methods which try to assure objectivity and criticism of evidence. The historian of Western music, being a member of the culture which he is studying, has not always had to be so concerned with objectivity, and the approach of the critic rather than the scholar is still felt in many of his publications. The ethnomusicologist's main potential contribution to the study of Western music is, then, the techniques which he has developed in the study of other musical cultures.

Trends in the History of Ethnomusicology

A definitive history can hardly be written for a field, such as ethnomusicology, which is so new that the majority of its exponents are still living and active. Several brief surveys of the history of ethnomusicology have appeared; those by Sachs (1962:5-32), Kunst (1959), and Nettl (1956:26-44) may be mentioned here. This history is actually the subject of our book and appears in its various aspects in each chapter. Our task here is to summarize the ideological trends in the history of ethnomusicology, something which is not easy to do because so many of the scholars are of the present rather than the past: their total contributions as well as their predominant points of view can hardly be evaluated since their views may change and their important contributions may be superseded by still more significant ones. Many trends can be felt in different countries at various times, and the emergence of individual scholars has occasionally wrought sudden changes in these trends because the field is so sparsely populated. Nevertheless, certain tendencies have been manifested, and the alternating influence of various disciplines has caused an alternation of emphasis and interest which is worth noting.

As a field concerned with the music of non-Western cultures, ethnomusicology is an old area of interest; but as a field with modern methods and equipment and with a name, it is relatively new. In some ways it goes back to the composers of the later Middle Ages and the Renaissance who used folk music and even some Asian material, which would have been considered very exotic, as elements in some of their compositions. The Renaissance humanists and the eighteenth-century rationalists were surely the spiritual predecessors of the modern interest in all aspects of man's behavior, and in the ways of men outside one's own culture. To the history of ethnomusicology belongs Jean-Jacques Rousseau, whose famous encyclopedia of music, first published in 1767, contains samples of folk, Chinese, and American Indian music. Descriptions of oriental music were written by missionaries in the late eighteenth and early nineteenth centuries. And an interest in European folk music has been conspicuous in the world of scholarship in early nineteenth-century Europe, particularly England and Germany.

Perhaps we can consider the descriptions of Chinese music by French missionaries (du Halde, Amiot) and the collecting of German folk song by philosophers and philologists (such as Herder and the brothers Grimm) as part of the same cultural tradition.   Different as were the backgrounds of these two groups of students, both were evidently motivated by a regard for the value of musical material foreign to themselves. It is curious to find missionaries, whose aim was to present Western culture and religion to the Orient, doing also the opposite, bringing oriental music to the West. But it was to be expected that the poets of Romanticism would take an interest in the songs of the rural population. The collections of individuals such as Herder (see Pulikowski 1933) and the theoretical treatises on folklore by what Dorson (1955) calls the first group of English folklorists were eventually to have considerable impact on the development of ethnomusicology. But there is actually not much connection between, on the one hand, the nineteenth-century collectors of folk song, the missionaries such as Amiot, and the historians of Western music who also delved into the Orient, such as Kiesewetter, and on the other hand, the founders of the discipline of ethnomusicology.

Whereas ethnomusicology is usually, by implication, considered much younger than historical musicology, the two areas, in the modern senses of their names, originated in the same decade. Musicology is usually considered to have started in 1885 with the publication of the *Vierteljahrschrift für Musikwissenschaft*, whose founders were Philipp Spitta, Friedrich Chrysander, and Guido Adler. These scholars distinguished between music history and the presumably more scholarly and in some ways scientific approach of musicology, which was to embrace not only Western music history but also the various aspects of "systematic musicology"—music theory, acoustics, psychology of music, and the synchronic study of the music of non-Western cultures. The second volume of the *Vierteljahrschrift für Musikwissenschaft* did indeed contain a milestone in ethnomusicology: Carl Stumpf's study of Bella Coola Indian songs (Stumpf 1886), which is considered by some as the first really ethnomusicological publication since it is a study of the musical style of a single tribe with emphasis on the structure of scale and melody (see also Chapter 2).

Jaap Kunst (1959:2-3) does not consider Stumpf as the first *bona fide* ethnomusicologist, but prefers to place A. J. Ellis in this honored spot. Ellis's major work (Ellis 1885) is close in time to Stumpf's and again shows the proximity in time of origin between historical musicology and ethnomusicology.

Kunst considers Ellis important because of his contributions to methodology—the so-called cents system of measuring intervals was devised by him—rather than because of his investigation of any individual musical style or culture. Whichever of these scholars is considered the real founder of our field, its beginnings belong properly in the 1880's, the time in which historical musicology also began.

Ethnomusicology was not the outgrowth of a single field; rather, representatives of several disciplines converged, roughly at the same time, but probably not by coincidence, on the music of the non-Western cultures. Carl Stumpf can perhaps be considered a representative of the field of psychology, which was one of the subjects on which he published widely, and both he and the outstanding Erich M. von Hornbostel were employed in the "psychological institute" of the University of Berlin. A. J. Ellis was a philologist and mathematician. Walter Fewkes was an anthropologist; while Franz Boas, the anthropologist who had such a great impact on American ethnomusicologists, brought to his field the methods of his first areas of study, geography and physics. The historians of Western music who were prominent at the time of the first ethnomusicological publications—Adler, Spitta, Chrysander—had an interest in and a respect for this new branch of their discipline, but their own contributions to it and their influence on it were relatively minor. In later times, and even during the 1940's and 1950's, ethnomusicologists seem to have been recruited less from the ranks of music historians than from those of folklorists and anthropologists, and when the field of music did contribute a scholar to the field, it was perhaps more likely to be a practicing musician or composer than a historian.

The large number of disciplines which have contributed personnel has made ethnomusicology a field with little centralized methodology. We cannot say that any single tradition led to our methods. A field which has the broad goal of understanding all of the world's music in its cultural context has of necessity had to draw on the experience of many fields of study.

The diversity of our origins has been more of an asset than a liability, even though it has at times obstructed clear communication. But in the early days of ethnomusicology, the importance of psychologically and mathematically oriented scholars had far-reaching consequences. Characteristically, the recognition by Ellis, that intervals must be measured objectively, and his invention of the cents system according to which each halftone is divided into 100 equal parts (the cents) gave impetus to the objective description of scales.

The importance of the invention of sound recording to the development of ethnomusicology cannot be overestimated. Right from the time of the earliest recordings, students of non-Western music began using this marvelous method of preserving the sound of a performance of music, as a way of collecting their raw material and as an aid to its analysis. It is generally believed that the first recordings of non-Western music were made by Walter Fewkes, who made Edison cylinders of Zuni and Passamaquoddy Indian songs in 1889. The phonographic recording of ethnic music was taken up by other American scholars, such as Frances Densmore, and shortly after Fewkes' beginning, the German pioneer Carl Stumpf also published a study of Indian music (Stumpf 1892) based on recorded material. The need for using recordings in the study of non-Western music was immediately obvious to the student. He was, after all, confronted by a kind of sound which may have seemed chaotic, which made no musical sense to his Western-oriented ear, and he needed repeated hearings in order to enable him to reduce this mass of strangeness to something which his mind could perceive as a system. In the area of folk music, the need for studies based on recordings was not generally accepted quite as early. Here the student thought himself to be faced by a kind of music with whose style he was already familiar through his acquaintance with Western cultivated music, and because folk songs had already been written down and published in collections for decades. It was not until the highly prestigious Béla Bartók (whose notations, based on recordings, differ so

greatly from those presented in commercial folk song collections) showed that ethnomusicological methods of notating music produced a page of music which looked quite different from
the pages of older folk song collections, and began to publish
his scientific studies of Hungarian and other Eastern European
folk music, that European folk song began routinely to partake
of the processes of field recording and transcription.

After the practice of recording became established at the
turn of the nineteenth century, many individuals not primarily
or particularly interested in music began to make recordings
of the music of cultures near which they happened to be. It
became evident that the processes of colonization and West-
ernization of all peoples was about to work changes in the
musical cultures of the world, and that many musical styles
would soon disappear. This applied also to Europe and North
America, whose rapid urbanization and industrialization threat-
ened to cause the traditional folk music styles to disappear.
Anthropologists and folklorists therefore took up the cause of
music recording, and since they required no special knowledge
of music in order to make these recordings, great numbers of
cylinders, and later, of disks, were produced and given to the
ethnomusicologists, who worked at home in the laboratory, for
transcription and analysis. Indeed, the bulk of the material
collected was too great for the small sprinkling of interested
ethnomusicologists to handle, so that the establishment of organized archives became essential.

The idea of having archives for storing, processing, classifying, and cataloging ethnomusicological recordings has become
basic in the field and has led to the development of a special
area of knowledge and skill within ethnomusicology. Archives
are, in a sense, equivalent to libraries in other disciplines insofar as their importance in research is concerned.

The most famous of the European archives is the Phono-
gramm archiv in Berlin, founded in 1900 by Carl Stumpf and
Otto Abraham mainly for storing cylinders brought by German
ethnologists. It functioned for several decades as the model for

archives established elsewhere, especially in the United States, where a former assistant in the Berlin archive, George Herzog, was later to build at Columbia University a similar collection which moved, in 1948, to Indiana University. Since World War II, the leading role among archives has been taken over by Herzog's institution, called the Archives of Folk and Primitive Music (and which in 1954 came under the direction of George List), and by the Library of Congress's Archive of Folk Song. For histories of the various European archives, see issues of the *Folklore and Folk Music Archivist,* also the works of Kunst (1959), Herzog (1936), and Hornbostel (1933). The history of archives is a fascinating one to which an entire volume should be devoted: we can mention only the most important individual institutions.

Most of the archives have recordings as their primary interest; background information of all sorts (see Chapter 3) is included, but notations are not usually part of the collections, although the Indiana University archive as well as the Berlin-Phonogrammarchiv have issued lists of publications based on their recorded holdings. Some of the European folk song archives, however, have consisted largely of transcriptions, and only lately have begun adding recordings to their holdings. Possibly the most prominent of these archives is the Deutsches Volksliedarchiv in Freiburg-im-Breisgau. Here are stored collected versions of the words and music of German folk songs in manuscript as well as on recordings. The disadvantages of manuscript collections compared to recorded ones, if not self-evident, are discussed in Chapter 4. But an archive such as that in Freiburg has the advantage of making possible a much more thorough indexing and cataloging of its material than does a collection consisting only of recordings. The Freiburg archive has a number of catalogues and indexes, making it possible to identify songs according to type, place collected, first phrase of the tunes, related tunes in European folk music outside Germany, inclusion in printed sources, etc. This type of cataloguing has not had a great impact on the archives which concentrate on non-Western music, but it should become, increasingly, an aspect of all ethnomusicological archiving. In summary, we should stress that the development of archives has been tremendously important. In the 1960's, national archives in many nations, regional ones in large countries such as the United States, and more modest institutional ones abound; and one of the future tasks of ethnomusicology will be to centralize the information regarding the holdings of all of these collections. The work of many ethnomusicologists has been oriented toward the individual piece of music, rather than—as some would wish —toward the musical behavior of cultures. And this fact has as its background the development of archives and their emphasis on identifying and creating approaches to the specific work of music. The fact that archives have, to a degree, neglected the cultural context of music is perhaps a factor in the relative neglect, until very recently, of this important phase of ethnomusicology.

Ethnomusicology in the United States

In the United States, ethnomusicology since 1900 has occupied a position of relatively greater prominence than it has in Europe. We have mentioned the early recording activities of Walter Fewkes, who was later to become the director of the Bureau of American Ethnology in Washington (an institution which was, throughout this century, to sponsor a great deal of research on Indian music including the tremendous recording activity of Frances Densmore). American students of non-Western culture soon began to realize that music is an aspect of human behavior worth including in any picture of culture; but their European counterparts, with few exceptions, have shown less interest in music beyond making field recordings—which is in itself, of course, a valuable contribution. In the United States, some of the anthropologists became active in the study of these recordings, in transcription, analysis, and so forth. And anthropological institutions were the ones which supported scholars working in non-Western music. This is probably due to the attitude of Franz Boas, the German immigrant who is generally considered the leader of the distinctively American approach to anthropology which emphasizes field work, the description of whole cultures, and an interest in psychology. Boas himself made field recordings on the northwest coast of the United States and Canada, and did a certain amount of transcribing. And he trained a number of investigators who were to become scholars of great prominence (among them George Herzog), and who were to emphasize the role of the arts in their work. This tradition of anthropological background in American ethnomusicology (in contrast to the prevailingly musicological background in Europe) continued into the 1950's. Of course the statement of this tradition should not be taken too literally, for it indicates only a tendency; exceptions abound, and many individual scholars cannot be classified as being on either side of this not-too-distinct fence. In his relationship to other scholars, the ethnomusicologist (according to Sachs 1962: 15) "sits on the fence between musicology and ethnology." But this is in a way only due to the coincidences which caused the field to be populated by individuals who began in one of the two main disciplines and then found the other attractive and necessary.

The American ethnomusicologists who approached their field as anthropologists did, indeed, frequently get into anthropology from the field of music. Some were practicing musicians (especially jazz musicians) who wished to delve into the folk and non-Western roots of their art. Others were students of Western music history who discovered the music of other cultures more or less by academic coincidences such as being required to take a cognate course in "comparative musicology." Some were students of anthropology who, hearing examples of African music, were motivated by the piano lessons taken in their youth to explore the exotic music further. Characteristically, it was the musician who in his student days was stimulated by anthropology, but who then returned to approach the field of ethnomusicology as an anthropologist. It has been rare for a student of culture to begin, as a graduate student, to show an interest in music, and to start from scratch to develop the knowledge of music needed for detailed ethnomusicological work. Perhaps the musical skill required for transcription and analysis must be acquired early in life, or at least cannot be gleaned from books but requires hours of laboratory training. At any rate, until recently, the American anthropologist who did not have a musical background of sorts was sometimes discouraged from making studies of music beyond simply collecting recordings in the field. Thus, while they have recognized the importance of music in culture and have encouraged the ethnomusicologists in their ranks, American anthropologists have not been very active in describing musical behavior themselves. But again, exceptions must be noted, and this is only a tendency. Since the 1940's, there have been efforts, especially on the part of Melville J. Herskovits, Alan P. Merriam, Richard A. Waterman, and others, to encourage anthropologists without a music background to study directly at least certain aspects of musical behavior which do not involve the technical analysis of music (see Merriam 1960).

Similar trends can be noted in European institutions in the 1950's. But in most cases, European scholars have been completely trained musicologists who later moved into ethnomusicology and digested the anthropological information which they needed when they were already mature scholars. Being historians of music, they frequently turned to the art music of the Asian nations, although they showed an interest also in the nonliterate cultures. Up to the 1950's, the American ethnomusicologists were mainly students of what they themselves called "primitive and folk music."

Since the early 1950's three important trends in American ethnomusicology have changed its image. Perhaps the most evident of these is the concept of bi-musicality as a way of scholarly presentation of the music of other cultures, and of active performance and even composition in the idiom of another culture as a way of learning the essentials of its musical style and behavior. This concept, fostered primarily by Mantle Hood at the University of California at Los Angeles, has had a great impact on the musicians in the United States and has taken the field of ethnomusicology to a degree out of the hands of anthropology departments in the universities and placed it in the music departments, many of which had previously been quite neglectful of it. Students of this new school of thought go into the field not so much as ethnological investigators but as pupils, and their desire is among other things to find competent native teachers who would teach them, as they would teach native pupils, the musical arts of their countries. Of course this approach is simplest in those cultures which have a way of talking about music, a system of music theory, and a tradition of music instruction. Thus it has been followed most frequently in the Asian high cultures. Pupils of Mantle Hood have begun teaching ethnomusicology at a number of American colleges, the result being that oriental music has begun to play a much greater role in ethnomusicology as it is practiced in this country. The more traditional, anthropological approach continues side-by-side with this new one, but even anthropologists, such as David P. McAllester, have been profoundly influenced by the idea that active performance, as well as passive observation, is of great use in studying a musical culture outside one's own background. We should add that while the performance or bi-musicality approach is obviously a great help, a student who has simply become accepted as a native Indian or Japanese musician has not yet, by virtue of this fact, become an ethnomusicologist, for at that point he has not yet made a contribution to our knowledge of world music: he has simply helped to prepare himself for making such a contribution in the future.

A second trend of the 1950's was the increasing concern of the ethnomusicologist with the contemporary music of other cultures. The tendency to look for "pure" or "authentic" material which had never undergone any influence from Western music has gradually given way to an attitude according to which musical material available in a culture is the object to be studied, and its presumed age or the degree to which it has been influenced by other musical cultures, while interesting, is not a criterion for inclusion in ethnomusicological study. An interest in the processes whereby the musical influence of the West is being brought to bear on non-Western musics, and, ultimately, in the ethnomusicological study of Western high culture, is becoming increasingly evident. Here ethnomusicology has followed the trend in American anthropology, according to whose views the anthropological methods must be used to study not only the cultures outside the investigator's background, but also his own culture. Since World War II, anthropologists in the United States have devoted increasing energy to studies of the American culture (see for example a special issue of *American Anthropologist,* vol. 57, no. 6, 1955), and investigators native to other cultures have worked in their own backgrounds. The emergence of musical scholars in those countries inhabited by some of the nonliterate societies has made it possible to accept the idea that the student of ethnomusicology can work in his own culture. Just as anthropologists have, in following this kind of an interest, collided with sociologists, historians, psychologists, etc., the ethnomusicologists may be stepping on the toes of their brother historians of contemporary Western music, of psychologists of music, etc. But many ethnomusicologists in the United States feel strongly that the methods and approaches which they learned in dealing with music outside their own culture can usefully be applied to Western art music, and that these methods can show things which the methods of musicologists at large cannot. Whether they are right remains to be seen; but especially in the area of comparison and in studies involving music as a universal concept can their point of view be useful. Just as some of the early ethnomusicologists came to the study of foreign cultures because of their desire to find out about man's musical behavior at large, which could not be determined on the basis of their own culture alone, the modern ethnomusicologist, who still wants to study man's musical culture, feels that he must include also the most complex culture of all along with the non-Western and folk cultures traditionally part of his discipline.

A third trend is the investigation of musical culture without the analysis and description of musical style, but through field work in which the role of music and of the individual's musical activity is researched. The impact of anthropology on this attitude has been mentioned above. We should indicate also another factor, the sudden growth of the recording industry, which has made available vast numbers of commercial records of non-Western and folk music, much of it of excellent research quality. One result of this sudden mushrooming of available sound has been a feeling of frustration on the part of the ethnomusicologist who must spend hours making a notation of one song, and a feeling that it is possible to analyze a considerable portion of musical behavior without the use of notation. Thus the emergence of mass recordings has tended to discourage the kind of detailed study of individual pieces which was formerly characteristic, and to reinforce the tendency, already present in anthropology, to describe musical behavior rather than musical style. It is to be hoped that the very laudable stress on the cultural context of music will not cause a substantial decrease in the technical study of the music itself.

The three tendencies mentioned here as being important during the 1950's and early 1960's are most evident in North America. The European ethnomusicologists have continued, largely, to work in solid traditions developed in the 1920's; and their contributions have been great. An interest in the typology of music, in the relationship of folk to art music, and in the geographic distribution of musical style have been among the noticeable emphases in European ethnomusicology since World War II. But since 1955, the amount of contact and the interdependence of European and American scholars so far as theory and method are concerned have steadily grown.

Bibliography

Chase, Gilbert (1958). "A dialectical approach to music history," *Ethnomusicology* 2:1–8.

Dorson, Richard M. (1955). "The first group of British folklorists," *Journal of American Folklore* 68:1–8, 333–340.

Ellis, Alexander J. (1885). "On the musical scales of various nations," *Journal of the Society of Arts* 1885.

*Herzog, George (1936). *"Research in Primitive and Folk Music in the United States, a survey.* Washington: American Council of Learned Societies, Bulletin 24.

*Hood, Mantle (1957). "Training and research methods in ethnomusicology," *Ethnomusicology Newsletter* 11:2–8.

———— (1960). "The challenge of bi-musicality," *Ethnomusicology* 4:55–59.

Hornbostel, Erich M. von (1933). "Das berliner Phonogrammarchiv," *Zeitschrift für vergleichende Musikwissenschaft* 1:40–47.

*Kolinski, Mieczyslaw (1957). "Ethnomusicology, its problems and methods," *Ethnomusicology Newsletter* 10:1–7.

*Kunst, Jaap (1959). *Ethnomusicology,* 3rd edition. The Hague: M. Nijhoff. Suggested reading, pp. 1–66.

Merriam, Alan P. (1955). "The use of music in the study of a problem in acculturation," *American Anthropologist* 57:28–34.

*———— (1960). "Ethnomusicology, discussion and definition of the field," *Ethnomusicology* 4:107–114.

Merriam, Alan P., and Linton C. Freeman (1956). "Statistical classification in anthropology . . . ," *American Anthropologist* 58:464–72.

*Nettl, Bruno (1956). *Music in Primitive Culture.* Cambridge: Harvard University Press. Suggested reading, Chapter 1.

*———— (1961). *Reference Materials in Ethnomusicology.* Detroit: Information Service.

Pulikowski, Julian von (1933). *Geschichte des Begriffes Volkslied im musikalischen Schrifttum.* Heidelberg: C. Winter.

*Rhodes, Willard (1956). "Toward a definition of ethnomusicology," *American Anthropologist* 58:457–63.

Sachs, Curt (1959). *Vergleichende Musikwissenschaft, Musik der Fremdkulturen,* 2nd edition. Heidelberg: Quelle und Meyer.

Schneider, Marius (1957). "Primitive music," in Egon Wellesz, ed.,

*———— (1962). *The Wellsprings of Music.* The Hague: M. Nijhoff. Suggested reading, pp. 1–16.

Ancient and Oriental Music. London: Oxford University Press (New Oxford History of Music, Vol. I), pp. 1–82.

Seeger, Charles (1961). "Semantic, logical, and political considerations bearing upon research in ethnomusicology," *Ethnomusicology* 5:77–81.

Stumpf, Carl (1886). "Lieder der Bellakula Indianer," *Vierteljahrschrift für Musikwissenschaft* 2:405–426.

——— (1892). "Phonographierte Indianermelodien," *Vierteljahrschrift für Musikwissenschaft* 8:127–144.

Wachsmann, Klaus P. (1961). "Criteria for acculturation," in International Musicological Society, *Report of the 8th Congress, New York 1961.* Kassel: Baerenreiter, p. 139–149.

*"Whither ethnomusicology?" (1959). Panel discussion. *Ethnomusicology* 3:99–105.

Chapter 2

BIBLIOGRAPHICAL RESOURCES
OF ETHNOMUSICOLOGY

THE PUBLICATIONS OF
the field of ethnomusicology have appeared in the books and
periodicals of a wide variety of disciplines. Since ethnomusicology has existed as a separate field, with its own Society, journals,
and bibliographies for a relatively short time, the bibliographer
of this field must be able and willing to work in the areas of
general musicology, anthropology, folklore, and other fields.
Moreover, a great deal of important source material for the
music of the world's cultures appears in publications dealing not
with music *per se,* but with various aspects of culture and language, and these must be identified by bibliographically uncon-
ventional means.

The purpose of this chapter is to acquaint the student with
the tools for bibliographic location of ethnomusicological materials, and to review briefly those publications and authors with
which each student of ethnomusicology should have at least an
acquaintance.

There is no book which could be called the ethnomusicologists' Bible, and perhaps this is fortunate, for orthodoxy is not
a good thing for a young discipline. Nor is there a standard en-
cyclopedic work whose authority towers over the rest. Instead,
there are a number of general books and articles which have
attempted to survey all or a selection of the materials which

comprise the field, each in a sense a pioneer work, in spite of the fact that the earliest of them antedates the latest by some fifty years. Perhaps the most useful of the general books is *Ethnomusicology* (3rd edition, 1959), by Kunst, first published in 1955, the main asset of which is its voluminous bibliography. The text part of the book is a solid if somewhat uneven survey and history of ethnomusicology. It contains a good deal of advice based on the author's thorough experiences in Indonesia, but its point of view is largely the result of Kunst's own interest in musical instruments and in scales. Although a product of the 1950's, the point of view is essentially similar to that of the German musicologists of the 1920's, Stumpf and Hornbostel. Kunst's *Ethnomusicology* also contains a section devoted to "Training Possibilities for Ethnomusicologists" which, while its accuracy is impaired by its tendency toward obsolesence, nevertheless can give the student of idea of the way in which ethnomusicology is taught, and of the institutions which specialize in it. And since Kunst was an enthusiastic photographer, he included in his book photographs of as many scholars as he could. But as already indicated, this book's outstanding feature is the bibliography of some 5,000 items, with indexes of authors, subjects, tribes, and periodicals. In spite of its great value, Kunst's *Ethnomusicology* cannot occupy the position of the standard work representing the entire field. It omits several important areas of music, and, especially neglects those aspects of music research which involve the role of music in the cultures of the world, and which treat music as an aspect of human behavior rather than as an organized group of sounds.

Two early works, *Primitive Music* (1893) by Wallaschek and *Die Anfänge der Musik* (1911) by Stumpf, are mainly important because of the place they occupy in the history of our field. Both deal with the music of nonliterate cultures as a unit, and both view their subject as important mainly because of the light it sheds on the prehistory of Western music. Stumpf's is by far the more useful book, for it takes into account a tremendous amount of material and manages, despite the early date of its

publication, to present an acceptable and generally accurate survey of "primitive music." A similarly historical point of view is
held by Lach in his *Die vergleichende Musikwissenschaft*
(1924), one of the early works which tried to state the problems
and methods of ethnomusicology and as such belongs to a series
of works to which several early researchers contributed, but
which has in effect been continued through the 1950's in the
pages of the journal *Ethnomusicology*. Similar to Lach in orientation are Sachs' *Vergleichende Musikwissenschaft* (1959), Wallaschek's *Primitive Music* (1893), Stumpf's *Die Anfänge der
Musik* (1911). Sachs' book follows a less single-minded approach
than the others, treating the music of other cultures first as an
aspect of Western music history, then as a field of study in its
own right, and finally as an aid to the study of cultural, psychological, and biological aspects of music. But more of Sachs' work
later.

Some Important Scholars of the Past

While a large number of early ethnomusicologists tried to set
down the approaches of their field—as well as survey its subject
matter—in a single volume, it is curious to find that the most
prominent and influential early scholar did not write such a
book. The bibliography of E. M. von Hornbostel's writings is
a large one, covering, geographically, more ground than any
other student's, and ranging over a tremendous variety of approaches and problems. But he never wrote a book in which he
condensed the vast amount of information which he must have
had at hand, nor one which states his credo of research and
scholarship. If all of his writings were woven into a single, large
book, the result would indeed be a compendium of world music
and a statement of approaches—musicological, ethnological, psychological, physical—which would exceed the most voluminous
surveys of later years. But perhaps because he was aware of the

great amount of material to be covered, and of the inherent
futility of surveys and introductory works with the degree of
oversimplication which is inevitable in them, Hornbostel never
published such a book. It is all the more necessary, therefore,
that the student acquaint himself with the landmarks of Hornbostel's publishing career. A complete list of his writings appeared in the *Ethnomusicology Newsletter* no. 2, 1954; there it
can be seen that many of his works were written jointly with
other scholars, particularly with Otto Abraham. Hornbostel and
Abraham's article "Tonsystem und Musik der Japaner" (1903)
is the first of a long series of articles surveying the music—mainly from the viewpoint of melody—of various cultures, and setting
down a method of describing music which has since been followed by many. The authors emphasize the scales, distinguish
between vocal and instrumental as well as between theoretical
and actual intonation; they pay less attention to rhythm, form,
etc. (as the title indicates), but give detailed information on the
measurement of intervals. A group of transcribed musical examples follows, with commentary on the individual pieces. After
several years, during which Hornbostel (sometimes with Abraham or Stumpf) produced similar studies of the music of Turkey, India, North American Indians, New Guinea, Sumatra, etc.,
he published two studies of special importance. His "African
Negro Music" (1928) attempts to distill, from a large variety of
styles, the broad characteristics of African Negro music, a kind
of approach not previously attempted by him. In another work,
"Fuegian Songs" (1936), he presents the music of one of the
simplest Indian tribes (on Tierra del Fuego) in previously un-
attained detail. These are the high points in Hornbostel's presen-
tations of individual musical styles and cultures.

Among the other landmarks in Hornbostel's bibliography we
must mention two works which are concerned with the problem
of transcription: Hornbostel and Abraham's "Über die Bedeutung des Phonographen für die vergleichende Musikwissenschaft" (1904) and "Vorschläge zur Transkription exotischer
Melodien" (1909). In Hornbostel's "Melodie und Skala" (1912)

we find a detailed statement of his theory of scale and the method of studying melody. The close relationship between the scale of a piece and its melodic contour, but also the points at which these two elements are not interdependent, are brought out here. Also of tremendous importance is Hornbostel and Sachs' "Systematik der Musikinstrumente" (1914), which is the basic classification scheme for musical instruments. This classification used the work of the Belgian instrument curator Victor Mahillon as its basis, and although Curt Sachs himself indicated to this writer his belief that it required considerable revision, it is still the only classification in general use today. After Sachs' death, and almost 50 years after its publication, it was translated into English, indicating that it had not outlived its usefulness. (See Chapter 7 for a sample of this classification.)

In certain of his publications, Hornbostel delved into the problems of musical prehistory and into theoretical problems involving diffusion and multiple genesis. Most of the time he tended to remain aloof from these frequently unrewarding speculations, in contrast to most of his contemporaries, who were eager to decide whether man was more likely to borrow ideas from his fellows or invent things independently several times, in different places. But a few of his works did enter into the controversy. For example, his "Über einige Panpfeifen aus nord-west Brasilien" (1910) involves the theory—later to become a catchword—of the "blown fifth" *(Blasquintentheorie)*, a theory which tries to show the diffusion of a musical concept through comparison of instrument forms and tunings in the Pacific, but which has not been generally accepted. While it is difficult, then, to pinpoint *the* works of Hornbostel whose significance is such that they must be known to the student, it is important that students be aware of this scholar's tremendous impact on the field of ethnomusicology, and be acquainted with a sampling of his publications.

Equally encompassing, and more accessible to the unspecialized reader, are the works of Curt Sachs. A man equally concerned with European music history and the study of non-Western music, Sachs produced several works of a general nature, and their impact on ethnomusicology has been great especially because they appeared in English and in a style suitable to the laymen.

An early work which concerns ethnomusicology as a discipline is Sachs' *The Rise of Music in the Ancient World* (1943), a history of ancient music which takes essentially an evolutionist view of music history and thus traces the course of musical development from the simplest styles of some South American Indians and of the Ceylonese Vedda through the music of the Oriental high cultures to the ancient Egyptians, Greeks, and Romans. (By an evolutionist view we mean one according to which all musical cultures are assumed to have passed through the same stages, from simple to complex; and the differences among musical cultures are partly reflections of the fact that we have observed them at different stages of this development.) To be sure, such an approach has its great disadvantages, for the evidence for musical evolution is circumstantial at best. But leaving aside these considerations, this work presents a fine summary of the styles of the world's music. Included also are some of Sachs' intriguing theories regarding the intimate relationship of music and culture patterns; and while these have not been generally accepted, they are interesting sidelights.

These theories are better developed in Sachs' *World History of the Dance* (1938), which includes a chapter on the music of nonliterate cultures. He believes, for example, that the general temperament of a people (and this he ascribes to the racial background) is specifically reflected in that people's music and dance. This is a theory which, in its general terms, is widely accepted, for music and dance are, after all, part of the same pattern of culture which determines other kinds of behavior. But Sachs believes that one can predict specific dancing and musical behavior from the general characteristics of a culture (Sachs 1938:188). He shows, for example, that the Zuni Indians use melodies as well as dances which exhibit great vigor, while the "tranquility" of the Marquesas Islanders is reflected in the sustained tones of their music and their sitting posture in the dance. Although *World History of the Dance* contains some controversial statements, it must be considered one of the landmarks in the study of the interrelationship of the arts.

Sachs, in *The Commonwealth of Art* (1946), pursues these interrelationships further, attempting to show that all of the arts in a given culture or historical period share the same basic characteristics. He also postulates several traits present in all art, for example, his "universal dualism" concept, from which he also derives his two basic types of music, logogenic (word-born) and pathogenic (emotion-born). Again we see the evolutionist approach, placing the nonliterate cultures at the beginning and equating them with prehistory, for the distinction between the two basic musical types appears only in the simplest styles. In more complex cultures it is blurred, and in the world's high cultures it disappears.

In his *Vergleichende Musikwissenschaft* (1959), first written several decades earlier, Sachs includes these theories also, but on the whole it is a much more matter-of-fact presentation of the findings of ethnomusicology. Sachs' love of typology and his evolutionist approach are evident here again, and his awareness of the role of music in culture is an important asset of this book. But throughout his work Sachs takes a lofty approach to the problems of the ethnomusicologist. He rarely goes into a detailed discussion of one culture and the various and manifold aspects of its musical life. The value of his writings is in his view of the woods—but he neglects the trees.

Curt Sachs' work covering ethnomusicology as a whole is his most recent one, *The Wellsprings of Music*, published posthumously (1962) and edited by Jaap Kunst. Here, in contrast to some of his other works, Sachs appears not as the voice crying in the wilderness, but as the leader and coordinator of his colleagues, whom he quotes frequently and whose views he praises or criticizes. He even abandons to a degree his evolutionist interpretation of music history, although vestiges of it are still evident in his chapter headings ("Early Music," "On the Way," "Progress?"). His interest in non-Western music is still motivated by what it may show of the early stages of Western music. In this last work, Sachs is less dogmatic and less inclined to propound special theories of musical development and of the relationship of music to culture at large than he was in his earlier work. The fact that he has turned from speculative to more descriptive statements is shown by his change of terminology; pathogenic music has become "tumbling strains," and logogenic, "one-step melodies."

A different aspect of Curt Sachs' work appears in his writings on musical instruments. Here the woods and the trees are given equal space, and his vast detailed knowledge of the world's organology comes to the fore. Sach's *Real-Lexikon* (1913) is still the authoritative encyclopedia of musical instruments, containing as it does etymology and equivalents in many languages for each instrument, as well as the expected information on structure and geographic distribution. And finally, his collaboration with Hornbostel in devising a universally accepted classification of instruments ("Systematik der Musikinstrumente," 1914) also belongs among the great landmarks of ethnomusicology. The writings of this many-sided scholar must be familiar to the student of ethnomusicology; but his theories should be accepted as guides and hypotheses rather than as hard and fast facts.

Since Sachs' main works are surveys of broad areas, it may be useful here to mention some other general works. Among the books which attempt a coverage of the music of nonliterate cultures are Bose's *Musikalische Völkerkunde* (1953) and Nettl's *Music in Primitive Culture* (1956). The latter approaches its field by describing the individual elements of music such as melody, rhythm, and form, and tends to concentrate on North American and African examples, giving a sampling of the kinds of things which are found in these cultures rather than attempting an all-encompassing theory of the type found in Curt Sachs' works. Bose's is less concerned with rhythm and form; it is greatly influenced by the work of Bose's teacher, Hornbostel, reflecting his concern with vocal technique, melody and scale, and the relationship between racial characteristics and musical style. Bose also presents a theory in which the basic differences between instrumental and vocal styles are explored and explained. The tone systems of the high cultures are contrasted with those styles in which scales without theoretical explanations or foundations are used. Bose states the hypothesis that truly instrumental styles are found only in cultures with a body of music theory. Bose's is also one of the few books in which the relationship of language and music is explored, and in which the problem of style, and of what constitutes "a musical style" is attacked.

One of the early investigators of the music of Oriental high cultures was Robert Lachmann. His work also should be known to the student. His most general book, *Musik des Orients* (1929), is the first to treat the music of the Oriental high cultures as a unit. The idea of melodic skeletons, called *patet* in Java, *raga* in India, *maqam* in Arabic, as the basic ingredients of Oriental composition was postulated there. Lachmann's is one of the most ingenious works in ethnomusicological literature, for it succeeds convincingly in reducing the vast detail of Asian music to an intelligible formula. But after a reading of Lachmann should come the reading of works which delve into these details.

Among the brief treatments of ethnomusicology we should also mention Haydon's *Introduction to Musicology* (1941), Chapter 7 of which surveys the methods and problems of the field in relation to other subdivisions of musicology. The approach is somewhat dated, however, especially since Haydon views the field essentially as an auxiliary science of historical musicology.

The first volume of the *New Oxford History of Music* (Wellesz 1957) is in a sense a compendium of knowledge in the field of ethnomusicology. Although it disclaims any intention of indicating that non-Western music is simply a stage in a development which leads to Western cultivated music, the tone of the book is largely historical. A long section on the music of nonliterate peoples by Marius Schneider presents that author's interesting but not always convincing theories. Schneider, of course, is a leading scholar whose works should be known to the student. He is similar to Curt Sachs in his determination to see the genesis of world music as a single, more or less unified development. He is equally interested in the structure of music and in its role in culture, but his writing abounds with hypothetical statements which are not provable and frequently are not even credible. His interest in historical processes in non-Western music is great, as is indicated by the sections on "Origin of Music," "Origin of Polyphony," and "Historical Development" (Wellesz 1957:1–82). As an introduction to the music of nonliterate cultures, Schneider's essay in this book can not be recommended because of its very specialized point of view. The other sections in the volume, each by a specialist, are summaries of the musical histories of the Asian high cultures (with occasional mention of folk music), concentrating on those aspects of music traditionally stressed by ethnomusicology—melody and scale. There is some variation in quality among these chapters, but all together they form a good survey of Asian art music.

Among the compendia of material, we should also mention *Das Europäische Volkslied* (Danckert 1939), an attempt to describe the folk music of Europe, nation by nation, according to the theoretical view of a group of German anthropologists usually called the *"Kulturkreis"* school. The description of the music is mainly a tool of the theory, but Danckert's work is still the best survey of its field. A briefer survey of European and American folk music, less detailed but without the rather controversial theoretical base, is Herzog's article "Song" (1950), which summarizes the most common features of its field and the methods of dealing with them.

Monographic Landmarks

Having attempted an evaluation of the most important scholars and general works in the field of ethnomusicology, we now approach a more difficult task, the selection and summarization of some of the most important specialized publications. Although many publications are discussed and referred to in this text, the following is an attempt to show how some of the better monographic treatments are put together, to designate a few model studies, and to survey briefly the work of some of the important ethnomusicologists whose work is not so world-encompassing as that of Hornbostel and Sachs.

Carl Stumpf has already been mentioned as the author of an early survey of primitive music, *Die Anfänge der Musik* (1911). He is also the author of what is considered to be the first article of significance on the music of one tribe, "Lieder der Bellakula Indianer" (1886). In this article, the stage is set for dozens of future studies with essentially the same organization: delimitation by tribe; emphasis on the melodic phenomena, especially the scales, and inclusion of transcriptions. Most of the members of the "Berlin school" of ethnomusicology—Stumpf, Hornbostel, Kolinski, Herzog, and their students—tended to organize their studies in this way. While such an organization might appear to be the obvious one to use, we should consider that the tribe is not necessarily always valid (or even convenient) as a musical unit, and that melodic phenomena are no more essential to music than are rhythmic ones. If Stumpf had taken a different approach to his work in 1886, perhaps the future of ethnomusicology would have been different.

As a model monograph in the Stumpf-Hornbostel tradition we may take Herzog's "A Comparison of Pueblo and Pima Musical Styles" (1938). Essentially, this study consists of separate analyses of the two musics, each subdivided by sections on vocal technique, melody, rhythm, over-all structure, and types. The comparison is brief, and is followed by a large section of transcriptions, which are evidently considered the main body of the work. The old emphasis on scales is indicated by a 14-page section at the end, juxtaposing the scales of the individual songs. Herzog's works, among the most important, tend to follow the Stumpf-Hornbostel tradition rather closely. The emphasis on the transcriptions, on analysis in terms of the individual elements of music (without disregarding the interactions among those elements), and the subdivision of the tribal style, once defined, into separate types, is characteristic. Herzog has also reflected the Hornbostel tradition in his breadth of interest. His publications deal with American Indian, African, Oceanian, and Western folk music, and he is less prone to explore the historical layers or the acculturational processes evident in the material. Generally he has been less interested in analyzing the effects of Western music on the indigenous material which he is studying.

Another student of Hornbostel's, Mieczyslaw Kolinski, tends to follow more in the theoretical footsteps of his teacher—Herzog's work being representative of the geographic and procedural approaches of Hornbostel. Although Kolinski is also the author of tribal monographs, and the publisher of innumerable transcriptions, he is most important because of his speculations involving the character of world music at large and his methods of dealing with it. Kolinski's general theory of tempo and of describing tempo, "The Evaluation of Tempo" (1959), is typical of this scholar's work. Kolinski proposes to measure this by indicating the average number of notes per minute. To illustrate his theory, he compares the music of several American Indian tribes and finds, for instance, that the Pawnee have 139 notes per minute on the average, the Yuma, 118, and the West African Dahomeans, over 150.

Also characteristic is "Classification of Tonal Structures" (1961), a classification of scale and melodic structure in a system which allows space for all possible combinations of tones which would appear in a chromatic arrangement. Intervals which do not fit, i.e., which do not appear in the tempered 12-tone scale, are assimilated to their closest equivalents. With this system of classification, Kolinski compares American Indian, African Negro, and Anglo-American folk melodies to show the number of different tone structures appearing in each culture. While Kolinski's approach is definitely directed at comparison of musical cultures—one of the primary aims of ethnomusicology—it has not found broad acceptance because the picture of world music which it yields does not seem to convey meaning beyond the bare facts it presents. But Kolinski has contributed greatly and importantly to the methodology of musical analysis and description, if not so much to the understanding of musical structure itself.

Among the followers of the Berlin school who later deviated from its aims and methods is Marius Schneider, already mentioned as a scholar whose work claims ardent adherents as well as bitter critics. His chapter on the music of nonliterate cultures in the *New Oxford History of Music* (Wellesz 1957) has been discussed above. Although his publications deal with a tremendous variety of subjects, his *Geschichte der Mehrstimmigkeit* (1934)—a history of polyphony—is perhaps best known and most representative. It involves a survey of polyphonic styles in "primitive" music and an attempt to show historical layers, somewhat in the fashion of the German *"Kulturkreis"* school. His works sometimes present theories which, while highly imaginative, are difficult to prove or even to believe. His writings usually include numerous transcriptions; and while these are evidently accurate, they lack certain basic information such as the number of performers, whether the transcription is an excerpt or a whole composition, etc.

Another German scholar of great importance is Walter Wiora, a specialist in German folk music whose interests have branched out beyond this area, and who has produced a number of monographs and articles on basic questions of ethnomusicology. Like Schneider, Wiora is interested in stratifying the musical cultures of the world in the fashion of a historian. Perhaps his main contribution is his ability to see the world of music as a unit and to evaluate properly the interaction between the art music and the traditional music of a culture. Wiora's most important work is probably *Europäische Volksmusik und abendländische Tonkunst* (1957), a history of music in western Europe which stresses the role of folk music in the fine art. His main strength is probably his thorough knowledge of both historical musicology and ethnomusicology.

Less exciting in terms of theory, but extremely solid in the presentation of detailed information on individual musical cultures, are two other ethnomusicologists of German schooling: Kurt Reinhard and Ernst Emsheimer. Reinhard's contributions have been in Turkish and Chinese music. His largest work, *Chinesische Musik* (1956), is a historical survey of Chinese music based on secondary sources. In recent years, Reinhard has devoted himself especially to the rebuilding of the Berlin Phonogrammarchiv, which was built up by Stumpf and Hornbostel but largely destroyed during World War II. In this capacity, Reinhard has written important articles on archiving methods and set a pattern for reporting holdings and progress in ethnomusicological archives (see his "Das Berliner Phonogrammarchiv," 1961).

Emsheimer's most important works have appeared in the periodical *Ethnos,* a Swedish anthropological journal, and concern musical instruments of peoples living in northern Europe and Asia. They are models of scholarship, approaching their subjects from physical, organological, and ethnological points of view, and they include considerations of musical style as well as structure of the instruments. Emsheimer's largest work, to date, is a description, with transcriptions, of the music of some Mongolian tribes, *The Music of the Mongols* (1943); but his later, more specialized studies, deal with instruments, and he is the coeditor of a projected handbook of European folk music instruments (with Erich Stockmann).

A towering figure among European ethnomusicologists was Béla Bartók, the famed composer, who considered his scholarly work in musicology equal in importance to his compositions. Bartók's most important works are his monographic collections of Hungarian, Serbo-Croatian, and Slovak folk songs (Bartók 1931, 1951, 1959). His main interest was the preservation and propagation of the songs of the peasant communities of eastern Europe, and his main works are indeed largely collections of his own transcriptions. Although his influence was great, his theoretical contributions are somewhat limited. They consist of 1) his great facility and care in transcription, and 2) a system of classifying melodies. His method of transcribing is discussed in Chapter 4, and while the care Bartók lavished on the notations and the ability of his hearing are awe-inspiring, the very extent of the detail causes problems. The method classifying melodies has been widely accepted as well—it is largely based on rhythm and on the number of lines and the number of syllables per line in the text—but it has also been severely criticized (see review by Bose in *Ethnomusicology* 5:62–63, 1961). Bartók can be considered the leader of a school of Hungarian and other eastern European folk music scholars, including the eminent Zoltan Kodaly, whose work is perhaps of equal or even greater theoretical value than Bartók's. Among the limitations of the Hungarian scholars' approaches we may mention a certain tendency toward cultural purism (present also in the work of many collectors of western European folk song), i.e., the focusing of interest on material presumed to be old and untouched by influences from the city, and a degree of scorn for acculturated material.

A number of other scholars are known mainly because of the collecting which they did, and because of their transcriptions and analyses of raw material. Each country has a sort of folk song collector laureate, and we would be hard put to discuss all of them and to evaluate their collections. Besides Bartók, however, the greatest impact on the English-speaking world was probably that of Cecil Sharp, a British collector whose importance in American folk music is second to none. Sharp's influence is felt mainly among the American and British collectors who wished to find songs of great age and were not interested in songs of recent origin. He is also among those who developed the classification of folk music according to the modes of Gregorian chant, believing that the modal character of the tunes indicated the early date of their origin, and that the modal system provided a good scheme for grouping tunes. His most important work, *English Folk Songs from the Southern Appalachians* (1932), contains a large collection of songs, analyzed according to mode but not according to other elements of music, with an introduction giving his rather special view of the modes. An outgrowth of Sharp's approach has been the tendency of American collectors to analyze songs, especially their scales, individually, without drawing a composite picture of an entire corpus of music and its style.

An excellent collection which goes further than Sharp's but follows the same general tendencies is Schinhan's *The Music of the Ballads* (1957). Here the songs are transcribed, the scales are classified, the over-all form of each song is given. But rhythm is not included. Despite their limitations, the collections which we can consider to have been produced under the influence of Sharp and Bartók, with their individual analyses of the melodic aspects of tunes, are greatly superior to the large number of collections, produced everywhere, in which no analysis is attempted, and in which songs are not grouped in a musically meaningful fashion.

In our survey of types of ethnomusicological publications we should also include an example of historical approach to individual elements of music. Sachs' *Rhythm and Tempo* (1953) is an attempt to find logic and to describe a worldwide historical development in what is actually a rather neglected element of music. A similar work in the field of melody is Szabolcsi's *Bausteine zu einer Geschichte der Melodie* (1959), in which it is assumed that certain basic laws govern the history of melodic movement everywhere. Szabolcsi's work is characterized by its attempts to explore musical history and to create a rather exact picture of the probable sequence of events, and by the author's thorough use of the extant literature on the subject. Some of Szabolcsi's conclusions must be disputed, but his book is one of the few which treats Western and non-Western music together and as such should be considered a classic in ethnomusicology.

We have attempted to mention those ethnomusicologists of

largely European residence whose works the student of ethnomusicology should know, and to single out a few of their outstanding publications. Obviously this procedure has its dangers: we have omitted some scholars who perhaps should have been included, and for this omission we can only apologize and repeat that we present only a sampling. Drawing lines is always difficult. We have been guided by two things: 1) the extent to which a scholar covered relatively large areas of ethnomusicology, and 2) the extent to which he, through a single important work, has influenced other scholars. For a more detailed enumeration of ethnomusicologists we refer the reader to Kunst (1959:63–66).

Important American Contributions

The following paragraphs attempt to do for American scholars what was done above for European ones. Perhaps the outstanding figure in terms of publication is Frances Densmore. Densmore specialized in North American Indian music and worked without being greatly influenced by the European and American ethnomusicologists who were her contemporaries. Through a long lifetime of research, her methods and views did not change appreciably, and as a result of the isolation from other scholars in which she carried on her studies, her publications do not have the degree of authority which they otherwise might. Nevertheless, Densmore's many books and articles (of which *Teton Sioux Music*, 1918, is perhaps the best) present a wealth of notations, backgrounds of individual songs,·and general information about Indian music. Her transcriptions are not as reliable as those of Bartók, Hornbostel, and Herzog (see Chapter 4), and she is weakest in her over-all conclusions and in her statistical summaries of Indian styles (see Chapter 7). But students of ethnomusicology are bound to use her publications.

Among the consistently important American students of
ethnomusicology is Charles Seeger, whose work, like that of Curt
Sachs, attempts to formulate theories on the music of all of the
world's cultures, and, more important, to devise methods for
studying all music. His interest in transcription and notation is
discussed in Chapter 4. His other theoretical writings involve the
relationship between historical and synchronic studies of music,
between the music itself and the words which must be used to
describe music, and between the musician and the researcher.

Several American ethnomusicologists have come from the
field of anthropology; they have been interested mainly in the
role which music plays in culture, and in the study of music
as human behavior. David P. McAllester, a pupil of George Herzog, has produced monographs in the field of North American
Indian music which can serve as models for the type of study
which concentrates on a body of music more limited than an
entire tribal repertory. McAllester's *Enemy Way Music* (1954)
is a study of cultural values as reflected in music behavior and
music in one Navaho ceremony, the Enemy Way. Although
transcriptions are included here, they serve primarily as illustrations for the ethnological approach which the author follows.
McAllester's *Peyote Music* (1949) is a study of a musical style—
the Peyote style—found in a specific selection of songs in each
of a large number of North American Indian tribes. Although the
music itself is somewhat more in the foreground here, this monograph also stresses the relationship of music to other activities
and to the Indians' value systems.

Alan P. Merriam has been among the most prolific and influential American ethnomusicologists. Mainly an Africanist, he
has also contributed publications on the music of the American
Negroes, on jazz, on North American Indian music, and on questions involving the problems of ethnomusicology as a science,
as well as bibliographies. All of his publications are quite sound
and authoritative, but it is difficult to pick out landmarks among
them. One representative work of his (Merriam, 1955) is an
attempt not only to use anthropological methods for ethnomusi-

cological purposes, but to use musical material for the purpose of solving problems in the field of anthropology. Merriam (1958) is also the author of the best summary of African music published thus far.

Richard A. Waterman, a jazz musician turned anthropologist and ethnomusicologist, has made important contributions to the study of West African and American Negro music as well as Australian aboriginal culture. An important contribution of Waterman's (1952) is a theory explaining the reasons for the partial acceptance of African musical traits in the American Negro repertory which has been widely judged as the fundamental statement on the subject.

Among the American scholars active in ethnomusicology we should also mention B. H. Bronson, a specialist in British-American folk music who has also pioneered in the objective classification and the exact study of genetic relationship among variants of folk tunes. *The Traditional Tunes of the Child Ballads* (1959), by Bronson, is a most important work, a tremendous compendium of the tunes collected for the so-called Child ballads—the British-American ballads presumably of popular (anonymous) origin—both in Britain and North America. For some ballads he gives over 100 tunes, and he indicates the genetic relationship of each tune to the rest as well as giving an analysis of scale and mode, but not of rhythm or form. Other publications of Bronson's involve the use of I.B.M. techniques (with punched cards) to sort melodies according to their characteristics.

Willard Rhodes, a student of American and folk music and of African music, has had considerable influence on the development of ethnomusicology in the United States. Besides producing a number of publications, he stands out as the teacher of many of this country's scholars and as the first president of the Society for Ethnomusicology.

Among the monographs which should be known to the student we should include *Japanese Music and Musical Instruments* (1959) by Malm. This very beautifully illustrated book should perhaps be considered the best over-all survey of the music of one high culture; its main weakness is its lack of musical examples. Rather than approach the subject chronologically or geographically, Malm gives brief historical sketches and descriptions individually of several types of Japanese music—religious music, Gagaku, Nohgaku—and then of several important instruments—Biwa, Shakuhachi, Koto, Shamisen—and ends with a discussion of folk music. This rather contrasts with Reinhard's *Chinesische Musik,* which is similar in size and includes separate discussion of instruments but is essentially chronological in its approach, and which does include a large number of examples. Malm's work is characteristic of American ethnomusicology of the 1950's in its interest in the contemporary scene, even though it does not neglect the history of Japanese music. Thus, Malm even gives a list of places "Where to Hear Japanese Music in Tokyo," as well as other useful appendices.

The Nuclear Theme as a Determinant of Patet in Javanese Music (1954) by Hood is another monograph of importance. It is a very detailed study of one aspect of Javanese music—Patet, a concept somewhat similar to mode in Greek and medieval European music. This book is based on the author's own practical study of Javanese musicianship, rather than mainly on informants or written Javanese sources. Hood's ability to perform the material is keenly felt; there is perhaps no other work analyzing a musical style of the Orient which shows the author to be so intimately familiar with the style.

A type of study which is beginning to appear in increasingly large numbers is the survey of past research, theory, and method. An authoritative representative of this kind of publication is *Anglo-American Folksong Scholarship Since 1898* (1959) by Wilgus, a searching study of scholarship in American folk song by American scholars in the twentieth century. Although most surveys of research are shorter and more strictly bibliographical, Wilgus' stands out as a model because of its lively treatment of the interrelationship of various ideas and theories. It reads, at times, like a play-by-play description of a sports event. Concentrating on scholarship involving the verbal texts of folk song,

Wilgus nevertheless considers also the music and especially also those studies involving both words and music.

Periodicals

The student of ethnomusicology should be acquainted not only with the most important periodicals in the field, but also some of those in adjacent fields which frequently include articles and reviews of ethnomusicological importance. Indexing services and other bibliographies of the contents of periodicals are described below in the section on "Bibliographies."

The most important journals are *Ethnomusicology* (Journal of the Society for Ethnomusicology) and the *Journal of the International Folk Music Council* (abbreviated *IFMC*). *Ethnomusicology* began in 1953 as a mimeographed letter edited by Alan P. Merriam, designed to establish contact among the scholars of this country and the world. Gradually it turned into a newsletter and, in 1958, into a full-fledged journal which appears three times per year. Its articles have dealt with the music of nonliterate and Oriental cultures and with questions of general import in the field, and occasionally with Western folk music. A group of articles outlining the problems and purposes of ethnomusicology, culminating in a special issue in September, 1963, devoted entirely to these matters, have been one of its main contributions. The inclusion of many musical examples is one of its features. Book reviews, record reviews, and a substantial dance section are worth mentioning, as are its special bibliographies. The "Notes and News" section contains information on work in progress, new publications, organizations, field trips, and conferences.

The *Journal of the IFMC* is an annual publication devoted about half to Western folk music and half to the music of nonliterate cultures. Its articles tend to be abstracts of papers read at the Council's meetings, although with the 1961 volume they have become more substantial in size. An important feature is the review section, which is much more comprehensive than that of *Ethnomusicology*, for it includes, besides book reviews, descriptions and evaluations of the contents of journals in the field and of individual articles from other periodicals. Among the periodicals in ethnomusicology now extant we should also mention the *African Music Journal*, published by the International Library of African Music and edited by Hugh Tracey. It contains articles and reviews on African and other Negro music, some written in ethnomusicological fashion, others concerned with questions such as the use of African material by African and Western composers and with "applied" problems such as the future of the African Negro music.

Among the earlier periodicals we should mention two: *Zeitschrift für vergleichende Musikwissenschaft*, a spiritual forerunner of *Ethnomusicology*, which was published from 1933 to 1935 by a German society, "Gesellschaft zur Erforschung der Musik des Orients," and which includes articles—in German, English, and French—by such leading figures as Hornbostel, Lachmann, Herzog, and Bartók; and another serial publication which had only a brief life, but great importance, *Sammelbände für vergleichende Musikwissenschaft*, which lasted only from 1922 to 1923 but which reprinted some of the important early works in the field.

Three further contemporary serial publications are devoted to ethnomusicology, including material of a specialized nature. The *Colloques de Wegimont* contains occasional volumes (two at the time of writing) devoted mainly to proceedings of sessions held at Wegimont, Belgium, under the leadership of Paul Collaer. The *Folklore and Folk Music Archivist* is a small journal published by Indiana University and devoted to news and problems of ethnomusicological and folkloristic archives.

Many periodicals in other fields have included information on the music of non-Western and folk cultures. These should be known to the student of ethnomusicology, whatever the discipline from which he approaches his field. Among the musicological periodicals, the American and German ones have been the most important: *Musical Quarterly, Journal of the American Musicological Society,* the Music Library Association's *Notes,* and, in Germany, *Musikforschung.* Some of the early German music journals contain the early classics in our field: in the nineteenth century, *Vierteljahrschrift für Musikwissenschaft;* later *Zeitschrift für Musikwissenschaft,* and, during the 1930's, *Archiv für Musikforschung.* Some organs of international societies should also be mentioned: the *Zeitschrift* and the *Sammelbände* of the Internationale Musikgesellschaft, and the contemporary journal of the International Musicological Society, *Acta Musicologica.*

Anthropological periodicals have not as frequently included articles on ethnomusicological subjects as have music journals. Nevertheless, some important works have appeared in these organs, especially in the American ones, most important of which are *American Anthropologist* and *Southwestern Journal of Anthropology.* The internationally oriented *Anthropos* (Fribourg, Switzerland) and the German *Zeitschrift für Ethnologie,* as well as the Swedish journal *Ethnos,* have had important contributions. More important than the anthropology journals, however, have been those in the field of folklore. Again, the American ones stand out in their interest in musicological subject matter. Most important has been the *Journal of American Folklore,* which has contained many of the landmarks of research on American folk and Indian music in the last five decades. Also to be mentioned are *Western Folklore, Midwest Folklore, Southern Folklore Quarterly,* and the *Bulletin* of the Tennessee Folklore Society. The *Bulletin* of the Folk Song Society of the Northeast (1930-37) contains many of the articles by Phillips Barry, a pioneer scholar in British-American folk music.

European folklore journals have not been as interested in musical folklore as have the American ones. But the British periodicals devoted to more practical aspects of singing and folk dance should be mentioned: *Journal of the Folk Song Society* (1889-1931) and *English Dance and Song* (since 1936). Of course many other periodicals have included occasional contributions of an ethnomusicological nature. This has been only a summary of high points, with a listing of those journals which the scholars in our field regularly scan.

Bibliographies

Just as ethnomusicologists must be acquainted with the journals of several fields, so must they be prepared to use the general bibliographies of musicology, anthropology, and folklore. But increasingly they will find that bibliographies including only ethnomusicological materials are becoming available. There are, indeed, a considerable number of specialized bibliographies on hand already.

Kunst (1959, with 1960 supplement) gives the largest and most comprehensive bibliography. It contains some 5,000 items, indexed by author, instrument, subject of a musical nature, tribe and nation, and periodical. It is strongest in Asian music and in the music of nonliterate cultures, and weakest in Western folk music. Bibliographic information is fairly complete, though at times certain details are omitted. Beyond Kunst, articles in magazines and journals can be located in *Music Index* (Detroit), which covers music periodicals in many languages from 1948 on, and which gives entries for authors and titles. For earlier materials, and for periodicals outside the field of music, the general periodical indexes are useful: *Reader's Guide* for general and popular articles, *International Index* for more scholarly ones. *Psychological Abstracts* includes some material, as do the large German indexes, *Bibliographie der deutschen Zeitschriftenliteratur* and *Bibliographie der fremdsprachigen Zeitschriftenliteratur*. Another general source of periodical information is the annual "Folklore in Periodical Literature" in the supplement of *Journal of American Folklore*. Some periodicals give lists of the contents of other journals; most useful here are two anthropolog-

ical journals, *Anthropos* and *Current Anthropology*. The bibliographic sources of ethnomusicology are also outlined and briefly
evaluated by Nettl (1961).

Bibliographies of specific subjects—usually limited geographically—are found for a number of areas only. The best one in
terms of quality done so far is that of North American Indian
music compiled by Joseph Hickerson (M.A. thesis, Indiana University, 1960; to be published by the Bureau of American Ethnology). It gives annotations, lists musical examples and their
sources, and—very important—locates material on Indian music
in publications devoted to broader ethnography. The location
of such musical information in general discussions of culture,
tribal monographs, field reports, etc., is one of the difficulties of
ethnomusicological bibliography. But this type of material is of
great importance as it is usually the best source for indicating
the cultural context of music. Thus Hickerson's work could serve
as a model bibliography for our field.

African music is covered by Varley (1936); his work was
brought up to date by Merriam (1951). A predecessor—less detailed but more inclusive (records and sheet music are included)
—of Hickerson's work is a monumental bibliography of North
American folklore by Haywood (1951), which was reprinted in
1961 with corrections. Rhodes (1952) gives a survey of the
trends in North American Indian music research. Thus, the areas
in nonliterate cultures best covered bibliographically are North
American and Negro Africa.

There has been, however, an excellent bibliography in the
field of Asian music mainly devoted to the cultivated music of
the Oriental high cultures, but including also the folk music of
these countries. Cited here as Waterman (1947), it appeared as
a series of articles in the Music Library Association's *Notes,* and
while covering largely the Western publications, it includes also
a good many which appeared in Asia itself. There is no over-all
bibliography of European folk music, although there are bibliographies for individual nations. Nor are there complete bibliographies for Oceanian and Latin American music (for the

latter, however, see the music section in the annual *Handbook of Latin American Studies).* Gilbert Chase's *Guide to the Music of Latin America* (Pan American Union, 1962), in its second edition, is also excellent for ethnomusicology.

For keeping abreast of the current publications in ethnomusicology, several periodicals are very useful. The best coverage is in the journal *Ethnomusicology.* Here a "Current Bibliography" section of some 400 items per year is given. Coverage is not very even, however, for perference is given to the music of nonliterate cultures and, secondarily, the high cultures of Asia. Folk music is rather neglected. But *Ethnomusicology* has made bibliographical work something of a specialty, presenting so-called "special bibliographies" of material on certain subjects and areas, or of the work of certain individual scholars, as a recurring feature.

Also of use in keeping abreast of current publications are certain periodicals which give the contents of other journals. The *Journal of the IFMC* is most intensive in this kind of coverage—it even gives brief reviews of the articles—but since it appears only once a year it is not really very current. We have already mentioned the lists of current articles given in *Anthropos* and *Current Anthropology* (since 1962). The *Journal of Music Theory* also lists current articles of theoretical interest, and some of these have ethnomusicological content. For books in our field the best continuing list appears after the book review section in the Music Library Association *Notes.*

Unpublished theses should also be covered by the careful bibliographical searcher. The most comprehensive source is Alan P. Merriam's list in *Ethnomusicology* (Merriam 1960, supplemented by Gillis 1962). Also of great use are the occasional lists published by the Joint Committee of the Music Teachers National Association and the American Musicological Society, entitled *Doctoral Dissertations in Musicology,* edited by Helen Hewitt (3rd edition, 1961, published by the American Musicological Society). Here the dissertations are classified by subject, and ethnomusicological materials have a section of their own.

Unfortunately, only a few musical dissertations done in anthropology departments are included. Of course the excellent *Dissertation Abstracts* published by University Microfilms (Ann Arbor, Michigan) is an indispensable tool in any field.

Personal bibliographies, i.e., lists of all of the publications of certain individual authors, are sometimes useful for the ethnomusicologist. Such lists have been compiled for some of the most prominent scholars in our field, and we mention the following as most useful: E. M. von Hornbostel, compiled by Alan P. Merriam *(Ethnomusicology Newsletter* no. 2, Aug. 1954, p. 9–15); Frances Densmore, compiled by Alan P. Merriam and others *(ibid.* no. 7, April 1956, p. 14–29); George Herzog, compiled by Barbara Krader *(ibid.* no. 6, Jan. 1956, p. 11–20); Andre Schaeffner, compiled by Barbara Krader *(Ethnomusicology* 2:27–34, 1958); and Curt Sachs, compiled by Kurt Hahn *(Acta Musicologica* 29:94–106, 1957); also a bibliography of the works of Jaap Kunst, issued in mimeographed form by the Royal Tropical Institute, Amsterdam, in 1961.

Related to the personal bibliographies are directories of various sorts, giving location of institutions, addresses and other information about scholars, etc. There is no comprehensive directory for the field of ethnomusicology. Kunst (1959) describes institutions in a section on "Training Possibilities for Ethnomusicologists," as well as giving brief sketches and photographs of selected scholars. *Ethnomusicology* offers occasional surveys of courses taught in the United States and other countries, and some information on institutions. *The Folklore and Folk Music Archivist* gives surveys of the history and contents of important collections of recordings. The *International Directory of Anthropological Institutions* and the projected *International Directory of Anthropologists* are valuable. Finally, Lawless (1960) gives biographies of professional performers of folk music in the United States—and some of these are also scholars and researchers.

While the dance is not a specific subject of this book, the close relationship between dance and music can hardly be ignored. Thus we should mention at least the best survey of dance research available, an article by Gertrude P. Kurath (1960), which contains an excellent bibliography. The "Current Bibliography" in *Ethnomusicology* includes a special section on current publications dealing with dance research.

Discography

Along with bibliography, the science of discography is increasing in importance to ethnomusicologists. The raw material of ethnomusicology is best preserved, after all, not in books but as recorded sound. Thus a knowledge of commercial recordings and the ability to locate nonprocessed field recordings in archives or private collections is an essential companion skill to bibliographic facility.

There is not, and there probably never will be, a comprehensive central guide to the contents of ethnomusicological archives. Occasionally this kind of information appears in print, but to a large extent the student must locate material of tribes, cultures, instruments, and song types in which he is interested through personal contact, or through the exchange channels of scholarly societies. Each of the important archives of folk and non-Western music is well cataloged, and direct inquiry will normally produce the desired information. In the United States, the Library of Congress' Archive of Folk Song is certainly the best source for field recordings of American folk music, and a good one for other kinds. The Archives of Folk and Primitive Music at Indiana University contains one of the best collections of North American Indian music, as well as rich samplings from all other parts of the world; it is perhaps the best all-around collection. The Laboratory of Ethnomusicology at Northwestern University contains, among other collections, a great deal of African and New World Negro music. The Ethnomusicology Archive at the University of California at Los Angeles specializes in Oriental music. The Phonogrammarchiv in West Berlin contains a large general collection especially strong in Turkish and other Near Eastern music. And other, only slightly less important archives also have their specialties. Here *The Folklore and Folk Music Archivist* gives useful information.

George Herzog (1936) published a survey of research in ethnomusicology in which the most important field collections made up to that time are enumerated, and their locations given. This survey is still valuable, although it should be realized that many of the collections listed do not have the value they had in 1936, having been superceded by others of greater scope and acoustic fidelity. Also, the location of many has changed. Reinhard (1961) gives a listing of the contents of the Berlin Phonogrammarchiv as it was built up after World War II. The International Folk Music Council in 1954 published an *International Catalog* listing archives. And the news sections of *Ethnomusicology* and the *Bulletin* (not the *Journal*) of the International Folk Music Council give information on important acquisitions of some of the large archives.

The location of commercial records of folk and non-Western music is, of course, less difficult, but their evaluation is equally hard. Until about 1952, few recordings of this sort were available; since then, the industry has mushroomed, and every month sees the release of several recordings intended to serve scholar and student, as well as many which are intended only as entertainment, but whose titles do not distinguish them from the more serious one. The first important attempt to provide the public with authentic material for oriental music was made by Hornbostel in 1928; a set of records, edited by Carl Lindström, illustrating Asian and North African high cultures, was issued and entitled *Musik des Orients*. About 1958 it was reissued by Decca with the title *Music of the Orient;* and in spite of the great competition from newer recordings, it is probably still the best survey of its area, containing as it does pieces which are well suited to attracting the layman to the large area of non-Western music.

The student of ethnomusicology will not devote much time to his subject before being confronted by the *Ethnic Folkways Library*, a series published by the Folkways Corporation which contains that company's output of greatest authenticity, in contrast to its large number of entertainment issues. This series contains many fine LP records accompanied by notes of varying quality. But it also contains some severe disappointments. Among the outstanding records of the *Ethnic Folkways Library* we should mention three from its early days: *Sioux and Navaho Music; Music of Equatorial Africa;* and *Hungarian Folk Music,* made from recordings taken by Béla Bartók and accompanied by a booklet of his transcriptions. Besides surveys of the music of nations and tribal areas, Folkways has also presented records of a more specialized nature, such as *Drums of the Yoruba of Nigeria,* edited by William R. Bascom, in which the various uses and styles of drumming are illustrated. Another series of importance is the *World Library of Primitive and Folk Music* edited by Alan Lomax and issued by Columbia. *The Sound of Africa,* a large set of LP records issued by the International Library of African Music and edited by Hugh Tracey, illustrates many African styles and is accompanied by detailed notes on cards. The pamphlets accompanying commercial records are sometimes tremendously useful, but sometimes they have been written by individuals who knew little about the conditions under which the recordings were made. The usefulness of a record is proportionate to the quality and amount of background information given in the accompanying notes. This point is further discussed in Chapter 3; but it behooves us here to speak briefly of the problems of evaluating commercial production of field recordings.

Record reviews in the general record magazines, such as *High Fidelity* are only moderately useful in most cases. These magazines do not include many recordings of ethnomusicological interest, and their reviews tend to emphasize the acoustic fidelity and the quality of the performance rather than cultural authenticity. The record review index section in the Music

Library Association's *Notes* contains folk and non-Western music once each year (see *Notes* 18, no. 4, Sept. 1961). Good reviews of records, written from the ethnomusicological point of view, appear in *Ethnomusicology, Journal of American Folklore* (usually essays giving concise opinions on each of a large group of records), and, beginning with its 1962 volumes, the *Journal of the IFMC*. A fine list of records was also published by Kunst (1959:24-36).

Evaluating records without the aid of reviews by specialists is difficult. We can, of course, ascertain whether a record contains a representative sampling of a culture's music or whether only a few nonrepresentative examples appear; but this does not help us in evaluating the usefulness of the individual pieces of music on a record. Among our criteria must be the following: Was the piece recorded in the field, or in a laboratory? By native musicians, whose performance would be accepted by others in their culture? Has the music been arranged for Western consumption by professional musicians? These questions cannot easily be answered by simply listening. Thus, the value of the record and the possibility of evaluating it are largely dependent on the presence and quality of the accompanying notes. These should give detailed information on the circumstances of recording and on the kinds and numbers of instruments and performers, and there should be at least a cursory description of the musical styles and of the forms of the compositions. Lacking such notes, even an excellent collection can be rendered useless. As Laurence Picken says in a review of the UNESCO *Musical Anthology of the Orient*, "an anthology that includes much interesting and beautiful music is reduced to a fraction of its potential value by slipshodness in documentation" (*Journal of the IFMC* 15:142, 1962).

Mere lists of recordings, without discrimination as to quality, are found in many places. Lawless (1960) lists a large number of American folk song records. The International Folk Music Council's *International Catalogue of Recorded Folk Music* (1954, with supplements published at intervals), is a list which, though large, can be considered to have the Council's recommendation. The Library of Congress' *Catalogue of Printed Books: Music and Phonorecords* contains reprints of catalog cards of recordings and a subject index, making it possible to locate the music of specific individual cultures. The Library of Congress catalog began including records in 1953. Finally, the Schwann LP record catalog, a listing of records available on the American market, has a special section on "folk music" which also contains the music of non-Western cultures, all arranged by country.

In spite of these many aids, there is no doubt that the field of ethnomusicological discography is not nearly so well developed as that of bibliography. It is evident that there are a great many important bibliographical aids, which were necessitated by the fact that ethnomusicological publications appear in the annals of several disciplines. But it is necessary for the student to be acquainted directly with the procedures for finding bibliographic information, with the most important landmarks in the history of research, and with the most important scholars in the field.

Bibliography

Bartók, Béla (1931). *Hungarian Folk Music*. London: Oxford University Press.

———— and Albert B. Lord (1951). *Serbo-Croatian Folk Songs*. New York, Columbia University Press.

———— (1959). *Slovenské ľudové piesne*, vol. 1. Bratislava: Academia Scientiarum Slovaca.

Bose, Fritz (1953). *Musikalische Völkerkunde*. Zürich: Atlantis.

Bronson, Bertrand Harris (1959). *The Traditional Tunes of the Child Ballads*. Princeton, N. J.: Princeton University Press.

Danckert, Werner (1939). *Das europäische Volkslied*. Berlin: J. Bard.

Densmore, Frances (1918). *Teton Sioux Music*. Washington: Smithsonian Institution. (Bulletin 61 of the Bureau of American Ethnology.)

Emsheimer, Ernst (1943). *The Music of the Mongols*. Stockholm: The Sino-Swedish Expedition, Publication 21.

Gillis, Frank J. (1962). "An annotated bibliography of theses and dissertations in ethnomusicology and folk music accepted at American and foreign universities, supplement I," *Ethnomusicology* 6:191–214.

Haydon, Glen (1941). *Introduction to Musicology.* New York: Prentice-Hall. Reprinted by University of North Carolina Press (Chapel Hill), 1959.

Haywood, Charles (1951). *A Bibliography of North American Folklore and Folksong.* New York: Greenberg. 2nd revised edition, New York, Dover Publishers, 1961, with added index of performers and arrangers.

Herzog, George (1936). *Research in Primitive and Folk Music in the United States.* Washington: American Council of Learned Societies, Bulletin 24.

———— (1938). "A comparison of Pueblo and Pima musical styles," *Journal of American Folklore* 49: 283–417.

———— (1950). "Song," in Funk and Wagnall's *Standard Dictionary of Folklore, Mythology, and Legend,* vol. 2. New York: Funk and Wagnall.

Hood, Mantle (1954). *The Nuclear Theme As a Determinant of Patet in Javanese Music.* Groningen: J. R. Wolters.

———— (1963). "Music, the unknown" in Harrison, Hood and Palisca. *Musicology.* Englewood Cliffs, N. J.: Prentice-Hall.

Hornbostel, Erich M. von (1910). "Über einige Panpfeifen aus nordwest-Brasilien" in Theodor Koch-Gruenberg, *Zwei Jahre unter den Indianern.* Berlin: E. Wasmuth, Vol. 2.

———— (1912). "Melodie und Skala," *Jahrbuch der Musikbibliothek Peters* 20: 11–23 (published in 1913).

———— (1928). "African Negro music," *Africa* 1:30–62.

———— (1936). "Fuegian songs," *American Anthropologist* 38:357–367.

Hornbostel, Erich M. von, and Otto Abraham (1903). "Tonsystem und Musik der Japaner. *"Sammelbände der internationalen Musikgesellschaft,* 4:302–360.

———— (1904). "Über die Bedeutung des Phonographen für die vergleichende Musikwissenschaft," *Zeitschrift für Ethnologie* 36: 222–233.

———— (1909). "Vorschläge zur Tanskription exotischer Melodien," *Sammelbände der internationalen Musikgesellschaft* 11:1–25.

Hornbostel, Erich M. von, and Curt Sachs (1914). "Systematik der Musikinstrumente," *Zeitschrift für Ethnologie* 46:553–590. English translation by Anthony Baines and K. P. Wachsmann in *Galpin Society Journal* 14.3–29, 1961.

Kolinski, Mieczyslaw (1959). "The evaluation of tempo," *Ethnomusicology* 3:45–56.

———— (1961). "Classification of tonal structures," *Studies in Ethnomusicology* 1:38–76.

Kunst, Jaap (1959). *Ethnomusicology*, 3rd edition. The Hague: M. Nijhoff.

Kurath, Gertrude P. (1960). "Panorama of dance ethnology," *Current Anthropology* 1:233–254.

Lach, Robert (1924). *Die vergleichende Musikwissenschaft, ihre Methoden und Probleme*. Wien: Akademie der Wissenschaften.

Lachmann, Robert (1929). *Musik des Orients*. Breslau: Jedermanns Bücherei.

Lawless, Ray M. (1960). *Folksingers and Folksongs in America*. New York: Duell, Sloan and Pearce.

McAllester, David P. (1949). *Peyote Music*. New York: Viking Fund Publications in Anthropology, no. 13.

———— (1954). *Enemy Way Music*. Cambridge: Peabody Museum Papers, vol. 41, no. 3.

Malm, William P. (1959). *Japanese Music and Musical Instruments*. Tokyo and Rutland, Vt.: C. E. Tuttle.

Merriam, Alan P. (1951). "An annotated bibliography of African and African derived music since 1936," *Africa* 21:319–330.

———— (1955). "The use of music in the study of a problem of acculturation," *American Anthropologist* 57:28–34.

———— (1958). "African music" in Bascom, William R., and Melville J. Herskovits, *Continuity and Change in African Cultures*. Chicago: University of Chicago Press, pp. 49–86.

———— (1960). "An annotated bibliography of theses and dissertations in ethnomusicology and folk music accepted at American universities," *Ethnomusicology* 4:21–39.

Nettl, Bruno (1956). *Music in Primitive Culture*. Cambridge: Harvard University Press.

———— (1960). *An Introduction to Folk Music in the United States*. Detroit: Wayne State University Press. Revised edition, 1962.

———— (1961). *Reference Materials in Ethnomusicology*. Detroit: Information Service.

Reinhard, Kurt (1956). *Chinesische Musik*. Kassel: E. Röth.

———— (1961). "Das berliner Phonogrammerchiv," *Baessler-Archiv*, Neue Folge, 9:83–94.

Rhodes, Willard (1952). "North American Indian music, a bibliographical survey of anthropological theory," *Notes* (Music Library Association) 10:33–45.

Sachs, Curt (1913). *Real-Lexikon der Musikinstrumente*. Berlin: J. Bard. Reprinted by Olms (Hildesheim), 1962, and by Dover (New York) 1963.

———— (1938). *World History of the Dance*. New York: Norton.

———— (1934). *The Rise of Music in the Ancient World, East and West*. New York: Norton.

———— (1946). *The Commonwealth of Art*. New York: Norton.

———— (1953). *Rhythm and Tempo*. New York: Norton.

———— (1959). *Vergleichende Musikwissenschaft; Musik der Fremdkulturen*, 2nd edition. Heidelberg: Quelle and Meyer.

———— (1962). *The Wellsprings of Music*. The Hague: M. Nijhoff.

Schinhan, Jan. P. (1957). *The Music of the Ballads*. Durham, N. C.: Duke University Press (The Frank C. Brown Collection of North Carolina Folklore, vol. 4).

Schneider, Marius (1934). *Geschichte der Mehrstimmigkeit*, vol. 1. Berlin: J. Bard.

Sharp, Cecil J. (1932). *English Folk Songs from the Southern Appalachians*. London: Oxford University Press. Reprinted, Oxford University Press, 1952.

Stumpf, Carl (1886). "Lieder der Bellakula Indianer," *Vierteljahrschrift für Musikwissenschaft* 2:450–426.

———— (1911). *Die Anfänge der Musik*. Leipzig: J. A. Barth.

Szabolcsi, Bence (1959). *Bausteine zu einer Geschichte der Melodie*. Budapest: Corvina.

Varley, Douglas H. (1936). *African Native Music; An Annotated Bibliography*. London. Royal Empire Society.

Wallaschek, Richard (1893). *Primitive Music*. London: Longmans.

Waterman, Richard A. (1947) and others. "Bibliography of Asiatic musics," *Notes* (Music Library Association) 4–8, 1947–51.

———— (1952). "African influence on American Negro music," in Sol Tax ed. *Acculturation in the Americas*. Chicago: University of Chicago Press.

Wellesz, Egon (1957). ed. *Ancient and Oriental Music*. London: Oxford University Press. (New Oxford History of Music, vol. 1).

Wilgus, D. K. (1959). *Anglo-American Folksong Scholarship Since 1898*. New Brunswick: Rutgers University Press.

Wiora, Walter (1957). *Europäische Volkmusik und abendländische Tonkunst*. Kassel: J. P. Hinnenthal.

Chapter 3

FIELD WORK

HAVING INDICATED SOMETHING of the nature and scope of ethnomusicology in Chapter 1, and having surveyed the most important of its published products in Chapter 2, we are now ready to discuss the various activities of the ethnomusicologist. Our order of procedure is that which the scholar himself must normally pursue—from gathering the raw material through the work of transcription and analysis to description of musical style and the study of music in culture. Thus we begin with the most basic and logically the first of these activities, field work.

Curt Sachs (1962:16) divides ethnomusicological research into two kinds of work, field work and desk work. Field work denotes the gathering of recordings and the first-hand experience of musical life in a particular human culture, while desk work includes transcription, analysis, and the drawing of conclusions. The distinction between these two kinds of work is shrinking. Perhaps it should not be made in the first place, for as we shall see, a great deal of the field work done by ethnomusicologists does actually require the use of a writing table and of the kind of seclusion implied by the term desk work, while the desk work is increasingly done as part of a field trip. Possibly the distinction came about at a time when the ethnomusicologist himself rarely went into the "field," leaving this to be done by a professional anthropologist who brought home material for the music specialist to work with at his desk.

Evidently it was once thought that field work is simply the gathering of raw material, done with a recording machine by a person who need know little more than how to switch on a recorder. It was an essential but hardly dignified portion of the ethnomusicological operation. But increasingly it has been recognized that much can be gained if the ethnomusicologist himself goes into the field, and failing that, if the ethnological field worker can learn what he needs to do in order to provide the music specialist with really useful material.

Just what is this "field" which the ethnomusicologist is to visit? In the days of idealized tribal life, we may presume that the field worker found out, by reading and heresay, the location of a tribe, and that he went there by whatever means of transportation was available and then found his tribe, neatly clustered in its group of villages, untouched by any contact with the evil West and its conventional music; he made friends, asked them to sing and play, and turned on his recording machine. After his friends had assured him that they had sung all they knew, he folded up his materials and went home again, his field trip completed. Unfortunately, it rarely works this way. The ethnomusicologist's "field" is a complicated situation, with more evidence of mixture with other cultures than of an ancient, undisturbed cultural lineage. It may consist of individuals unwilling or unable to sing, of inhibition, ignorance, and technical difficulty, and deception by commercialism. On the other hand, if the ethnomusicologist considers himself the student of music in all cultures, his "field" may also be his own environment, and he is part of it. Thus the concept "field work" includes more than just a rather standardized visit to a primitive village.

Because the world's cultures are complicated and because musical life in the world consists of many different kinds of phenomena, the student's approach to field work must be careful and circumspect. He must prepare himself, and he must have some ideas of what he will do, even if on arrival he may change these ideas. With the amount of emphasis placed by recent scholars on the quality of field work (see Merriam 1960:110-11), one would think that a great deal of literature regarding the methods to be followed and the pitfalls to be avoided would have appeared. Actually there are few such guides, perhaps because ethnomusicological field work, in addition to being a scientific type of activity, is also an art. It involves the establishment of personal relationships between the investigator and the people whose music he wishes to record and whose thoughts about music he wishes to uncover, and such relationships cannot be built by resorting to written instructions. It might seem advisable, therefore, to urge students to go into the field and to do the best they can, without further outlining their behavior for them. But this would probably yield, for most students, rather poor results. Let us instead outline the kinds of field work which have been and can be done in ethnomusicology, the kinds of things which should be observed and gathered, and let us indicate some tools—technical and intellectual—which may be of help. These directions should be taken as hints; no outline or how-to-do-it guide can be given for this most personalized aspect of ethnomusicological research.

The usual assumption is that the ethnomusicological field worker will bring back from a trip some physical material—recordings, and perhaps notes. In one type of field work, however, the most important product of the work will not be a physical record but the field worker's ability and knowledge in the musical culture which he is visiting. This kind of product is envisioned in the type of ethnomusicological work which has the development of bimusicality as its immediate goal. The individual who wishes to learn to be a competent musician in another culture must ordinarily approach his field work in a way quite different from that of the anthropological field worker who wants to develop a high degree of insight without going native. And it is the work of the latter type of field investigator which we shall discuss on the following pages.

Some components of field work are the same in every type of culture, but in practice there have been great differences in the approaches taken toward folk cultures, nonliterate cultures, and Asian high cultures—to say nothing of the approaches to field work in the realm of Western cultivated music. It would seem that the ideal of a field worker is to learn all (or as much as possible) about all musical aspects (or as many aspects as possible) of a culture. This ideal is clearly beyond our reach, and thus it is necessary to limit the projected work. It is probably easier to come close to the ideal in a tribal community than in a folk or a high culture. Thus the ethnomusicologist who spends one or two years with an Indian tribe stands a better chance of learning something about all phases of musical culture than the student of, say, Japanese music or Spanish folk music. It may be proper to say that limitation of field work in a tribal culture is mainly geographical and demographic; the area to be investigated is small, and so is the population. Even so, only the luckiest of field workers can say, after spending a year with a small tribal community, that he has recorded samples of all types of music, has made observations on all types of musical behavior, and, in a word, has completed the musical research which can be done on that tribe at that time. In a Western folk culture the chances of accomplishing such exhaustive coverage are much smaller, because the culture usually contains more communities, individuals, and contacts with other cultures. Only in a few cases, then, would field projects without some kind of prepared limitation seem advisable. There are proponents of a school of thought according to which the best approach is simply to turn on the tape recorder and bring home whatever sounds occur; but the chance of providing good cultural background information with such an approach is not great, nor is that of providing a meaningful collection of recordings which represents some phase of culture. On the other hand, it is not especially advisable to come into the field with preconceived ideas of what kind of recordings one will make, and what kinds of songs will be available. Thus, the student of old British ballads who tries to collect such material in Newfoundland would find some appropriate songs, but he would perhaps be disappointed; and if he were determined to record only old English ballads he would be missing a vast treasure house of sea shanties and Irish songs. Thus, while a collector should have some kind of program for his work, he should not allow it to blind him to unexpected kinds of material with which he could also concern himself.

Types of Field Trips

The most common kind of field trip is that which has as its goal the making of a general sampling of a community's musical culture. Usually—in tribal cultures—this can be extended beyond a single community, possibly to the entire area inhabited by the tribe. The general sampling approach is manifested in the publications of Frances Densmore, who followed it in her work with some twenty tribes. Thus, Densmore's study of Teton Dakota music (1918) includes, according to her table of contents, songs of ceremonies, old ceremonial songs, songs connected with dreams or visions, songs belonging to societies, modern war songs, council and chief songs, dance songs, game songs, children's songs, love songs, and honoring songs. Of course, some categories of music are not included (no Ghost Dance, Peyote, or flute songs), but the majority seem to be represented. To some extent, Densmore also collected material involving the role of music in the culture, but this was done in a manner more incidental to the recording than as an object in itself.

An overview of the role of music in culture is given in McAllester's study of the Navaho Enemy Way ceremony (1954). Here, although the musical examples given are taken from only one Navaho ceremony, a considerable portion of the monograph is devoted to a study of Navaho cultural values as expressed in music, indicating that the latter aspect was stressed in McAllester's field work. We can imagine field trips in which a general treatment of one of several phases of musical life is sought—the musical material itself, the role of music in the culture, or musical instruments. But except for investigations in which only recordings are sought, such sectional overviews seem to be rare, judging from the extant literature. It is more common to find investigators trying to limit their activities by the type of music or informant they work with.

The opposite of the cultural overview approach is one in which the entire musical repertory, or perhaps the entire musical experience, of one individual is collected. Many field workers who attempted to collect a sampling from an entire tribe or an entire folk community found that their mainstay was a single informant—a player or a singer. But few have consciously gone into the field with the purpose of using one informant as their unit of work, without concerning themselves with other members of the culture except to find out more about the one main informant. In anthropology, the idea of learning about a culture from detailed autobiographical data of individuals has long been valued (see Lowie 1937:135); capturing the musical biography of an individual through his reminiscences as well as through recording his musical content, as it were, has been followed occasionally. Schiørring (1956) provides an example of such an approach, though it did not (and perhaps no such study can) result from only a single field trip. Parenthetically, recording the musical biographies of ordinary individuals in Western culture would seem to be one way in which ethnomusicology methods could be applied to Western civilization to find information which conventional musicology has not made available.

Sachs (1962)—and everyone writing about the subject—stresses the importance of prolonged contact with members of another culture. To say that the purposes of ethnomusicology cannot be accomplished by tourist-like visits is unexceptionable. But there are types of field work for which short visits, particularly series of short visits, are very useful. For example, in studying the material of one informant, it would seem useful, after a prolonged visit, to visit the individual repeatedly, first in order to collect material which may have slipped his memory on the first occasion, and second, in order to observe the changes which may, over the years, have been imposed on this repertory and style of performance. There have been cases in which the informants of deceased or retired field workers were revisited by younger scholars, with most interesting results.

Concentration on special aspects of a musical culture is characteristic of relatively short field trips, of investigations in the music of high cultures, and of trips following an initial, general investigation. For example, one might undertake a trip simply to record the songs of children or of women; or to investigate a specific instrument and the people who play it (this has been done, for instance, for the Guatemalan marimba and its marimberos). Or one might investigate the music of one ceremony, as was done by McAllester for the Peyote songs of the Comanche.

While a great many field trips have been undertaken for the study of one branch of a culture's music, and while this kind of limitation seems to be advisable, we should mention another type of selective collecting which, while on the surface it may be similar to the kind of trip just described, is really of a different nature and may result in the defeat of the field worker. This is the kind of investigation in which one type of material is selected from among others, but the difference between it and the culture's other material is evident only to the collector, not to the members of the community which provides the informants. An example is the search for "old" material. While most non-literate cultures have been, in recent years, influenced by either the Western or another high civilization, and while the process known as acculturation is very much in evidence in most areas of the world, some collectors have tried to segregate the material which existed in a tribe before acculturation took place. Some cultures recognize the distinction between this "old" material and the new, which was created under the influence of other cultures, but others ignore it. To ask informants for old material may not provide results, and to disparage the new material, which to an informant may seem much superior compared to the old, may cause problems in the investigator's personal relations with his informants. Moreover, a field worker may, contrary to his own beliefs, not be in a position to identify the old material, and certainly in imposing his own distinction—preacculturated versus acculturated—he may be doing violence to or ignoring the distinctions which exist in the culture itself.

The kind of selective field work not based on the informant's own criteria of distinction has been practiced in great quantity by collectors of the folk music of Western cultures. Many collectors, who have been termed the "purists" of the profession, have urged their informants to avoid giving them songs whose composers are known, or songs which were brought from urban sources, etc. In British-American collecting, the search for ballads in contrast to other song types has led to a curious confusion (see Wilgus 1959:167–73). Informants cannot define ballads, and even scholars cannot do this easily. Thus, within the ballad "canon," particularly that of James Francis Child, are some songs which can only by a stretch of the imagination be considered ballads, while similar ballad-like songs languish outside the select circle. Going about the countryside collecting only the Child ballads and searching for informants of whom it is said that they know versions of "Lord Randall" or the much sought-after "Edward" is exciting, but does not tell us much about the folk music culture of the rural United States, nor about the musical idiolect of individual informants. Thus, while vast numbers of Child ballad versions have been recorded and published, we know very little about the other songs in these singers' repertories, or about their thoughts on music and folk song.

There are two types of collecting which are done under circumstances different from the conventional "field trip." One involves the ethnomusicological investigation of the scholar's own surroundings, either the folk culture which exists in the countryside neighboring his academic institution or the ethnic groups which populate his city. Such work—in which the scholar lives, as it were, right next to his field—can produce excellent results, although it has not been carried out in large volume. Some European scholars whose academies are located in small towns have maintained constant contact with informants over a period of years. Others make regular vacation visits to the villages and are accepted by their informants as a part of life. A folklore project (which included folk song) carried out at Indiana University in 1960 involved a series of short trips to informants in Brown County, twenty miles from the campus. Work of this sort is especially recommended to students before undertaking more extensive field trips.

Field work in which the field is part of the worker's regular and more or less constant environment is involved in a study of the investigator's own culture. Little has been done in this newest branch of ethnomusicology, and many would surely deny that investigation of one's own culture is ethnomusicology at all, since the idea of comparing other cultures and styles with one's own, and the principle that one can be more objective about other cultures than about one's own, are important fundamentals of our field. But native students of non-Western music have been accepted as ethnomusicologists for some time by their Western colleagues, and their work has frequently been of great value. Even in the nineteenth century, Franz Boas (Lowie 1937:135) experimented with American Indians, whom he trained in anthropological method and theory, and who gave important and objective accounts of their native cultures. Accepting the descriptions of Japanese scholars, such as Shigeo Kishibe, of Japanese music, or the studies of West African tribal music by African scholars, such as J. H. Kwabena Nketia, has become perfectly acceptable to Western ethnomusicologists. Indeed, Nketia (1962) seems to believe that the outsider, i.e., Westerner, does not have as good a chance of bringing out the essentials of a musical culture as a trained, native, insider. If this is the case, there certainly does not seem to be any reason why a Western ethnomusicologist should not make a field investigation of his own surroundings. In doing this he must, of course, maintain the same standards and safeguards which he would have to accept if he were working in another culture. He must be critical of his own observations, make complete records of his findings, and preserve (in his own thinking) the distinction between himself as investigator and his neighbors as informants.

A second way of collecting which does not involve field trips is collecting by mail. This practice has limited value in a group of folk cultures, and probably has no value at all unless reinforced by real field work. But some important collections have been made partly through the mail, so that this approach is worth a brief commentary.

Folklore societies and academic institutions have from time to time sponsored collecting projects by mail. Individual scholars who are widely known to the general public are also in a position to do such collecting. The procedure is simply to publicize the fact that material of a certain nature is desired—folk songs in general, ballads, etc. Individuals who have such material frequently respond with great enthusiasm. Of course it is difficult to find out whether the material thus collected is in oral tradition, whether, in some cases, it is not copied directly from published sources, or whether it was written down by a relative of the correspondent but is known to the correspondent only in writing, etc. The famous American collector Vance Randolph received some material in this fashion, as did Frank C. Brown, who amassed a vast quantity of North Carolina material. Collecting only by mail is probably not advisable. In the case of music, few of those who write in giving material are competent transcribers, and while they may write in the appropriate words, the melody may be taken from a book. Informants by mail may get local musicians, music teachers, etc., to transcribe tunes from their singing, but such musicians may not be competent to transcribe for ethnomusicological research. Collecting by mail may, however, serve as an approach to informants who might otherwise be hard to locate in a community of thousands. Visiting the informants after they have indicated by letter that they know material would seem the wisest solution, and the collector who is interested in finding versions of one particular song, say of the ballad "Edwaid," or of certain types of instrumental music, may find that the initial approach by mail or through radio or television may be the most comprehensive. On the other hand, published collections which contain a great deal of material sent by mail are probably useful mainly insofar as they indicate the types of songs available rather than in the accuracy with which the versions are reproduced.

A combination of laboratory and field conditions exists when informants are brought from their homes to the ethnomusicologist's recording laboratory. Under such circumstances, it is often possible to get more of an informant's time and attention for recording, and there is greater opportunity for re-recording, eliciting of special kinds of information and music, discussion of musical terms and ideas, possibly with the use of other informants' recordings, etc. On the other hand, bringing an informant to the laboratory has the disadvantages of making him perform under unaccustomed conditions, of failing to have available the kinds of instruments required and the correct kinds and numbers of performers, and of making him perform materials which he might, at home, not normally sing or play. Again, it would seem that investigation of this sort is most effective when combined with actual field work; it might, for example, be useful to bring to the laboratory some of the best informants a year or two after their community had been visited by a collector. Some of the most important archives, however, have been built to a substantial degree with materials collected in the laboratory; this is true mostly of folk music archives, and includes the Archive of Folk Song in the Library of Congress.

As we have seen, there is great variety in the approaches to field work and in the types of field investigations which can be carried out in ethnomusicology. We should mention briefly also the approach which takes a single village as its unit, with all of the complexities that the musical life of a community can present; an example is the work of Brailoiu (1960). We should also mention the general ethnographic field trips of anthropologists who gather information on musical culture and instruments without recording any music on tape.

Some Suggestions for Field Work

Our next paragraphs attempt to discuss some of the essential information which nonmusicological anthropologists can bring home about music, and what kinds of recordings can best serve the desk-working ethnomusicologist. Needless to say, it is impossible to guide the field work of any individual without knowing in detail the culture which he will study. The following paragraphs, then, give the kinds of information which, under ideal conditions, would be desired for thorough ethnomusicological research.

1) *General material on a musical culture.* Among the questions on music which could be answered by both a specialist and a general ethnographer are the ones listed below; their general nature and their place in this outline does not indicate, however, that their answers should be sought first; on the contrary, it may be necessary to do more detailed work on individual kinds of music, and the recording work itself, before the broader questions can be broached.

a) What is music? Is there a word which encompasses all music? What is the purpose of music?

b) What kinds of music are there? What is singing used for?

c) How is music evaluated? Is there good and bad music? Is it possible to distinguish between the quality of a song and the quality of the performance? What makes a good song? And what makes a good singer or instrumentalist?

d) Do all people know songs? Who performs most of the music?

e) Where did the people's music come from? Does anyone make up songs? How are they made up?

f) How are individual compositions identified? Is the composer of a song remembered? Is there a distinction between the words and music of a song? Do people know how the words and the music separately came about? Do different people sing in different ways?

g) Does anyone own a song? Who is allowed to learn songs? Are there certain songs which may be sung only by certain individuals? Can one inherit or buy songs?

h) How do people learn songs? Do they rehearse? What happens when people make mistakes in singing songs?

i) Is there a way of telling the old from the new music? Which is better?

j) Does the community have contact with the music of neighboring tribes or communities? Or with Western popular or classical music? What do they think of it? Do they ever learn songs from neighboring tribes? Can they tell the difference between these kinds of music? How do they distinguish them? How do they react to songs sung to them by the investigator, or played on a tape?

k) Does anyone get paid for making music? What are the names of the best singers and performers? What are the names of the people who know the most songs?

(Many other questions can emerge from these, of course. This section is not intended as a questionnaire for informants, but rather for the investigator himself. Besides these general kinds of questions about musical culture, the following more specific aspects should be considered.)

2) *About each kind of music or the music in each native category, the following information should be made available:*

a) Use and purpose of the type of music. When may it be performed?

b) Amount of material; is there a set number of songs? Are all of the pieces of the group performed on each occasion?

c) Who may and who may not perform this music?

d) Does the culture have a way of describing the style of this music and of distinguishing it from its other styles?

e) What individual or individuals are the best performers of this music?

f) In what other ways is this music distinguished from the other kinds of music which are used in this culture?

g) Some of the questions given in the above section, on the musical culture as a whole, should also be used here.

3) *About each informant, the following information should be included:*

a) Name, age, sex. Some general observations about personality and some biographical information.

b) What kinds of music or songs does he know? What kinds does he like best?

c) What instruments does he play?

d) Does he make up music? How does he go about it?

e) Where does he learn songs? Does he learn any from anyone outside his community? Does he ever "dream" songs?

f) How does he remember songs? What does he use to help him? When he learns songs, does he practice them? Does he change songs after he learns them? Can he sing songs in a particular way as sung by other persons?

g) The questions under no. 1 above, which apply to the culture at large, should in several cases also be applied to individual informants. Indeed, the answers to those questions are largely dependent on the answers to the questions about the individual informants.

4) *About each informant, but from persons other than himself.*

a) Is he a good musician? What makes him so?

b) Does he do anything different from other singers or players?

5) *About each song or piece.*

a) Native designation; and observer's designation, if different.

b) Time and place of recording. Speed of recording machine.

c) Was music performed especially for recording, or was recording made during an ordinary performance?

d) Name(s) of performer(s). Number of performers per part, or numbers of instruments of each type used.

e) Was any special eliciting technique used?

f) Where was the piece learned?

g) Refer to other recordings of the same composition made by the same or other investigator, if known.

h) If a song, what are the words? These should be dictated in a spoken version to the investigator, or recorded on tape, with translation. Can the informant tell anything about the difference between the words as spoken and as sung?

i) If the instruments used have fixed pitch (such as xylophones, panpipes, wind instruments with finger holes, etc.), indicate all possible pitches by having the informants—if this is possible—play all of the notes of each instrument, in scale form, on a recording.

j) What does the song mean to the informants? To the listeners? Is it a good song? Does one ever perform it differently? Is the performance which was recorded a good one?

k) What kind of activity accompanied the performance? If a dance, detailed information is necessary, and a sound film is ideal. Otherwise a description including notes on the steps, gestures, costumes, etc., should be provided. Some knowledge of dance notation is of great value to the ethnomusicologist as well as to the general ethnographer; material on this subject is provided by Kurath (1960).

6) *Musical instruments.* (Detailed information about instruments, whether they are used in recordings made by the investigator or not, is highly essential.)

a) What kinds of instruments are there? Does the culture have a classification of them? Is there any symbolism in the terminology?

b) The linguistic aspects of instruments' names should be investigated. Questions cannot be listed here, but we refer the readers to studies in which the structure, etymology, and cultural background of Haussa instruments are investigated. (See Hause 1948).

c) Name, general description by ethnographer of each instrument.

d) Photographs from various sides of the instrument, with a ruler placed next to the instrument in the picture, so that size can be easily ascertained.

e) The tuning of the instrument should be recorded.

f) Do neighboring cultures have similar instruments? What are their names for the instrument? Where did the people being investigated learn to make it?

g) How is the instrument made? Here, if the investigator can watch the entire process of making an instrument he may come upon valuable information. Otherwise, a detailed description by an informant must suffice. Are there any special rituals involved? Why may make such an instrument? To whom does it belong? How long will it last?

h) Who may play the instrument? Why? Who may hear it?

i) How is it played? Are there various styles of playing it? What makes for a good performance? Who are the good performers on the instrument?

j) Can it be played with other instruments? With others of its kind? With singing?

k) Who makes up music for the instrument? Is it possible to improvise? Is there a set repertory? Can one play on it any compositions which can also be sung, or played on other instruments?

It is evident that a tremendous amount of information must be gathered in order for a clear and detailed picture of even a simple musical culture to emerge. Many aspects of a musical culture might escape scrutiny if this questionnaire were the only means used for acquiring information; it is intended only as a guide to the field worker, and as an indication to the student of the kinds of material which are needed. Other information will also be found, and many of the questions given here will probably not be answered in any individual community. We have omitted completely the kinds of theoretical questions one might ask of an informant in a high culture who is a trained musician. The questions are most applicable, perhaps, to non-literate and folk cultures; to an extent, however, they can also be applied to art music, especially if directed toward informants who are not professional musicians. If an informant is a professional musician, the investigator is perhaps better off in the role of a pupil than of a questioner.

A very useful questionnaire which is directed to the informant, unlike the one above, which is directed to the collector, was devised by David McAllester (1954:91–92) for work with the Navaho. The use of a questionnaire with informants certainly seems wise insofar as it allows the investigator to control the questions and their order with each informant. If he is in a culture whose members are not disturbed by this technique, or if he is not dependent entirely on random conversation, such a questionnaire may be useful. McAllester evidently found the questionnaire valuable even though "the questionnaire itself broke down as far as any strict control over the interview went. Often several questions yet to come were answered in response to an earlier question" (1954:91). But if a questionnaire is devised, it should probably be formulated only after some contact with the culture has been established. McAllester had indeed had previous field experience with the Navaho, and directed the questionnaire specifically to them, so that the questions would be relevant to their particular musical culture. Since few such questionnaires have been published, it seems relevant to reproduce McAllester's.

QUESTIONNAIRE

FIRST LEVEL OF SPECIFICITY

1. Do you like to sing? Why?
2. Some people beat a drum when they sing; what other things are used like that?
3. What body parts are used in singing?

SECOND LEVEL OF SPECIFICITY

1. When and where is a drum (rattle, etc.—whatever the informant has listed) used?

2. In what ways may a drum (rattle, etc.) be beaten (sounded)?
3. How do you feel when you hear a drum (rattle, etc.)?
4. How old are children when they learn to use a drum (rattle, etc.)?
5. Is the drum (rattle, etc.) beaten the same way now as in the old days?
6. What makes you feel like singing? At what times?
7. Is there any time when you are not supposed to sing? (When you do not feel like singing?)
8. How many different kinds of songs are there?
9. Do these kinds sound different from each other?
10. How do the different kinds of songs make you feel when you hear them?
11. Are some kinds of songs hard to learn and others easy?
12. How old were you when you learned to sing? (How old were you when you could sing well?)
13. What did people say when you learned to sing?
14. Do you know some old songs that most people have forgotten?
15. Are there new kinds of songs being sung today? (What do you think of them?)
16. Are songs changing now? (Why?)
17. What do you think of American (Mexican) songs? (Why?)
18. Do you know any of either? (Do you wish you did?)
19. Are there other Navahos who do? (Are there any who did not go to school who do?)
20. Why do you think they (nobody) learned them?
21. Are there different ways of making the voice sound when we sing?
22. When do you use these different ways? (If any were described.)
23. Do people make their voices sound in new ways nowadays? (What?)
24. What do you think of the way American voices sound?
25. Are there any Navahos who make their voices sound that way when they sing?

Third Level of Specificity

1. Is there a kind of singing besides ceremonial singing? (What is it?) Suggest: lullabies, gambling songs, work songs, etc.
2. Is there a difference between the way ceremonial songs and other songs sound?
3. Are there ceremonial songs that can be used outside the ceremony?
4. Would you hear the show-off way the young men sing in a ceremonial?
5. Do you have a different feeling when you hear ceremonial songs and when you hear songs that are not ceremonial?

6. Do you feel differently about it when you hear a song in a ceremony and the same song *outside the ceremony?*
7. Are there special songs for working?
   Are there special songs for riding along?
   Are there special songs that go with games?
8. Are there songs people sing just to be funny?
9. Are there dirty songs the Navahos sing? (What do you thing of them?)
10. Are there special songs for good luck?
11. Are there songs to make people stop what they are doing and behave better? (Songs for teasing people?)
12. Are there songs that make you feel happy?
13. Are there songs that make you feel angry?
15. Did you ever make up a song? (Was it a happy song? sad? angry?)
16. (Here an experiment in mood and music was introduced. I sang, without words, and with as nearly identical facial and vocal expression as possible, two songs, "The Happy Farmer," and "Pore Judd is Daid." Of course, the former is fast in tempo and the latter is slow. Informants were asked to identify which was supposed to be the happy song and which the sad one. They were then asked to give their reasons.)
17. Do you know any songs about love?
18. What do you think of American songs about this?
19. Are there songs that are especially pretty?
20. What is it about a song that makes it sound pretty?
21. Are there songs you think sound ugly? (Why?)
22. Can you say a song is pretty the way you say a girl or a good rug or a bracelet is pretty?
23. What kind of singing do you like better: (illustrate with narrow and wide vibrato, plain and nasal tone).
24. What kind of melody do you like better: (illustrate with a chant-like melody and a more varied melody).
25. Are there songs you like just because of the melody? (What is it about the melody that you like?)
26. Are there songs you like just because of the words? (What is it about the words that you like?)
27. Are there songs for children only?
28. Are there songs for men only?
29. Are there songs for women only?
30. Are there songs for old people only?
31. Is it a good thing for you to know songs? (Why?)
32. Do you teach songs to your children?
33. How do you teach them.
34. Do you give them something for learning songs?
35. Do you scold them if they do not learn songs?

36. Did your parents act like that with you?
37. How old are children when they learn to sing?
38. Why do you want children to learn to sing?
39. Do the children around here sing? (What do they sing?)

Eliciting

The field worker who records music as it is performed in a ceremony, at a dance, or otherwise in its normal cultural setting, has no problem in eliciting music from his informants. He needs only to switch on his recorder and let it absorb the music. But the acoustic results are not often satisfactory in this procedure, and while the field worker is urged to make recordings of the music as it is actually performed in its context, it seems advisable also to make recordings in which laboratory conditions of a sort are approximated in the field. After all, the conditions for certain ceremonies may not be present at the time the collector is in the field, but he may wish to record this material nevertheless. Or a certain chant may be performed while the performers walk or dance over a large amount of space, and the collector may not be able to follow them with his microphone. Laboratory conditions can be approximated in a small hut or house, and individual informants as well as groups can be recorded. This kind of field work, however, requires the use of elicitation, and the degree of refinement with which the collector elicits may have great bearing on the substance of his collection. It behooves us, therefore, to discuss the problem of eliciting.

The collector who is faced by an informant who is said to be able to perform songs may be in the position of the adult who is asking his child to sing for grandpa. The child knows the song, but he may be unwilling to sing it, and even when he does finally sing, it is in a manner quite different from that of his usual rendition. Thus it is necessary to make the informant feel at ease, to give him confidence, to allow him to sing in his "normal" way, and to recognize when he is not doing so. The col-

lector may find, for example, that the informant does not know
how to begin. It may be necessary to jog his memory or to stimulate it by mentioning types of songs. It may be necessary for
the collector to sing songs from his own culture for the informant, and to begin swapping songs, as it were, so that the informant feels at ease. In some cultures, financial reward for singing
is very acceptable to informants; in others it is a dishonor. Its
use should be understood by collector and informant.

A pitfall in eliciting is engendered by the collector's desire
for a certain type of material or for a certain song. Thus an
informant may begin singing, instead of Indian songs which
show no influence of Western music, some of the recent songs
which have English words; or, instead of Child ballads, versions
of music hall songs. To show displeasure to an informant may
mean to seal a good source of material. Informants may frequently begin by singing recent material even though they know
older songs; and only gradually do they realize that the collector
is more interested in those older ones which otherwise stand in
disrepute with the informant's fellows. So, while a collector is
probably better off by limiting his project and thus searching
for certain types of material, he must be patient with his informants and accept whatever they have to offer, guiding them without pressure, never arguing even when he knows that an informant is misinformed. Anthropologists have long believed in
the adage, "the informant is always right."

Some important information about musical cultures can be
obtained by re-recording material previously recorded. For example, the collector may wish to record songs collected previously from other informants. In a typical European or American
folk culture, he can elicit such songs simply by referring to their
titles or first lines, or by giving the subject matter of the text.
In some cultures, however, there seems to be no specific way of
referring to a musical composition. Indeed, there may not be
such a concept as a "piece" of music, which is the basic unit in
Western musical culture. In such cases, eliciting songs may be
problematic one solution is to play for the informant some re-

cordings of the same song as it was previously collected, or to sing bits of the song for him, and then ask the informant to sing his own version of the song. The results thus obtained are sometimes baffling, for what the informant considers variants of the same song may not at all be what the collector expects; and informants may refer to two evidently similar songs as different entities, while insisting that two obviously different tunes are really versions of the same song. Nevertheless, eliciting with the use of recordings or with singing may influence the informant unfavorably; he may believe that versions of songs especially similar to those played are desired by the collector, and he may omit others which exhibit greater degrees of variation.

A good way of eliciting is to bring together two or more informants and to stimulate them to sing for each other, giving different versions of the same song; this brings about renditions in which the informant sings for his fellows, not for the collector. Re-recording and finding various versions of one musical item makes possible studies of the degree of standardization in musical performance, in the concept of musical units, of musical memory, of communal re-creation, and of many other aspects of musical culture.

Eliciting can also be used to explore the difference between significant and meaningless distinctions in a musical style, and the points at which legitimate variation becomes unacceptable error. In matters of intonation, for example, each culture presumably has a range within which variation is tolerated. Even in Western civilization, in which exactitude of melodic and harmonic intervals is stressed and an ideal of correct intonation exists in theory, a great deal of variation in pitch is acceptable, but intervals outside this range are said to be out of tune. This sort of distinction presumably also exists in nonliterate cultures, although the amount of permissible variation may be greater. Possibly the amount of pitch variation allowed correlates with the size of the intervals, more exactness being required where the intervals are smaller. At any rate, the study of such distinctions where a theoretical system is absent can be approached behaviorally by ascertaining the actual pitches used and the degree of variation present in the actual recordings. It may also be studied (but with great difficulty and with a need for great care) by inviting the informant's criticism of the collector's renditions of songs. One can perhaps train the informant to be the collector's teacher. The collector will sing back to the informant the songs which the latter has recorded, but with mistakes intentionally inserted at controlled points. This may enable the informant to state which mistakes, that is, which deviations from his own version, are acceptable to him. The technique is difficult to use, for it requires an informant who is willing to be honest in evaluating the collector's performance, and it requires a collector who is able to control his performance adequately so that he can make mistakes only where and to the extent to which he wishes to. This kind of technique has been used in linguistics, but only rarely in ethnomusicology.

Special problems in eliciting appear when the musical structure is complex, especially if a performance is by several singers, instruments, etc. The collector may wish to clarify the structure for purposes of analysis and transcription by allowing his recording machine to do some of the preliminary analysis or breaking down of the complexities into their components. For example, it is almost impossible to transcribe a record on which several xylophones of equal size are playing together if one does not know the number of xylophones. Even when the number and size of the instruments is known, it is extremely difficult to notate what each individual one is playing. It may be possible to reproduce the over-all acoustic impression, but this may be misleading. Thus it is possible that the melodic line is performed not by one of the instruments—with the others accompanying—but by all of them, alternately, in hocket technique, that is, each performing only one tone and playing only when it is time for that tone to be heard. The collector can try to move his microphone near each of the players in repeated renditions, or in a piece which consists of many repetitions of a short bit of music. This is likely to produce recorded material which has at least a good chance of being authentic, i.e., performed as it would be were the collector not present. The acoustic results may not be as satisfactory for the transcriber, because there will still be the background of the other instruments, which are not being featured in the recording at hand, to confuse him. Moreover, in some cultures it might be difficult to record three renditions of a piece of music, each with the microphone near a different performer, which are close enough to identical to be used as individual parts of a single composition. An acoustically better rendition, but one more difficult to obtain and less reliable in terms of authenticity, can be produced by asking each performer separately to perform his own part. Many singers and instrumentalists in non-Western and folk cultures cannot do this because they are so accustomed to performing only as participants. Even if they can perform their own parts individually, they may not be able to do so in a way which is close to identical with the way they would perform in ensemble. But either of these ways of eliciting parts is desirable in a collection, if recordings of the entire ensemble performing the same music are also made. Besides being a help to the transcriber, they may provide clues to the culture's musical thinking.

Finally, in the area of eliciting, we should mention the practice of recording without the informant's knowledge or consent. This is not recommended. In some cultures, for example, it is believed that a song taught to another person represents loss or harm to the song owner's soul; recording seems to be viewed similarly in such cultures. In a more rationalistic setting, members of a community may wish to discuss with a chief or elder the advisability of recording for a field worker, and these wishes should be respected. Throughout, dealings with informants must be honest, and what they do not understand must be patiently explained. Communities and prize informants have been rendered silent by the improper or unfair treatment accorded them by certain field workers.

Simple Collecting versus Comprehensive Field Work

In ethnomusicological thinking there seem to be two main approaches to field work. One stresses the concept of collecting, the other that of experience with a whole musical culture. Collecting, as such, implies an emphasis on the musical works which are collected and brought back to the laboratory. The kind of thinking which engenders the "collecting" concept may also be concerned with the informants as members of a culture, and with the role of music in culture, but it need not be. The basic notion of a "collector" is to find music previously not found and to hold on to it. His attitude implies the existence, in the world, of a limited corpus of tribes and communities, or, more frequently, of songs and pieces, and his job is to collect as many of them as possible. He is interested in organizing his work so that it will contain as large a proportion of the limited corpus as possible, and he feels strongly the preservative role of the field worker. He is most interested in older material, and he realizes that many musical items will either disappear or change greatly almost before his eyes if he does not make recordings of them. This type of field worker is mainly found in the area of folk music, although the Asian high cultures and the non-literate cultures also provide a field for him.

The other approach emphasizes music as behavior. The field worker still collects songs and is aware of his importance as a preserver. But he also believes that the world's musical corpus is not limited, that music is constantly being created, and that the chances of making exhaustive collections is small. He is more interested in observing all of the musical phenomena in a given environment.

In these two approaches we can find embodied the two main purposes of field work: the preservation of a cultural heritage before it changes, and the observation of cultural forces whether they remain constant or change. The second of these approaches is much more recent and has not produced a great volume of collectanea. Techniques for studying musical culture are not well developed, and at any rate they are bound to be more complex than those which involve merely collecting. The preservative approach to field work, on the other hand, has yielded vast collections of folk song, as well as of the music of certain non-literate cultures such as the North American Indians and some of the tribes of southern Africa. Theory and method for this approach is to a great extent dependent on the discipline of folklore, which has always emphasized the collecting aspect of field work, and which—in contrast to ethnomusicology—has a body of literature on collecting. Among the most interesting readings about the collecting of folklore is the first of *Four Symposia on Folklore* (Thompson 1953). Here the problems of European, American, and some Asian collectors are frankly and informally discussed, and the special devices which some of them have developed for dealing with informants, eliciting, and assuring even and exhaustive coverage, are stated and criticized. Most evident in this symposium is the emphasis on collecting, on finding the artifacts rather than on observing a culture and one of its aspects in action. The idea of mapping a geographical area to be covered, of collecting systematically from all informants, village by village or block by block, is extensively discussed as a desideratum; again, such coverage has been given only in the field of European folk music, and there only in a few isolated areas. During the last decade, collectors in Hungary, Romania, and some other East European areas have been collecting in teams in order to cover their nations quickly and comprehensively, largely with the idea of preserving the materials rather than studying them in their settings. In some of these nations, ethnomusicological field work has become a government concern. Where this is not the case, the organization of field work and systematic collecting has not usually been possible. On the other hand, the entry of government agencies into the collecting activity may tend to be detrimental to the product which is collected and to the attitude of the informants, especially if the government is interested for reasons other than scholarly ones.

Equipment for Collecting

The recording equipment which ethnomusicologists have used has usually lagged, by a few years, behind the products developed for commercial recording firms. For example, in the 1920's, when cylinders were no longer used commercially, some folk music collectors were still using them; in the early 1950's, when wire recording was no longer generally used, collectors were still depositing wire recordings in ethnomusicological archives. But on the whole, the history of field recording devices follows that of recording in general. Recommending equipment to the collector is difficult at a time when new products are constantly being placed on the market. At the time of writing, and for some years no doubt, tape recording will be the most efficient. Recording on disks is cumbersome and both fidelity and durability are lower. Some scholars still prefer transcribing from disk to using tape, and a good ethnomusicological laboratory should have equipment for cutting disks; but for most transcribers, tape has proved to be a great boon because of the ease of locating spots by means of the measuring device on most recorders, and because repeated playing does not harm the fidelity.

Wire recordings have advantages over disks, but they have lower fidelity than either disks or tapes and are most useful for conversation. The advantage of wire over disk is the greater length of recording time available for recording before changing the supply of the medium. While it is difficult to list specific tape recorder brands which are most useful, partly because such a list would be outdated very quickly, it seems desirable to list some of the requirements which an ethnomusicological field worker would place on his equipment; knowledge of these requirements will make selection of equipment easy. A detailed discussion of such requirements appears in Merriam 1954; and while this discussion is a decade old, it is still almost completely relevant.

The speed at which the recorder feeds the tape is important. There are recorders which feed tape as slowly as 1⅞ inches per second, but this speed is usually not satisfactory, so far as the fidelity of the reproduction is concerned, for music recording. For speech and perhaps for monophonic music 3¾ inches per second is satisfactory, but not for more complex material. Probably the most satisfactory service is given by tape running at 7½ inches per second. Large tape recorders, used in professional recording laboratories, are sometimes geared to 15 inches per second, but this speed usually consumes the tape too quickly for economy. Two-speed recorders are common, and it seems advisable to use a machine which feeds tape at 3¾ and 7½ inches per second.

Merriam (1954:6) emphasizes the importance in field work of getting a recorder which is simple to operate and to set up. Frequently it is necessary to prepare for recording very quickly, and the simpler a machine is, the more likely it can be repaired by the field worker himself. Simpler machines also tend to be more durable in the field. Before going into the field, the investigator should become thoroughly acquainted with his recording equipment, so that he can repair minor damage; field trips have been ruined because equipment broke down and could not be repaired by the field worker himself.

Many recorders have apparatus for recording on two edges of the tape, known as dual-track recording. While the use of such a recorder is not itself harmful, it is not advisable to use both tracks in recording unless absolutely necessary. The possibility of the sound from one track being audible, in the form of "ghosts," is still considerable, and having to splice the tape at a point where the breakage is hardly noticeable on one track may create a grave transcription problem on the other track. Other points of importance in a recorder are the presence of high-speed rewind and forward mechanisms (most models have these) and a good erasing mechanism. The latter enables tape to be used many times; if it is inadequate, sounds from one recording may still be audible when the next recording is made on the same spot. Some poor machines make it possible for the recordist to turn on the erasing mechanism by mistake; this sort of error would obviously be a calamity to a field worker, so he should protect himself against it by using a machine on which a special effort must be made to turn on the erasing mechanism.

Microphones are usually included in tape recorders, but the lower priced models are frequently furnished with inferior microphones, so that the purchase of a better microphone (with the tape recorder's own one available for emergencies) seems advisable. Long extension cords—a minimum of 50 feet of cable —are also very useful, since the source of power and the strategic placement of the recorder or the microphone may be some distance apart.

A source of power may not be available in the field, so it is advisable for the collector to bring his own. Even when power is available, a convertor may be needed to apply American machinery to foreign outlets. An electric generator is usually bulky and noisy, so that it must be placed a good distance from the microphone. It does, however, provide a degree of steadiness not quite as easily found in car batteries, which are the second alternative. If a regular car battery is used, it must be fitted to a convertor which changes the 6 or 12 volts to the 110 normal in American recorders. The battery must, of course, be recharged periodically; this can be done with an automobile generator, if a car is available, or by a service station with a charger, if this is not too distant. In most cases, the battery with convertor seems more convenient than the generator.

Recently, battery-operated tape recorders have come into use. The battery supplies power for the magnetic recording head, but the reels are operated by a spring which is wound manually. These recorders are excellent for work in which a small or moderate amount of recording is done. They do have some disadvantages—fidelity is not so high, speed is not quite as constant

—but their mobility makes them excellent traveling companions. The tiny, transistor-powered recorders do not seem adequate for ethnomusicological use as yet. But their development promises to broaden the variety of equipment available and to make a wider selection of types for the special needs of the field worker.

Among the kinds of tape available, plastic-backed is to be preferred to paper-backed (which is no longer available in most places) because of its greater fidelity and durability. Various kinds of tape of even greater strength have been made available within the last few years. The field worker must balance quality against cost; he may not be able to afford the best kinds of tape, which are consumed mainly by radio stations and record companies; but he should guard against accepting the least expensive brands since these, because of their lack of fidelity and their tendency to tear, make both preservation and transcription problematic.

Techniques of recording with tape are not difficult to master. The amateur has a tendency to hold the microphone too close to a singer's mouth; it should be no less than twelve inches away, much more if an instrument or a group of singers is involved. Tapes should be numbered, and items on each tape numbered as well: a number arrangement for the tapes combined with a letter arrangement for individual items will yield notations such as 3d, 6f. If dual-track tape is used, it is necessary to specify, for each item, on which track it is recorded. It is advisable to note such matters in good order as soon as recordings are made, and to keep written records collated with the recordings. Field workers may be tempted to leave such details until later, but they are risking the frailty of memory. Each item on a tape should be recorded on paper and an announcement giving its number should appear before it on the tape. Information about an item can be spoken onto the tape as easily as written. The collector should keep careful track of the speed of the tape for each reel, and he may find it useful to record some standard for pitch measurement—with a tuning whistle or fork—before each recording, for control of the speed, which may be subject to variation depending on the power supply. In order to perfect his recording technique the collector should practice recording his own voice before approaching informants, and he should be thoroughly acquainted with the various controls on his machine so that he need not be embarrassed by failures when the time for actual recording is at hand.

Archiving and Storage

Many field workers will wish to keep their collected recordings in their own homes or offices, and to study, transcribe, and analyze them. Those who are not specialists in ethnomusicology, or whose collections are too extensive for one person to transcribe and analyze, and those who for some reason wish to make their recordings available to others, may wish to place them in one of the various archives established for the purpose of assembling field recordings. Some of the great archives in the United States and in Europe have been mentioned in Chapters 1 and 2. Smaller archives are present in many institutions which have an interest in ethnomusicology, and indeed, an archive of some sort is almost indispensable to an institution which teaches advanced courses and accepts graduate work in our field. Thus the field of ethnomusicology has had to develop certain techniques which are loosely termed as "archiving," and which have gradually developed so as to have a small degree of standardization. In some ways these are akin to the techniques of librarianship; in others they are unique.

The basic unit of an archive is usually the collection, which is normally the product of a single field investigation by one collector in one culture, recorded on one medium. It is subdivided, of course, into a number of items, such as songs or pieces. The simplest procedure, beyond making a listing of the collection itself and depositing it as a unit in the storage space available, is simply to accept the collector's own numbering and arrangement. An archive of this sort would, ultimately, consist of a number of collections, each with its own system of numbering the songs. Beyond keeping the collection as a unit, there is a great variety in the number of things which can be done in an ethnomusicological archive; those with modest means may find it best to leave the materials as cataloged by the collector himself, making only a simple catalog listing collectors, tribes, and languages, and keeping whatever notes the collector furnishes with his recordings. Archives with more elaborate facilities will wish to do a great many more things. The following procedures may be interpreted to be in order of priority: the things mentioned first should be done by all archives, those given later by those which find it possible after fulfilling the first obligations.

1. Materials should be stored in a cool, dry place. Plastic-backed tapes develop a stickiness in warm temperatures, and eventually the adjacent portions of tape begin to stick together. Storage in a steel cabinet should protect tape or wire from the accidental rearrangement of the magnetized particles which is occasionally (but rarely) caused by an electric storm.

2. Notes, transcriptions of texts, and other written material based on a collection should be kept with the collection or in a filing cabinet, but labeled so that their relationship to the recordings is clear.

3. All material should be clearly numbered and labeled.

4. Catalogs—usually on filing cards—should be kept according to the following entries: collector, language or tribe, and shelf, i.e., according to location.

5. Specific agreements with the collectors, stating what rights the archive has and what rights the collector reserves for himself, must be made. Failure to do this has caused institutions considerable embarrassment and even legal difficulties. Some collectors are prepared to give their material to an archive outright; others make an indefinite loan or lend the material for a specified period. In either case, the collector should have the

right to use the material himself for research, and to have prior rights of publication. Some archives request depositors of material to fill out a form on which they indicate whether their recordings are available only for listening—this is of great value to students—and for classroom use, whether they may be used by students to practice transcription, and whether such transcriptions may be published. It should be specified, also, whether the materials may be duplicated (some collectors insist that they be duplicated if any intensive listening or transcription is to be done), whether copies may be given to other institutions in exchange, and to whom the material reverts if the archive should be disbanded. In the absence of copyright laws for recordings and for materials in the public domain, it is necessary to protect the ethnomusicological field worker so that he may have maximum control of the products of his work even while he makes them available to others. Protection of informants' rights is an even more complicated question; usually it is a contractual matter between the collector and his informant, and it is up to the collector to see that the informants' moral and legal rights are not abused.

6. If an archive is able to go beyond the basic steps given above, it may wish to make a duplicate recording of its entire collection; the duplicate collection would be used for listening, transcribing, and all other operations, so that the originals would remain untouched as much as possible, and would be available for return to the collector if this were necessary. Duplication of a collection whose originals are on disk, cylinder, and wire, onto tape is likely to cause problems in labeling and cataloging. Once the entire collection is duplicated on tape, it becomes possible to standardize the cataloging to a greater degree than when the collection exists on various media.

7. The archive may wish to go beyond the cataloging supplied by the collectors, unifying the entries and making separate entries for each of the individual musical items included. Then it becomes possible to have a catalog of types of songs and music, such as war songs, love songs, etc., another for instru-

ments, a third for stylistic categories such as polyphony, and even one for first lines or titles of songs—especially in collections featuring Western folk culture.

8. In order to make the archives' holdings even more useful to researchers and teachers, it might be advisable to analyze songs briefly so that a catalog of specific stylistic features—especially unusual or unexpected ones, such as peculiar scales and rhythmic patterns—could be set up. Such analysis has not, to my knowledge been carried out at any archive. Only a collection containing a large variety of material could provide the basis for the comparative work needed to establish such a catalog. With it, the archive could single out recordings with specific musical traits for demonstration and for the comparative work of specialists in various areas of ethnomusicology, much as a library, through its subject headings, can identify publications according to their content and character.

9. Finally, of course, an archive could make available part of its content in published recordings. Again, archives are in a unique position to make the selection of appropriate items because they have at their disposal large amounts of raw material from which to choose the most characteristic or the most attractive.

Archiving is, then, a middle ground between field work and desk work. As we have seen, much desk work is done in the field, and much field work is done close to the desk. Some archives, besides being middle ground, engage in field work themselves. Analysis of the type indicated in numbers 7 and 8 above is obviously already in the category of post-collecting research. The archive which does this is performing some of the work normally carried on by the individual researcher, but it can often do this better than the individual if it has a competent staff. Many archives also engage in collecting on their own, and, indeed, some consist largely of collections made by their own staffs (this is true of the Deutsches Volksliedarchiv in Freiburg) or under its own instigation (Library of Congress Archive of Folk Song). The steps outlined above are intended for an ar-

chive which contains all sorts of ethnomusicological materials.
But of course many archives specialize, accepting only materials
in a given area (again, the Deutsches Volksliedarchiv, which
contains German folk song and little else) or seeking certain
types of material while accepting others as well (the Archive
of Folk Song, which seeks American materials but accepts others
if they are offered). Such archives would certainly use procedures which specifically fit the kind of material which they
include. Some archives contain, in addition to recordings, manuscript transcriptions of music; cataloging these and integrating
them with recordings poses special problems. So does the inclusion of commercial recordings along with field recordings, although commerical records may contain material of great use.
The field of archiving in ethnomusicology and in folklore at large
is a relatively new one. The student interested in learning about
the contents and arrangements of various archives is advised to
read the issues of *The Folklore and Folk Music Archivist,* a small
periodical, published since 1958 by the Research Center for
Anthropology, Folklore, and Linguistics of Indiana University,
which describes a separate archive in each issue. For further
readings we suggest Thompson's *Four Symposia* (1953) and
the descriptive brochure issued by the Deutsches Volksliedarchiv
in 1956.

Bibliography

Brailoiu, Constantin (1960). *Vie musical d'un village.* Paris: Institut
    universitaire roumain Charles Ier.
Densmore, Frances (1918). *Teton Sioux Music.* Washington: Smith-
    sonian Institution. Bulletin 61 of the Bureau of American Ethnolo-
    gy.)
Das deutsche Volksliedarchiv (1956). Brochure describing the ar-
    chive. Freiburg.
Hause, Helen E. (1948). "Terms for musical instruments in Sudanic
    languages," Supplement 7 to the *Journal of the American Oriental
    Society* 68, no. 1, January–March 1948.

Kurath, Gertrude P. (1960). "Panorama of dance ethnology," *Current Anthropology* 1:233–254.

Lowie, Robert H. (1937). *The History of Ethnological Theory.* New York: Rinehart.

McAllester, David P. (1954). *Enemy Way Music.* Cambridge: Peabody Museum Papers, vol. 41, no. 3.

*Merriam, Alan P. (1954). "The selection of recording equipment for field use," *Kroeber Anthropological Society Papers* no. 10. Berkeley, Calif.

———— (1960). "Ethnomusicology; discussion and definition of the field," *Ethnomusicology* 4:107–114.

Nketia, J. H. Kwabena (1962). "The problem of meaning in African music," *Ethnomusicology* 6:1–7.

Schiørring, Nils (1956), *Selma Nielsens viser.* Copenhagen: Munksgaard.

Slotkin, J. S. (1952). *Menomini Peyotism.* Philadelphia: Transactions of the American Philosophical Society, new series, vol. 42, part 4.

*Sachs, Curt (1962). *The Wellsprings of Music.* The Hague: M. Nijhoff. *Recommended* reading, pp. 16–20.

*Thompson, Stith (1953). *Four Symposia on Folklore.* Bloomington: Indiana University Publications, Folklore series, No. 8. Recommended reading, pp. 1–88.

*Wilgus, D. K. (1959). *Anglo-American Folksong Scholarship Since 1898.* New Brunswick, N. J.: Rutgers University Press. Recommended reading, pp. 123–239.

Chapter 1

TRANSCRIPTION

THERE ARE TWO MAIN approaches to the description of music: 1) we can analyze and describe what we hear, and 2) we can in some way write it on paper and describe what we see. If human ears were able to perceive all of the acoustic contents of a musical utterance, and if the mind could retain all of what had been perceived, then analysis of what is heard would be preferable. Reduction of music to notation on paper is at best imperfect, for either a type of notation must select from the acoustic phenomena those which the notator considers most essential, or it will be so complex that it itself will be too difficult to perceive. But since human memory is hardly able to retain, with equal detail, what was heard ten seconds ago along with what is being heard in the present, notation of some sort has become essential for research in music. This does not imply that analysis and description based on sound—on what the researcher hears—is unessential; quite the contrary. But such analysis must almost always be supplemented by analysis of the material as it appears in notated form. In ethnomusicology, the process of notating sound, of reducing sound to visual symbol, is called transcription.

The idea of putting music on paper is based on certain assumptions which need not be generally accepted. According to Charles Seeger (1958a:184):

Three hazards are inherent in our practices of writing music. The first lies in an assumption that the full auditory parameter of music is or can be represented by a partial visual parameter. . . upon a flat surface. The second lies in ignoring the historical lag of music-writing behind speech-writing, and the consequent traditional interposition of the art of speech in the matching of auditory and visual signals in music writing. The third lies in our having failed to distinguish between prescriptive and descriptive uses of music-writing, which is to say, between a blue-print of how a specific piece of music shall be made to sound and a report of how a specific performance of it actually did sound.

Seeger (1958a) has distinguished between two purposes of musical notation, prescriptive and descriptive. The former has as its aim the direction of a performer, and the adequacy of prescriptive notation is judged by the adequacy of the perform-ance, or by the degree to which a performer perceives, through the notation, the composer's wishes. The symbols of prescriptive notation may be no more than mnemonic devices, as seems to have been the case in the medieval neumes which indicate little beyond the general direction in which the melody is to move. Exact pitches and rhythms were presumably known to the performers, or they were left to their discretion. The West-ern system of notation—and the various Oriental systems as well—was developed in order to be prescriptive, and while the amount of detail which it shows has gradually increased, it is still essentially a mnemonic device. There are many things which a composer expects the performers to know and to take for granted. Curiously, of course, the fact that composers do take certain performance practices for granted is responsible for the many disagreements among scholars regarding the precise man-ner of performance of early music. If composers had been, or could have been, more specific, the work of many music his-torians would be unnecesssary. In this chapter we are concerned not with prescriptive but with descriptive notation. Historically, descriptive notation developed along with the prescriptive. Descriptive notation, after all, is intended to convey to a reader the characteristics and the details of a musical composition which the reader does not already know. The Baroque com-

posers who used folk songs as the basis of polyphonic compositions performed both descriptive and prescriptive notation. As
long as notators of folk songs insisted on fitting the folk styles
into patterns of cultivated musical styles, there was not much
difference between the two kinds of notation. Only when the
great differences among the world's musical cultures began to
be evident, and when the purposes of the two notations became
distinct in the thinking of musicians and scholars, did external
differences between the two also begin to appear. And these
differences are not great, since most transcription, for better or
worse, is produced in Western notation. The advantages and
disadvantages of this are discussed below.

Transcription is performed in several ways. Earliest, and
perhaps least adequate, is field transcription, that is, writing
down a song as one hears it; it is difficult to write down a song
even in musical shorthand in one hearing, especially if it is in
a musical style which is strange to the investigator and inimical
to Western notation. But early students of non-Western music
had to use this very moderately accurate method, and even
after the invention of recording, field workers without recording equipment brought home field transcriptions. In spite of all
the obvious disadvantages of notating an African song while it
is being sung and danced to, with all of the confusion of the
situation tending to distract the transcriber, such a method is
presumably better than that of the anthropologist who tried, in
an apocryphal story, to learn an Australian aboriginal song and,
through long practice on the way home to Europe, made such
changes in it that it was transformed into a German folk song.
Such a lamentable fate would not have overtaken this song if
the anthropologist had become "bi-musical." But for the field
worker who did not specialize in music, or whose period of
contact with the culture he was investigating was short, field
transcription was the best way of bringing home musical material. Related to transcription of music as it is performed in a
bona fide cultural context is the transcription of a piece from
an informant in the laboratory. In such a situation it is possible

to ask a singer to repeat songs many times, or even to single out parts of songs for repetition. And while a singer cannot (by physical and physiological necessity) sing a song twice in exactly the same way, he can come reasonably close, and he will usually be accurate in those matters which are, to him, the most significant in the song. This is presumably what was done by Carl Stumpf in his 1884 study of Bella Coola music.

With the invention of recording, transcription done directly from performance, in the field or the laboratory, became obsolete. Nevertheless, techniques developed for laboratory transcription with an informant may still be used profitably in conjunction with transcription from recordings. Transcribing involves consideration of what is significant and what is incidental in a music—considerations which are related to problems faced in the study of language. Ethnomusicologists have made some use of the theory and techniques of linguistics for approaching some of these problems, and the use of an informant for transcription in the laboratory is one of these. The informant may be asked to comment on the accuracy of the recorded performance, and to identify insignificant or unintended sounds, for example. As recording progressed from the relatively primitive forms of cylinder and disk in the late nineteenth century to the more sophisticated wire and tape recordings in the post-World War II era, transcription became more convenient as well. The main advantage of transcribing from recordings is, of course, the possibility of hearing a piece many times in a single rendition, of comparing sections which are separated by intervening material, and of returning, day after day, to the same piece.

A more fundamental revolution than the development of recording has been the invention of electronic devices which perform transcription automatically. Such devices have always been both the dream and the terror of many ethnomusicologists. They would save the ethnomusicologist hours of labor and agonizing decisions while increasing his accuracy, but they would also allow him less control over his own work and make him the slave of elaborate machinery which produces graphs and similar communications of no interest to musicians, and they might, in-cidentally, put some of the techniques which he has laboriously learned out of business. At the time of writing, these devices have fulfilled neither their promise nor their threats, but they are being improved, and there is no doubt that they will soon play a considerable role. They are discussed below, but we mention them here because their existence leads us to examine some very fundamental assumptions regarding transcription by humans.

Transcribing music by hand and ear, as it were, is hindered by the situation in which the transcriber is a native of one musical culture trying to write down the music of another cul-ture, a transcriber using a notation system devised for one cul-ture and foreign to the styles in others. Thus, a concept such as the note, which forms the basis of Western musical thinking, might be erroneously applied to another musical culture in which the glides between notes are the essential feature. Slight deviations from pitch, hardly audible to Western ears used to the tempered scale, might be essential distinctions in another music. Again, several obviously distinct pitches could be con-sidered merely different versions of a single tone. The point is that human transcribers, using a notation which is always to some extent selective of the musical phenomena it reproduces, and having a background in a specific musical culture which is also selective of the musical phenomena which it uses as com-munication, might have great difficulty in first perceiving and then reproducing on paper the music of another culture in such a way that the essential distinctions are indicated in a way comparable to that which would be required by descriptive notation. Assuming that no human transcriber could reproduce all of the acoustical phenomena of a musical utterance, he should reproduce those which are essential, and deciding this is prob-ably the most agonizing part of transcription. Electronic devices which transcribe probably cannot be made selective in this way. They record everything regardless of its importance, and selec-tion of the essentials must be made later by the scholar. Thus,

even with machine transcription, the informed human interpreter must be available; conversely, even the best human
transcriptions can be improved by machines.

Approaches to Transcription

The inadequacy of Western notation as descriptive notation
is readily admitted by most authors on the subject, and its failures are vigorously attacked by Seeger (1958a). Nevertheless,
even as strong a champion of change as Seeger was prepared
to recommend that Western notation and graphs (see p. 126)
be used concurrently. The practical advantages of transcribing
in a system at least based on Western notation are considerable.
Transcribing music is itself an excellent way for the scholar to
learn the details of a musical style. There are other ways of
doing this — studying by means of performance is one — but
transcribing imposes on the student a kind of discipline which
could hardly be exacted by mere listening to recordings. Thus
transcribing has also an educational function. Until electronic
notation devices are readily available and perfected, transcription with some sort of manual notation system remains one of
the indispensable tools of the ethnomusicologist. And although
attempts at providing other notation systems have been made,
the Western system has traditionally been preferred.

The transcriber is usually faced by musical phenomena too
detailed to be notated, and by others which do not fit the
notation system. For the latter, special symbols have been devised; for the former, however, there is basically no solution.
After all, musical sound (as it appears in the stroboscope, for
example) is extremely complex. The slight fluctuations in pitch
which occur when a singer performs one tone—the vibrato; the
tones he moves through when gliding from one note to the next;
the slight differences in length among notes of approximately
the same value: all of these should be perceived by the tran-

scriber. Whether they should be written down or not depends on the possibility of distinguishing, in a musical style, between the essential and the nonessential phenomena. Assuming that music is a form of communication, there must, in each musical style, be signals which communicate something to the initiated. Just what it is that is communicated we need not discuss here; it may be a nonmusical message or something intrinsically musical. But we can assume that a song sung, say, by a Blackfoot Indian and heard by one of his fellow tribesmen communicates something to the latter, and that this "something" is not perceived by an outsider who is totally unacquainted with Blackfoot songs. Now we may also assume that certain aspects of that song must remain as they are in order for the song to retain its identity for the singer and the native listener, but that there are other aspects of the song which can perhaps be varied in a way which will not disturb the song's identity.

The problem is similar to one in linguistics, where the distinction between phonetics and phonemics has long been recognized, the former being the study of speech sounds as they occur and the latter being concerned with those distinctions among speech sounds which produce, in a given language, distinctions in meaning. A transcription of speech may be phonetic or phonemic—and there is a theoretical possibility that it could be both. The student of an unwritten language will normally begin by making a phonetic transcription, i.e., noting all distinctions in sound which he can, and then try to deduce the phonemic system of that language from the distribution of and relationships among the phonetic symbols. Presumably a similar approach could be followed in transcribing music. It should be possible to move from transcription of all musical phenomena perceived by the transcriber to another transcription which gives only the essentials. But one element of language which is a great aid to the linguist is absent here: meaning, in the lexical sense. For in transcribing music, one can usually do little to persuade an informant to distinguish between (to him) correct and incorrect renditions of songs, phrases, or intervals. Nevertheless, linguists can sometimes deduce the phonemic system of a language without recourse to meaning; they can identify particles of speech from their structure and distribution alone. Similar procedures ought to work for music, at least to a degree.

Actually, little progress has been made toward developing a phonemic method of transcription for music. But in examining transcriptions by authoritative scholars it is possible to distinguish those who have tried to notate all aspects of a musical utterance in detail from those who evidently were willing to commit themselves to the difference between essential and unessential distinctions. To be sure, one cannot blandly assume that a transcription full of detail is "phonetic" while one with less detail is "phonemic." The former one may indicate a style whose minute distinctions are essential, while the latter one may be disregarding important details without having deduced a "system" for the style. Finally, before examining specific examples and methods, we must emphasize that details which are not "phonemic" in a language or a music are not, of course, unimportant. They may be unessential to communication, but they still contribute to the character of the style. Their non-phonemic quality—and their omission in a transcription which is based on phonemic principles—is the result only of the fact that their presence can be predicted from their environment.

Those ethnomusicologists who have written about the methods and problems of transcription have not, to this writer's knowledge, identified themselves with the so-called "phonemic" approach, that is, they have not omitted features of music because these were unessential; at any rate, they have not called such features unessential. That many have (consciously, we must assume) made such omissions is evident from their transcriptions. Among the best transcriptions done—evidently—with the phonemic approach are those of George Herzog, who, while not neglecting details which characterize a musical style, avoids including such a mass of detail as to make a song unintelligible to the eye. An opposite approach appears to have been taken by Béla Bartók, who included all of the details he could, and who believed that it was the small, barely audible effects produced by the voice which actually characterized a musical style. Here of course we encounter a flaw in the analogy between music and language as objects for visual transcription. For while those elements in a language which are so characteristically present as to be predictable in their occurrence and location are considered nonphonemic, in a musical style it may be those very elements which give the style its character and which must be represented in a transcription. For transcriptions of music must do two things: they must include the elements which serve to distinguish musical utterances so far as their communicated content is concerned within their style or their musical culture; and they must contain those features which distinguish a whole musical style from another. Only the first of these needs is present in transcription of language.

At any rate, Bartók's transcriptions are exceedingly difficult to comprehend, and they are examples of descriptive notation which could at the same time be used as prescriptive notation. There seem to be times when Bartók was conscious of the phonetic-phonemic distinction. In at least one of his works (Bartók and Lord 1951) he gives detailed transcriptions above which he places less detailed versions of the melody which presumably represent songs as they appear in the listener's first impression.

Instructions and advice to the beginning transcriber are not lacking in the literature, and much of this advice may well be heeded today. Otto Abraham and Erich M. von Hornbostel (1909/10), in an early paper, admit the deficiencies of Western notation but advise the ethnomusicologist to use it because it is so widely known. They recommend modification of that system where it definitely does not fit the musical style which is being transcribed, and they present a table of supplementary symbols which have since been widely used and generally adopted. The main contents of that table are reproduced in Fig. 1; some symbols generally used but not included in Abraham-Hornbostel are also given.

↑ or +   above a note—approximately a quarter tone higher than written

↓ or −   above a note—approximately a quarter tone lower than written

These two signs used next to a key signature mean that the modification occurs consistently throughout the song; if they are in parentheses next to a signature, the modification is only occasional.

(♩)   pitch uncertain

♩, ♪   pitch quite indefinite, in the neighborhood of where the stem ends

♪   grace note

♩ ♩   dynamically weak tone

ρ̈   long pulsating tone without actual breaks

⌐ρ ρ   strong tie

ρ, ρ ρ   glide, glissando

⌢   above a note—tone slightly longer than noted, the lengthening being no more than half of the value indicated

⌣   above a note—tone slightly shorter than noted, but shortened by no more than one-third of the value indicated

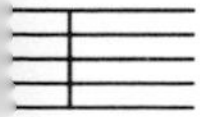

≣   major structural subdivision

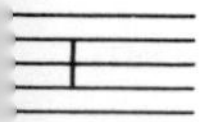

≣ or ⦂≣   minor structural or rhythmic subdivision

FIGURE 1. *Supplementary symbols frequently used in transcription.*

Hornbostel and Abraham also suggest some procedures. For instance, when a tune or phrase with three tones is identified, but the intervals among the tones are not clear, they suggest using a staff of only one line and placing the three notes, respectively, above, on, and below it, until more exact measurements can be made. In transcribing polyphonic music, they say it is sometimes advisable to give the over-all melodic impression, even when this is not the product of a single voice. They also recommend, for indication of small intervals, the insertion of additional lines within the staff:

And in spite of the early date of their work, they recognize the importance of graphs as they were then used by the American scholar B. I. Gilman.

In a pamphlet designed to standardize transcription of folk music, the Committee of Experts of the International Folk Music Council (International Music Council 1952) gives directions. Recommending the use of the Western staff, the pamphlet suggests the use of special symbols identical or similar to those of Hornbostel and Abraham. It suggests dividing the intervals in a song into two groups, those which remain constant, "implying the existence of a definite scale," and "those that vary" (p. 1). Here one might ask whether we can justly make this distinction. Two intervals will appear as separate units in either arrangement, and in the case of intervals which remain constant there will still, in most cultures, be considerable variation among different renditions. The Council recommends a footnote arrangement for variation among the different stanzas of a song, and it urges the transcriber to retain the original pitch of the performance rather than transposing to a more convenient pitch level.

Jaap Kunst (1959:39–41) gives valuable advice to the transcriber. In contrast to the present writer, Kunst believes that absolute pitch is an important part of the ethnomusicologist's gift. He believes, also, that the availability of the words is a great asset in transcribing vocal music, not only because of the value of the text for research, but because its structure may illuminate and thus facilitate perception of the rhythmic structure of the song. He cautions the student (1959:38) to work with the realization that the transcriber cannot know whether a given rendition by a member of a nonliterate culture sounds as it was intended to sound, and he presumably would not have subscribed to the concept of "phonemic" described above. He believes that the best procedure is to perceive the rhythmic structure of a piece by repeated hearings, then to notate all of the different pitches which occur (in a single scale), and then to proceed to transcription of the piece itself. Although admitting the value of mechanical and electronic devices for transcription, Kunst does not consider that such devices can be used alone. He considers them rather as occasional aids to be used when special problems arise.

Estreicher (1957), in a detailed essay which is presented in condensed and translated form by McCollester (1960), describes some problems encountered by him in transcription, and proposes solutions and procedures. Emphasizing the need for adapting the processes of transcription to the particular characteristics and difficulties of the style of music which is being researched, he recommends the use, essentially, of the Hornbostel-Abraham techniques described above. He makes use of controlled sounds superimposed on the music to help him perceive details not easily noted by the Western-trained listener. For example, he suggests the use of a steady tone signal to indicate changes in pitch level, and of devices such as the metronome to measure changes in tempo which may otherwise be too gradual to be noticed. He suggests to the transcriber that he prepare the tape he is transcribing by measuring it and indicating the points (by number of feet) at which certain key events of the music are heard. He thinks tape essential and will not work with disks. He makes considerable use of slowing down the tape to half speed; this transposes the music down an octave and causes some distortion of sound and timbre while clarifying some of the details which occur too quickly for grasp at ordinary speed. Parenthetically, we should say that the slowing-down technique is more useful for instrumental than for vocal music. In the case of music in which a single motif appears repeatedly, Estreicher recommends writing these various versions of the motif below each other for easier comparison.

Ethnomusicologists certainly vary in their approaches to transcription. While the techniques of one scholar may not be useful to another, it is interesting (and unusual) to find the procedures followed by one individual described in detail in print. Estreicher (1957) does give us a record of his own work, and students who are faced with the task of transcribing and are having difficulty in deciding how to attack the job may profit from his statements. Estreicher (as quoted by McCollester 1960:130)

prefers working with stylistically homogeneous recordings wherever possible in order to pick up early in the game typical traits within the musical style. He suggests working at the same time each day for several hours of intense concentration, and arranging the musical sections to be transcribed that day into homogeneous groupings from the simplest, that is to say easiest to grasp and most elementary stylistically, to the most complex, often the beginning of pieces where one finds statements more richly ornamented and rapid for example than interior passages. He advises the researcher to listen to the separate sections many times before arranging them in a working order.

Estreicher also suggests working first with the tape recorder at regular speed to get broad outlines, then at half speed for checking details, and finally returning to the regular speed. He is concerned also with the transcriber's psychological reactions to his own work; spending many hours on what would appear to be a simple and trivial matter can greatly discourage a scholar, and the use of autocriticism, constant revision, and patience are essential. It goes without saying that a transcriber will use a pencil with an eraser rather than a pen! Laying aside a transcription for days or weeks and returning to it is also a useful technique. Altogether, Estreicher's techniques are probably similar to those of most ethnomusicologists. All may not, however, agree with his theoretical assumptions in which there may be confusion between what he calls "reproducing an acoustical phenomenon" and transcriptions which "could reveal the full musical style" (McCollester 1960:131). He does face, of course, the problem of reproducing all acoustical details as against providing a transcription which can be understood by the Western-trained listener acquainted only with Western notation. But he does not indicate the relationship between the essentials of a musical style, that is, the phenomena which communicate and which correspond to the phonemes of languages on the one hand, and to the nonessential, "phonetic" ones, on the other. Perhaps an orientation toward this useful distinction would help to solve the dilemma, for it is a dilemma which grows as the possibility of an absolute transcription of phonetic-musical phenomena grows with the increased use of machine transcription.

Hints for the Transcriber

Estreicher's recommendations are of great value; a few directions should be added to them. It is useful, when transcribing a piece, to listen to it or to portions of it several times before setting pencil to paper, and to note the over-all form, possibly with the use of letters. The latter can be put on the music paper, spaced approximately, so that the details of the transcription—the notes—can be filled in. As transcribing begins, it is often good to transcribe the first phrase or short section in great detail, so that many of the kinds of problems to be met in the piece can be encountered and surveyed early in the game. The use of descriptive notes and whatever information accompanies a recording is of course indispensable, and the information included should be digested before transcription begins in earnest. After doing one phrase in detail, the transcriber may write down the remainder of the piece in more schematic form so that the outline of the entire structure emerges. After that, the details should be worked out. In the case of monophonic music with rhythmic accompaniment, it is frequently advisable to transcribe the accompaniment first. In general, short bits of music (perhaps six or eight notes) should be transcribed at a time and replayed many times in the process.

Among the mechanical aids which can easily be used by anyone is the tape loop. If a short section (not more than two seconds at 7½ in. per sec.) is very difficult to comprehend, it can be cut out temporarily and made into a loop which continues to replay so that the pauses caused by rewinding are avoided. Transcribing, as is now obvious, is a very time-consuming task. Even a simple song lasting from ten to twenty seconds may easily take one or two hours, distributed over several sittings, to transcribe. The first piece in a style is likely to be by far the most difficult for the transcriber, and students are advised to learn the technique by working on a body of compositions in one musical style rather than trying to sample the world's musical cultures in individual pieces. Students should also be cautioned against working too long at a time; there seems to be —at least for this writer—a decrease in accuracy after one or two hours of work.

If the student is beginning transcription without having a corpus of material which he collected in the field, he would do well to begin with a European folk style. This should be followed by one of the relatively simple, monophonic styles from a nonliterate culture, such as North American Indian. As a start, styles with strophic song structure are more easily transcribed than others. The student learning transcription should try to do so by concentrating, for a year or two, on a few contrasting musical styles, and by working on each one intensively. Polyphonic material should not be attempted until after a good deal of monophonic music has been transcribed.

Here the availability of field notes is extremely important, and the student should not throw himself at polyphonic material for which he does not know the number of singers or the kinds and numbers of instruments. Acoustic distortions, overtones, combination tones, etc., are likely, in the case of vocal polyphony especially, to put hazards in the way of the transcriber unless he knows a good deal about the circumstances of a performance. In all cases, transcription with tape recordings is to be preferred to work with to other media. Tape does not wear out with constant replaying, as do disks. It is easier to find one's place on a tape than by dropping the needle on a disk; and when it breaks, tape can be spliced rather easily. Some of the slower-moving recorders tend to break tape less easily than those which rewind at high speeds. Using single-track recordings and machines is usually preferable to those with dual tracks, since the former avoid the possibility of "ghosts" from the other track being audible on the track being transcribed. And speaking of the problems involved in breaking and splicing tapes, plastic-backed tape is more durable than paper tape, some of the professional brands developed since 1958 being almost impossible to tear.

The exact measurement of pitches and intervals is a special problem which has long interested ethnomusicologists. Identification of the individual tone in terms of cycles per second is the first step. In the laboratory, the oscilloscope and the strobo-scope are time honored devices, but they are not frequently available to the private ethnomusicologist or student. Hornbos-tel's *Reisetonometer* was a whistle with a slide which was gradu-ated in terms of cycles. Here the ability of the scholar to judge the identity of simultaneous or successive pitches is an essential factor. This is true also of Jaap Kunst's monochord (see Fig. 2a), which consists of a stretched steel string over a board which is calibrated to vibration rates, and a movable block of wood used for stopping the string. Pitch can be identified by ear and then "measured." The monochord was also expanded into a composite

FIGURE 2. *(a)* (OPPOSITE). *Kunst Monochord for determining frequencies.*

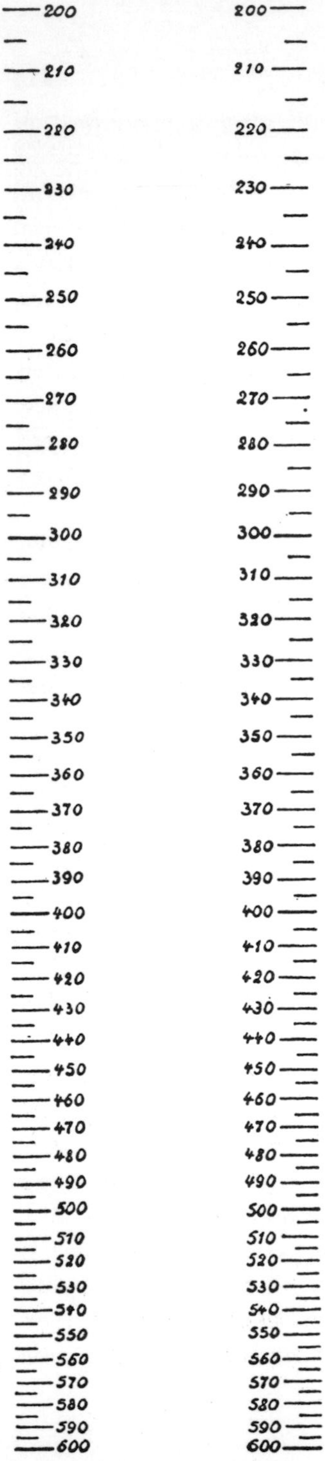

FIGURE 2. *(b) Bose Nomogramm for converting frequencies to cents.*

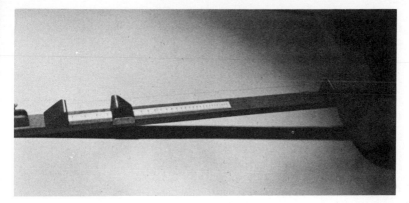

device consisting essentially of twelve such monochords so that a scale or tone system can be reproduced. The monochord seems to be a device of only moderate use to the transcriber, but successful transcriptions have resulted from its use (see, for example, Brandel 1962). And it is very useful to the teacher who wishes to demonstrate scales and intervals.

Having found the vibration rates of tones by any of these methods—the Melograph, Kunst's monochord, Hornbostel's *Reisetonometer*—the transcriber will need to convert his figures to expressions in terms of intervals. The system most widely used is the *cents* system devised by A. J. Ellis. Conversion of cycles to cents makes necessary the use of logarhythmic tables. A cent is one-hundredth of a tempered semitone, so that a minor third would be 300 cents, a perfect fifth, 700 cents, and an octave, 1,200 cents. Since the series of vibration rates progresses according to the logarhythmic principle, Sachs (1962:25–26) gives a table according to which the log of an interval as expressed in cycles can be converted to cents. The superiority of cents as a means of expressing intervals is obvious. Two numbers must be used to express intervals in terms of cycles, while in the cents system a single number is used. Morever, a difference in vibration rates such as 400 could be any interval, depending on the absolute pitch level, while a number of cents expresses a specific interval, i.e., the same ratio of cycles, at any pitch level. But conversion by means of Sachs' tables, while exceedingly accurate, is complicated. Several shortcuts have been devised; among them, that of Bose (1952a:297) is perhaps the most adequate (see Fig. 2b), though it is a bit too gross for very detailed calculation. But since the human ear evidently does not discriminate beyond perhaps 1/14 of a tone, the margin of error inherent in Bose's shortcut is perhaps insignificant.

Bose's method requires the use of a ruler with centimeters and millimeters marked. Each centimeter indicates a tempered half-tone, i.e., 100 cents. Thus, if we wish to find the interval between two cycles, we simply measure the distance in terms of centimeters. For example, we may wish to find the interval between 370 and 505 cycles; measuring, we find that it equals 5⅓ cm., or 533 cents, which is very slightly more than a perfect fourth. Again, we may wish to find the vibration rate for a neutral third, i.e., 350 cents (half-way between a major third, 400 cents, and a minor third, 300 cents), above middle-*c* (256 cycles). We measure 3½ cm. from 256 and arrive at 312.

A method of transcribing by ear, measuring intervals by the use of Kunst's monochord, and converting these measurements to cents, has been used by Brandel (1962). Her transcriptions, which use ordinary notation augmented by the conventional symbols, are accompanied by charts which give the specific distances between the tones in terms of cents. Thus, for the one transcription (Brandel 1962:252), she uses the pitches *g*, *f*, *e*-flat, *c*, and *a*, but finds that the distances among these tones are actually 191, 227, 283, and 279 cents, respectively. If the intervals were those of the Western tempered scale, they would have equalled 200, 200, 300, and 300 cents, respectively. Here, then, we have a method which uses Western notation but assigns to each tone a pitch which differs from that which it would have had in the tempered scale, and which indicates exactly the pitch actually used in the piece. But deviation from a "tone" is not accounted for in Brandel's method. Thus we must assume that the distance between *a* and *c* is, in this piece, always 279 cents;

this obviously cannot be the case, but we have no indication of the amount of variation from this standard.

It is often difficult to distinguish between formal divisions of a piece and the larger metric units. Thus, full bar lines are, in many transcriptions, intended to separate the small divisions of the over-all form. Differentiation between major divisions

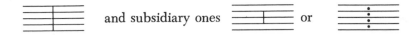 and subsidiary ones or

can be made, and both kinds of bar lines taken together would then provide a proper picture of the metric structure of the composition involved. Above all, care must be taken not to force the music into an isometric structure of the type common in Western cultivated music. If the transcriber encounters difficulty in deciding on the location of rhythmic divisions, he may do best by omitting bar lines entirely. In Western notation, bar lines are, after all, among the most obviously prescriptive features.

The individual differences among transcribers, their ears and methods, and even the differences between the ways in which a recording will sound to a transcriber at different times, are translated into considerable discrepancies when different transcriptions of one piece are attempted. Thus, the song in Fig. 3a and 3b is given in two transcriptions, one (3a) made by the collector, Frances Densmore (1939:228), the other (3b) by the present writer. This example shows the need for recourse to devices which are more accurate than the human ear steeped in one musical tradition. But in transcribing into Western notation, the student can at least eliminate some of the devices which are useful only for Western high culture music, for example, the use of key signatures which indicate sharps or flats for tones which do not occur during a song. Thus, the F-sharp in the Densmore transcription of Fig. 3 is quite unnecessary.

Since rhythm involves the relationship among small segments such as note values but also the temporal relationships among larger formal divisions, it is difficult sometimes to identify

Figure 3. *(a) Nootka Song, transcribed by Frances Densmore.*

Figure 3. *(b) Nootka Song, transcribed by Bruno Nettl.*

rhythmic and metric divisions and to draw bar lines at sensible places. It is advisable to use small formal units as well as stresses in drawing bar lines, and it is essential to make clear to one's self the criteria being used for each type of bar line.

A Suggested Procedure

While individual differences among transcribers and among musical styles to be transcribed require modification of any set procedure, the following one might perhaps serve as a point of departure.

1. Listen to the piece carefully; read all notes and available material about it, determine the number of singers, instruments, etc. If the piece is strophic in structure (i.e., if it consists of repetitions of a fairly short segment of music), determine the strophe to be transcribed first. The first one on the recording may not be the best one for starting, since it may deviate markedly from the rest.

2. Decide on the broad structural divisions, and note them with the use of some kind of letter scheme. (Doing this is more properly part of the description of style, but it is useful as a preliminary step to transcription because the transcriber benefits from having the over-all outline of a piece in mind before becoming immersed in its details.)

3. Determine the number of pitches and kinds of intervals. Transpose the piece to a key requiring few accidentals or leger lines, but indicate the actual starting pitch somewhere.

4. Notate the first phrase in detail. Make special note of points which present unusual difficulty.

5. Notate the rest of the piece or stanza in less detail. If several strophes are recorded, variations of the later ones from the first can be indicated by a kind of footnote arrangement.

6. If words are available, fill them in. Then use them, wherever possible, to help solve problems of rhythmic detail.

7. Slow the tape to half speed, and check the entire transcription, especially the points found to be problematic in step 4.

8. Using normal speed, check the transcription again; then go on to another piece.

9. A day or two later, check the transcription again, but begin at a point other than the beginning. Possibly one should start with the parts which presented difficulty, or with the ending. Rechecking of this sort should, ideally, be undertaken several times. But care should be taken not to negate, at a moment's notice, what was done at the beginning of the transcription procedure. This writer has occasionally made changes in a transcription and continued revising it until he finally returned to what he had originally transcribed.

Sometimes it is useful to make a rough, undetailed transcription of several songs or pieces in a style, and then to return for more thorough work. Acquaintance with a style in advance of transcribing is, of course, important; this can be gained in the field or by thorough listening to the collected recordings which are to serve as the basis for transcription.

Automatic Transcription

Among the objections to the use of Western notation for transcription is the view that it was invented as a tool for prescription, and that possibly the concept of "note" is not a valid one either for description of music or even for prescription of music in other cultures. As a remedy, the use of hand graphs has been advocated. Seeger (1958a:188) cites the advantages of graphs over notes in detail. According to him, graphs have far greater potential for achieving accuracy even when they are drawn by hand with the use of the same methods as those ordinarily applied by the transcriber in making notation. Exact measurement of tempo, rhythm, and pitch can be more easily approached if the transcriber can cast aside the concept of the articulated note as the main point of order. Rhythm can be represented better in a system which does not depend on dividing units into halves as does Western rhythmic notation. The phenomena between the "notes" can be better indicated in graphs than with notes. Fig. 4 shows a hand graph.

But a hand graph would not indicate the musical features such as timbre and vibrato which Western notation also fails to include. Here the use of electronic or automatic transcribers is important. The two reasons for using graphs—the failure of the Western notation system as a descriptive tool, and the ease of adapting graphic techniques to automatic transcription—should not be confused. The second reason is responsible for a long, and by far not yet complete, history of technical development to which ethnomusicologists, psychologists, physicists. and engineers in several countries have contributed.

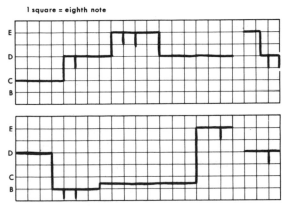

FIGURE 4. *Hand graph based on transcription in Fig. 3b.*

Among the first attempts to transcribe with electronic apparatus was that of Milton Metfessel (1928), who worked in the 1920's in association with the famed music psychologist Carl Seashore. By using a stroboscope which indicated vibration rates and photographing the oscillation of the pitch against a control frequency, and finally superimposing a graph against the photograph, he was able, by calculating each pitch, to arrive at a sort of graph notation. The method was complicated and expensive, and except for the work of a few scholars, it went largely unnoticed. Another attempt, using an oscillograph which eliminated the need for detailed calculations, was made by Juichi Obata and Ryuji Kobayashi (1937). According to Dahlback (1958:8), this apparatus registered pitch, rhythm, and intensity, but was unsatisfactory for lower frequencies.

In the case of Metfessel and some other attempts, the automatic transcription device was invented not for the purpose of transcribing *per se,* but for studying some special aspect of music performance. Metfessel wished to show significant differences between Negro and white singers, an idea also pursued in a project initiated by Fritz Bose (1952). In the latter, an attempt was made to measure differences in vocal tone color with the use of apparatus similar to that used by Obata and Kobayashi (1937). Bose (1952) describes his apparatus in some detail. His device, evidently a rather primitive one, does not seem to have played an important role in the later and more successful developments in machine transcription.

The two most important developments in automatic transcription during the 1950's were those resulting from the work of Charles Seeger and of the Norwegian Folk Music Institute, Oslo, under the leadership of Olav Gurvin. Seeger, who has pioneered American work in this area since Metfessel, began his attempts in the 1930's, and in 1950 he presented a paper describing a rudimentary "instantaneous music notator" (Seeger 1951). He describes the structure of the apparatus, which is based on the principle of a frequency net provided by an oscillograph.

According to Dahlback (1958:7), Seeger's work is based on principles similar to those used by Obata and Kobayashi. The recorder produces separate curves for frequencies and amplitude (melody and rhythm). The recorder in Seeger's first model was a Brush Development Corp. Double Channel Magnetic Oscillograph, BL-202. The pen of the oscillograph moved up to 120 cycles per second. This model, which could reproduce only whistling, served as the basis of a more advanced type: the addition of filters has made possible the transcriptions of singing as well. According to Seeger, his device, later named the Melograph, is superior to the Norwegian apparatus discussed below in its "directness, speed, and simplicity of handling" (Seeger 1953:63). But according to another statement of his, the device awaits various developments. Its accuracy and discrimination are much greater than those of the typical Western-oriented ear, and its recording of material on graphs allows much greater accuracy than does Western notation. Indeed, the Seeger frequency analyzer has "a top discrimination of about 1/14 tones" (Seeger 1958a:188–89). Rhythm and tempo can be reproduced in ways which also show changes with a margin of error of only 1/100. Accentuation can, on the graph, be indicated for the time being only by "manual superscription of notational symbols, such as, for example, of meters, bars, etc. But it can show, with surprising accuracy, the fluctuations of a basic pulse so symbolized" (Seeger 1958a:188–89).

The Norwegian method is described by Dahlback (1958:7–17) in what is so far the most detailed report on a project involving machine transcription. The project was an attempt to study the singing style of 125 Norwegian folk singers. For this chapter, the equipment used in the project is of greatest interest; but the importance of the project in the history of ethnomusicology should be emphasized as well, for it is unique in its detailed coverage of personal singing style and in its dependence on automatic transcription apparatus. The Norwegian device consists of a double cathode ray tube, the lower ray of which measures frequencies and the upper, amplitude. The series is projected on a screen, which has logarhythmic gradations to approximate the tempered scale, and is then filmed. A period meter marks seconds. Three filters allowed the fundamentals to pass but cut out other frequencies. It is the filtering system of the Norwegian method which enables it—in contrast to the early Seeger Melograph—to record singing as well as whistling. And it is the problem of distinguishing between fundamentals and other frequencies (overtones) on a machine which is the main stumbling

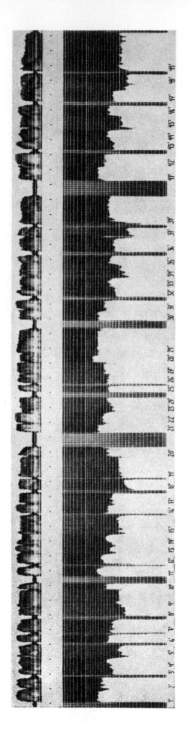

FIGURE 5. *Automatic transcription graph according to the Norwegian method.*

block in the development of really practical automatic transcription. According to Seeger (1960:42), the superiority of the Norwegian device consists largely of the elaboration of the filter system. Fig. 5 is a sample of automatic transcription made by the Norwegian method.

In spite of the very considerable accomplishments made to date, the field of automatic transcription must be said to be in its infancy, awaiting great achievements which are bound to come in the near future. Ethnomusicologists have reacted variously to these developments. Seeger hails them as bringing about a revolution in musicology, saying that "from now on, field collection and study of music of whatever area, occidental or oriental, and of whatever idiom of primitive, folk, popular, or fine art cannot afford to ignore the means and methods of the work outlined" (Seeger 1960:42). Herzog, while admitting the importance of the Seeger Melograph, writes in a somewhat less enthusiastic vein: "But the profusion of detailed visual data will have new problems of their own . . . and all this will have to be re-translated into musical reality and musical sense" (Herzog 1957:73). He also questions the utility of graphs in publications which are intended to convey information about non-Western and folk music to readers who are members of a public acquainted with Western notation but who would balk at the idea of reading graphs. Kunst (1959:38) is even less optimistic:

It is possible, by applying a mechanical-visual method of sound-registration. . . to carry the exactitude of the transcription to a point where one cannot see the wood for the trees, so that the structure of the piece transcribed has got completely out of hand. In my own view, the transcription by ear, in European notation, as nearly exact as possible, combined with the measurement of the actually used intervals, is nearly always sufficient for ethnomusicological purposes.

The "Committee of Experts" of the International Folk Music Council took a decisive stand in 1950 in favor of Western notation:

The deficiencies which this system presents for the notation of folk music can be overcome by the use of supplementary signs. This is all the more necessary because a notation tending to mathematical exactitude must necessarily depend on physical principles and would therefore entail the use of signs intelligible only to the specialists (International Folk Music Council 1952:1).

The Future of Transcription

Speaking very broadly, one cannot assert that the automatic transcription devices have made a great or obvious impression on the ethnomusicological literature of the 1950's. Except for the Dahlback study and Seeger's papers, which are primarily descriptions of apparatus, there have been few publications based on these devices and techniques. It is possible that the developments in automatic transcription have had a negative effect on the publication of transcriptions, for there has been, since about 1950, a decrease in the amount of printed music published by ethnomusicologists in their research papers. Possibly this is also due to the increased expense of printing music, but there is at least a possibility that the degree of perfection in transcription which is promised by the inventors of automatic devices has discouraged scholars from making transcriptions by ear. Such discouragement is not warranted. To be sure, the automatic devices cannot be ignored; they must be used whenever and wherever possible. The Seeger Melograph promises eventually to be only moderately expensive, so that many institutions could obtain it when it is generally available. Neverthless, at the time of writing only one institution in the U. S. possesses the Melograph. Seeger himself, the most outspoken champion of machine transcription, recommends that the two kinds of notation—conventional and graph (by which he presumably means both hand graphs and automatic graphs)—be used concurrently for the foreseeable future (Seeger 1958a:188). The value of transcribing as a learning device has been mentioned above, and its importance in this function should be stressed in view of the possibility that students of the future will rely on the relative ease of the automatic approach. In a sense, transcription by ear amounts to careful listening which is organized so that various aspects of a musical style can be perceived in some kind of order. Listening to a piece without the aid of transcribing it is, in a sense, like hearing a lecture without taking notes—something which has its values but which results in a more general, superficial impression than does the intensive listening with the help of paper and pencil. Thus we can, for all times, recommend the use of the long established custom of transcribing by ear as a method for students to absorb styles of music even if they will later transcribe the same pieces with automatic devices. Transcribing by ear does not, of course, preclude using a hand-graphing technique rather than that of conventional notation. But few publications of the past have made use of hand graphs to a significant degree. Some of those which have done so have used the graph not as a device to inject greater accuracy and greater detail into the transcription but in order to reduce to its essentials and thus to simplify the picture gained from the use of conventional notation. (See Densmore 1918:519 as an example.)

Besides the two main purposes of transcription, as a way of putting music down on paper for facilitating analysis and as a way of enhancing the information gained from listening, we must take into consideration a third purpose, the presentation of material in published form for consumption by the nonspecialist. This is perhaps the most problematic of the tasks faced by the transcriber. In the early days of ethnomusicology, transcription was the main vehicle for presenting the music of the world's cultures to the musician, the music historian, and the music-loving but not ethnomusicologically specialized anthropologist, folklorist, linguist, psychologist, and interested layman. Today, much of this function is taken over by good commercial recordings. The layman can satisfy his interests through such recordings much more easily than by laboriously reading notations which do not, after all, reproduce some of the most obvious features of the sound such as tone color (though these can sometimes be described in words). But the layman or the musician who wishes a closer acquaintance than recordings can afford could gain great insight from a notated transcription. He can analyze the material from viewpoints which cannot be accommodated by listening. Thus the publication of transcriptions in Western notation is of use here. There is, moreover, considerable demand for published notations of a combined prescriptive and descriptive character, i.e., collections of folk songs which can be both analyzed and sung. Here the ethnomusicologist can render considerable service, for his transcriptions, arrived at by ear and limited in accuracy and discrimination, are still of vastly greater value than the notations of certain laymen who have no interest in reproducing a song as it was collected from an informant.

Regarding transcription as a whole, we may, then, conclude by saying that automatic transcription is ideal, but that it does not allow the student to make the detailed personal discovery of a music which can come only from transcription by ear. It also does not provide the nonspecialist with material he can readily absorb; this applies, of course, to the specialist as well, but it is up to the professional ethnomusicologist to train himself rapidly to absorb the information from automatic graphs. Transcription by ear can also be done with the use of the hand graph, but no graph system is as elaborate or as widely understood as the Western notation system; thus the use of hand graphs can be recommended only for special problems. Western notation, on the other hand, incorporates some of the characteristics of Western cultivated music and tends to accommodate the transcriber's subjectivity which is usually rooted in Western cultivated styles. But Western notation can be modified and, because of the facility with which it can be used, it offers the most practical method of presenting new musical data in visual form. It forms the best basis for analysis and description of music.

Each ethnomusicologist should be well versed in the art of transcription by ear, but he should be aware of, and make clear in his publications, the limitations of this technique. And he should acquaint himself also with the apparatus and techniques of automatic transcription which, in the decades to come, will have to become increasingly prominent in his work.

Bibliography

Abraham, Otto, and Erich M. Von Hornbostel (1909–10). "Vorschläge für die Transkription exotischer Melodien," *Sammelbände der Internationalen Musikgesellschaft* 11:1–25.

Bartók, Béla, and Albert B. Lord (1951). *Serbo-Croatian Folk Songs.* New York: Columbia University Press.

Bose, Fritz (1952). "Messbare Rassenunterschiede in der Musik," *Homo* 2, no. 4.

——— (1952a). "Ein Hilfsmittel zur Bestimmung der Schrittgrösse beliebiger Intervalle," *Musikforschung* 5:205–208.

Brandel, Rose (1962). *The Music of Central Africa.* The Hague: M. Nijhoff.

*Dahlback, Karl (1958). *New Methods in Vocal Folk Music Research.* Oslo: Oslo University Press.

Densmore, Frances (1910). *Chippewa Music.* Washington: Smithsonian Institution (Bulletin 45 of the Bureau of American Ethnology).

——— (1918). *Teton Sioux Music.* Washington: Smithsonian Institution (Bulletin 61 of the Bureau of American Ethnology).

——— (1939). *Nootka and Quileute Music.* Washington: Smithsonian Institution (Bulletin 124 of the Bureau of American Ethnology).

Estreicher, Zygmunt (1957). *Une technique de transcription de la musique exotique.* Neuchatel: Bibliotheques et Museés de la Ville de Neuchatel. (See McCollester 1960 for translation in summary form.)

Gurvin, Olav (1953). "Photography as an aid to folk music research," *Norveg* 3:181–196.

Herzog, George (1957). "Music at the fifth international Congress of anthropological and ethnological sciences," *Journal of the International Folk Music Council* 9:71–73.

*International Music Council (1952). *Notation of Folk Music; Recommendations of the Committees of Experts.* Geneva.

*Kunst, Jaap (1959). *Ethnomusicology,* 3rd edition. The Hague: M. Nijhoff. (Pp. 7–11 and 37–46 are suggested reading.)

*McCollester, Roxane (1960). "A transcription technique used by Zygmunt Estreicher," *Ethnomusicology* 4:129–132.

Metfessel, Milton E. (1928). *Phonophotography in Folk Music.* Chapel Hill: University of North Carolina Press.

Obata, Juichi, and Ryuji Kobayashi (1937). "A direct-reading pitch recorder and its application to music and speech," *Journal of the Acoustical Society of America* 9:156—161.

———— (1938). "An apparatus for direct-recording the pitch and intensity of sound," *Journal of the Acoustical Society of America* 10:147—149.

*Sachs, Curt (1962). *The Wellsprings of Music*. The Hague: M. Nijhoff. Pp. 20—33 are suggested reading for this chapter.

Seeger, Charles (1951). "An instantaneous music notator," *Journal of the International Folk Music Council* 3:103—106.

*———— (1953). "Toward a universal music sound-writing for musicology," *Journal of the International Folk Music Council* 5:63—66.

———— (1958). "Singing style," *Western Folklore* 17:3—11.

*———— (1958a). "Prescriptive and descriptive music writing," *Musical Quarterly* 44:184—195.

———— (1960). Review of Dahlback (1959) in *Ethnomusicology* 4:41—42.

Chapter 5

DESCRIPTION OF MUSICAL
COMPOSITIONS

Analysis of music in
the American music curriculum denotes mainly the description
of the over-all structure of a piece of music, and of the interrelationship of its various sections. In most cases, indeed, it is
the fitting of this structure into a preconceived mold. The typical
textbook of analysis does not set out to teach the student the
principles and procedures used in describing music; rather, it
attempts to teach him the characteristics of certain specific forms
and then to show how well—or how badly—individual compositions fit these forms. The fact that relatively few pieces fit the
formal outlines which they are supposed to has not deterred
the writers of texts and some teachers of "form and analysis" from
continuing this approach. The result is that there is little methodology available for analysis of the over-all forms of musical
compositions, and even less for descriptions of smaller segments
of music such as scale, melody, and rhythm, and hardly any for
the description of timbre, dynamics, and tempo. The absence of
methodology in this case would seem to be a great handicap
in the study of Western musical culture, in which composers
have written about their own methods and intentions, and in
which a body of music theory in writing has long existed to
guide the interpreter of music. How much greater a handicap
must be the absence of such methology to the student of music

in other cultures, in which preconceived ideas as to the intention of composer or performer are likely to do infinitely more damage than they do in the description of Western music. This chapter does not attempt to provide the methodological foundations which we need. It will attempt to survey the approaches which are evident in ethnomusicological descriptions of music, to evaluate the contrasting work of a few scholars, and to provide some guidelines for the student who wishes to undertake the description of individual pieces of music and of entire musical styles.

We are faced with description of two kinds of musical units: the individual composition, and the corpus of several compositions. Of course the description of the single composition comes first, both logically and methodologically. Before undertaking the discussion of descriptions of bodies of music, we must study the problems of describing individual compositions. And before a scholar can describe, statistically or impressionistically, a body of music, he must describe the individual compositions in that body. To do otherwise would be to invite gross errors and false conclusions. The problem is, of course, that an infinite number of things could be said about a piece of music, and that we would like to restrict our statements to those things which are somehow relevant to discovering the essentials of a style, and to distinguishing it from that of other composers, nations, historical periods, or cultures. We are faced with two processes: first, the inspection and analysis of the material, in which objectivity and reliability are the primary requisites; second, the description of the music, which results from the analysis, and which must, above all, be communicative, and which must make some concessions to the reader's frame of reference.

In recent years few have been so concerned with the problems involved in the description of music as Charles Seeger. His publications (1951, 1953, 1962) have probed the fundamental problems and the underlying assumptions of musical analysis, and while they do not present blueprints for the practical side of our work, they are invaluable as critiques of the thought processes of musicology. Seeger is concerned with the distinction between music as an event and music as part of tradition (1951), and between the knowledge which one may gain from music directly ("music-knowledge") and the knowledge which comes from talking or writing about music ("speech-knowledge"). He shows a healthy degree of pessimism about the possibility of using language to make musical sense:

There have, I must say, always seemed to be excellent grounds for a hearty distrust of all talking about music. On the other hand there is the inescapable mandate of modern scholarship that there is nothing that cannot be talked about, provided only it be done in the right way. The musicologist is the one who obeys this mandate and tries to find the right way. (Seeger 1953:370).

Seeger summarizes a set of 21 working hypotheses for describing music, hypotheses which seem lofty and remote from the mundane work of counting notes and intervals, but which help to present the musicologist's work in broad perspective. Among these hypotheses are such safeguards of logic as his direction to exploit the various possible approaches in terms of opposites, i.e., to make a "structural" as well as a "functional" analysis; to use quantitative as well as qualitative criteria for data.

Seeger (1962) is also concerned about the problem of vocabulary in musical description. While his publication of "Concepts and conceptual operating techniques" necessary for describing musical tradition does not include terms which can be used in musical description itself, it does emphasize the need for clear thinking and for defining the basis and the limits of the work under consideration. It is hard to disagree with Seeger, for it cannot be denied that the terminology of musical description is inadequate. Based on terms used by composers, and approaching its object from a prescriptive rather than a descriptive view, this terminology has become hopelessly muddled so that communication among musicologists has suffered greatly. And in ethnomusicology, a field in which no prescriptive terminology from cultures under investigation is to be expected, the use of terms and distinctions based on the thinking of Western practical musicians seems to make even less sense than in the study of Western music history. It is a temptation to throw up one's hands, to say, "never mind describing the music, just let it speak for itself." And this may be a solution for those who wish to understand individual musical events without reference to their cultural environment, and without reference to the other musical events in the same and in other cultures. But where comparison, and even the possibility of comparative work, are intended, it is necessary to reduce the musical information to a form of communication which is readily understood and in whose terms comparison can be made. Thus Seeger's distinction between "music-knowledge" and "speech-knowledge" may perhaps be applied as follows: Music-knowledge may be sufficient for the understanding of a piece or a body of music in itself; speech-knowledge is necessary for comparison.

Instead of using speech, we might find the use of mathematical symbols a useful possibility, and, to be sure, the use of nonlinguistic symbols, such as letters and graphs, for musical description is widespread and should be encouraged. But mathematics as a way of communicating is not nearly as widely understood as language and, in the same way that music-knowledge must be translated into speech, mathematical symbols might have to be translated again, making it necessary to resort, as before, to the use of words. Inadequate as language may be for describing a nonlinguistic form of communication such as music, we find that it is still the most promising tool.

The typical textbook in analysis does not intend to give the student a tool whereby he can describe music however he may find it. Rather, it describes a body of music in terms which are applicable especially to it, assuming that the best way to introduce a student to musical structure is to allow him to see description of one kind of music in terms which apply to the style of that music. It seems to be taken for granted, in the best of these books, that different styles will cause the student to evolve different terms and methods. This seems unexceptionable; but students of other musics must be blamed for having used the methods derived from several European styles on the non-Western musics for which they should have derived (presumably from their "music-knowledge" of these musics) terms and methods appropriate to them. It would seem to be the task of the ethnomusicologist to derive a method which is equally applicable to all music.

Three Approaches to Description of Style

In the next group of paragraphs we will describe three approaches to the description of music. These three, labelled here "systematic," "intuitive," and "selective," appear in many publications, yet it is often difficult to identify them. The reason for this difficulty is that we cannot always tell, from a published description of style, what approach the author actually took in analyzing, and that combinations of approaches are perhaps the overwhelming majority. The approaches as outlined here are, to an extent, abstractions, but it is useful to distinguish among them as an introductory procedure.

The Systematic Approach. One approach to describing music is to identify all possible, or many, or, for practical purposes, a selected group of aspects of music, and to describe each of these aspects in an individual composition, or in a body of musical composition which, for one reason or another, are assumed to have something in common justifying their description as a unit.

The usual procedure in this method is to divide music into a number of so-called elements. In the teaching of music theory these are, most frequently, melody, rhythm, meter, form, and harmony or polyphony. In musicological studies a less practical but more objectively scholarly arrangement can be made; none is generally agreed on, but the following outline reflects the tendencies found in the majority of descriptions of musical style:

Pitch	Rhythm	Interrelation of pitch and rhythm
scale (enumeration of tones)	scale of note values (enumeration)	relationship of parts thematic material
intervals (melodic and scaler)	meter	polyphony
melodic contour	sequences of values	texture
formulas	tendencies	
timbre	tempo	

Many studies of bodies of music are devoted to only a few of the elements of music enumerated here; but the exhaustive studies touch on all of these (except where a given musical style does not contain material relevant to such description, such as a style without polyphony, or a study based on written notations in which no indication of timbre is given).

Many scholars are of the opinion that one would be able to produce an adequate description of a whole composition by religiously describing the elements of music of the composition in the form of this outline. Since the possibility of the analyst's being absolutely exhaustive is remote, there have been some attempts to analyze music with electronic computers. No doubt such an analysis would be exhaustive if properly programmed, but it would, in turn, have to be translated into ordinary musicological language. There is, moreover, no way of knowing whether a computer could distinguish between characteristic and noncharacteristic aspects of the music unless the programmer were able, in advance, to make the distinction himself. IBM punch cards have been used to identify tunes in the British folksong repertory which are genetically related (Bronson 1949), and this approach indicates that computers and other information-storing devices could be of limited use in the description of music. It is necessary to remember that description of the individual elements of music, without a consideration of the interrelationships and the points of correlation, among them, could give a misleading total impression. This applies, of course, whether mechanical aids are used or not. It is conceivable, for example, that two musical compositions produce exactly the same description without being identical except in certain super-ficial ways. Similarly, it is possible to find, in a statistical analy-sis, that 60 per cent of the compositions in a given corpus have a certain type of scale, and that 60 per cent have a certain type of rhythm. But this statement would not indicate that only 20 per cent of the compositions have both the rhythm and the scale indicated, and that the presence of both in the same song is an exception rather than a rule.

The Intuitive Approach. An alternative to the systematic, elements-of-music approach is one which attempts to identify the most striking, the most important aspect of a piece of music, or of a musical style. This procedure seems to be most rewarding in Western music, in which one can sometimes identify the com-poser's wishes and intentions. The question "What was the com-poser trying to do?" can be answered either by recourse to the composer's own statements or by the informed listener who, as a member of the composer's own culture, may be in a position to make valid statements about his music. To adopt the pro-cedure of describing the most striking feature of the music would seem less advisable for non-Western music (or any music outside the student's frame of reference), since one would in-evitably be struck by features in the music which either conflict or coincide with his own frame of reference. For example, he may be struck by the peculiarity of the scale, which may sound out-of-tune to him; or he may be struck by the fact that the kind of polyphony found is similar to a kind which he knows, etc. It is doubtful that a reliable description of non-Western music can be produced with this method; moreover, it would be difficult to be sure that such a description is correct. On the other hand, the intuitive approach may function as a check on the more reliable, but perhaps impersonal, systematic approach. Thus the student who has described the elements of music in a composition, one by one, could then proceed intuitively to find important features in the music which may have been omitted.

The Selective Approach. Many ethnomusicological studies

do not attempt to describe a piece or a body of music in its entirety but, instead, analyze only one or a group of related aspects. There are studies of scale and melody in the music of a given tribe (e.g., Brandel 1962), or of rhythm (e.g., Hendren 1936), or of melodic formulae (e.g., Hood 1954). Some of these studies are purposely selective of the aspect of music which they treat; others are selective because their authors have assumed certain aspects of music to be more fundamental than others. While no scholar can be blamed for studying one aspect of nature or culture which interests him, and nothing else, it is perhaps appropriate to criticize the selective approach as regards its contribution to ethnomusicology at large. The student who is beginning to work in the field of ethnomusicology, or the scholar who is trying to get a broad view of the musical culture of a people, fares better with a systematic, holistic approach to description of music. His great interest in rhythm should not allow him to neglect description of the melodic aspects of music, and the fact that a people exhibit in their music an unexpected kind of polyphony should not blind the student to the intricacies of the melodic formulae. The interrelationship among the various elements of music should be constantly kept in mind. After practice in systematic description of all aspects of a musical style, the student may wish to go into yet more detail in an individual aspect of the style. But this should, in my view, be done only as a part of what must, at least ideally, constitute a broader approach. If scholar A describes the scales of a music and leaves all else, he should at least approach these scales from the point of view that either he or scholar B will some day also study the rhythm of that music. To assume that successful and relevant study of one element of music can be accomplished is to neglect the overweening fact of the close interrelationships among the various aspects of music. Thus a description of only the scales of a musical culture tells us very little about that music. Scales do not live by themselves, and selective approaches to musical description should be considered selective for practical reasons only, not on the basis of scholarly principle. The manner in which selective description was done during the first decades of ethnomusicology indicates the great interest of the early scholars in melodic aspects of the music. And while considerable light was thrown on the music of non-Western cultures by this approach, the fact remains that a somewhat false impression was frequently given. Notions such as the inevitable simplicity of rhythm in non-literate cultures, the lack of classification of polyphonic styles, and the almost complete absence of terminology for description of timbre are partly the result of this selective approach to description of musical style.

Some Published Examples of Descriptions of Style

One way of learning about the description of music is to examine some of the analyses of and commentaries on non-Western and folk styles. Thus, before discussing the terminology of musical description and proposing some specific procedures, we should have a look at some of the publications which describe musical style. We are mainly concerned, here, with descriptions of style in which attention is paid to the individual composition; descriptions of the styles of groups of compositions is the subject of Chapter 6. Our task in this section is to see how descriptions of style in individual songs have been presented and how some scholars arrived at their techniques of description. The type of description with which we are concerned has been made almost exceptionally for vocal music; for that reason we are omitting the discussion of descriptions of instrumental music, but these could be expected to follow the same principles.

It is possible that an examination of published descriptions of musical style may not be indicative of the kind of work which is generally done in musical analysis. After all, few scholars are able, for reasons of space, to publish the complete results of their musical analysis. Few scholars would even wish to publish their complete analyses: a great deal of musical analysis (done by the student with the purpose of simply understanding the music) involves features which can easily be seen or heard, and the purpose of most published descriptions of music is the enlightenment of the reader or listener who will find some of the simpler aspects of the description unnecessary. This is especially the purpose of most analyses of individual compositions. As we move from analysis of single songs to descriptions of bodies of music, less can be found out through simple inspection of transcriptions, and the results of analyses, digested, are more essential to the reader. The following paragraphs are a discussion of certain selected published descriptions of music, beginning with description of individual compositions.

The tendency to describe each composition within a large collection is most evident in studies of folk music, particularly that of the British and British-American traditions. Cecil Sharp (1932) already made use of this practice, although on a selective basis. Each of the tunes in his classic collection of English folk songs found in the mountains of Virginia and neighboring states has the description of its mode and scale, in abbreviated form, according to Sharp's special system. Other aspects of music are not described, however, and it is obvious that Sharp, like many of his contemporaries, was most impressed by the relationship which the melodic structure of these tunes seems to bear to that of medieval music.

A more nearly complete description of individual tunes by Schinhan appears in a collection (Schinhan 1957) of songs similar in style to those published by Sharp (1932). Schinhan, after each tune, gives the scale (according to his system of classification), names the tonal center, and gives an indication of the interrelationship of the sections of each song with the use of letter-schemes widespread in musical literature. At the end of his collection, he goes into greater detail in describing the melodic structure, reproducing the scale of each tune, and indicating the number of times each tone is used in the song.

This very thorough description of scale (without accompanying description of melodic movement, formulae, etc.), forms a curious contrast to the neglect of the rhythmic aspects of the music. It is indicative of trends in ethnomusicology that Sharp's collection does not go beyond description of the mode of each tune, while Schinhan summarizes the individual descriptions in tables and statistical charts.

Flanders (1960) publishes analyses modeled largely after Schinhan's procedure, but with some added features. The structure of each tune is given according to the usual letter-scheme, and the relative lengths of the individual sections or phrases are stated by formula. Rhythmic structure is classified according to five main types which appear in the British-American ballads treated here. A combination of note-value relationships and meter is used as the basis for this classification. The melodic contour is described by a key word, such as "arc," "pendulum," "undulating." The scale, transposed so that the tonic will be *G*, is reproduced for each tune.

In each of these examples, British-American folk song tradition is involved, and the form of the description of the tunes conforms to the general style of the music. Thus, it is possible to classify rhythm and meter as falling in one of five main categories (corresponding essentially to poetic meters); it is possible to show the interrelationship of sections, since the songs can easily be divided into sections of approximately equal length, corresponding to poetic lines, and since there is considerable repetition or recurrence of individual sections so that letter-schemes are meaningful.

It is more difficult to describe the style of individual compositions in non-Western music, in which the concepts developed in Western music-theory, which form the basis of the descriptions given above, are not as easily applied. Perhaps it is for this reason that printed collections of non-Western music are not as frequently accompanied by the kind of tune-by-tune musical description as are those of folk songs. Roberts (1955) has published a collection of Nootka Indian songs containing what is essentially song-by-song description, even though the arrangement is such that the analyses do not appear with the transcriptions. Ninety-nine songs are involved. Roberts has concentrated on scale and over-all structure, paying less heed to rhythm. In contrast to the students of American folk song, she seems to be most interested in the form of the songs, giving the letter-scheme for each tune at least twice, first in a tabular arrangement in which the number of sections, phrases, or parts is the main criterion, and again near the end of the book, where the form of each song is laid out in even more detail. Finally (p. 209) a table giving the characteristics of each of the ninety-nine songs is presented.

Another example of non-Western music described song-by-song was published by Christensen (1957) in a study of music in New Guinea. Rather than relying on the formulaic presentation of Schinhan (1957), Flanders (1960), or Roberts (1955), Christensen gives a commentary on each of his fifty-two songs. He includes mention of over-all form, melodic contour, scale, rhythm, and—this is somewhat unusual—manner of singing, timbre, and tempo. This information is given again, in terms lending themselves more easily to comparison, in an appendix consisting of tables.

The examples of descriptions of individual songs discussed here are all more or less in the systematic category, i.e., they examine various aspects of the music one by one, giving their interrelationship but avoiding an impressionistic statement of what is most striking or what the composer was trying to do. Perhaps a reason is that the intuitive approach, applied to individual songs, may result in statements which have more the ring of "criticism" than of description. When this approach is applied to a body of music, it may be more valid, since it contains at least the statistical validity of numbers. An example of this critical sort of approach to description of individual songs is provided by Peacock (1954). Here, a "musical analysis" of nine songs is presented. Song no. 1 is described as follows: "Mode of G (Mixolydian); tonic G. This is a short song of a fisherman.... The melody consists of a single phrase, very pretty, but of a more restricted scope and with fewer ornaments than the other songs. Its bucolic color comes from the use of the Mixolydian mode (G)" (Peacock 1954:135). Rhythm is not mentioned, and the form is given only by implication. Emphasis is on the mode, which the author obviously considers the essential element of this song. But his song no. 3 is described in different terms: "Mode of D (Dorian); tonic D. The form of this love song is similar to that of the song which follows A-B-A. Here however the second phrase varies as it is repeated, with pretty ornaments, and, at the end, the theme A comes back slightly altered." Aside from the value judgments ("pretty"), this description is objectionable because of the discrepancy between the elements of music described in the two songs. If song no. 1 has bucolic color caused by the Mixolydian mode, what color is caused by the Dorian mode in song 3? Can the author be sure that he is describing elements of music which are actually the important ones, or is he simply reflecting his own background and interests? Since he probably could not tell what the composer was trying to do, he might have produced a more successful description by using a systematic outline. The intuitive analysis in Peacock (1954) is, we should say, probably indicative of earlier practices than his date of publication indicates. While the intuitive approach to analysis may occasionally show important features of music which do not turn up in more systematic descriptions, it is evident that, at least in music outside the Western cultivated tradition, it must be used in conjunction with the systematic.

It is obvious, from an examination of the systematic, song-by-song descriptions of musical styles cited here, that each description is made in a frame of reference based on the describer's knowledge of what the style is at least likely to contain. Making a successful and communicative description of a song without some presuppositions, without some things which are taken for granted by describer and reader alike, seems impossible. Attempts would probably founder on the elaborate terminology needed for establishing concepts and units, beginning with questions such as "What is a tone?" "What is meter?" etc. That such questions should be asked, and, indeed, that they have not been asked or answered sufficiently, cannot be denied. But if the task at hand is the description of music, then such fundamental questions may get in the way. The ethnomusicologist must take advantage of one of the universals of culture: he must take for granted that his reader will know what music is, and his description must fall within that frame of reference. But he should not take for granted is that he and the reader can correctly identify the relevant, the significant units and distinctions in any musical style.

Here again we face, as we did in considerations of transcription (Chapter 4), the distinction between music as a conglomeration of sounds, and music as communication with meaningful and nonmeaningful units and distinctions, and operationally, between the phonetic and the phonemic approaches. There is little that can be advised in a general way to solve this problem and to give direction to the student. It may be possible to differentiate between the phonetic and the phonemic distinctions in music, but such differentiation must come before actual description, rather than resulting from it. Perhaps one example of such differentiation may show its importance in description of style. Let us consider the environment of the individual unit. In the case of scales, it is not enough, for example, to state the number of different pitches which occur, or, in the case of rhythm, the number of note values. Attention should be given to the environment of each, to the notes which come before and after each one, to see whether the occurrence of one cannot be predicted from that environment. Thus, in examining certain eighteenth-century pieces, we find that the raised seventh degree in a minor scale occurs only when followed by the higher tone, while the lowered seventh is found when followed by a lower degree. The two sevenths, used alternately, could thus be considered different manifestations of one tone, not two separate tones, and while each has its distinct function, each is a complement of the other. Obviously, for this reason the two sevenths are considered simply the seventh of the melodic minor scale. Similar but also much more complex situations may be found in non-Western musical styles.

General Terminology and Procedure

While there is no generally accepted set of terms, or definition of these terms, in ethnomusicology, a large proportion of the literature does conform to an approximate standard in terminology. It seems appropriate to comment briefly on some of these terms and concepts.

Tonal Material. The procedures for describing the tonal material are fairly well established. First comes description of the scale, i.e., the tones which appear, without consideration of their role in the melody. (Ethnomusicologists have used the word "scale" to mean something rather different from what it means in traditional music theory. But since ethnomusicologists have also used the word to mean several different things, let us for our purposes define it as those tones—and the intervals among them—which are used in one or a group of compositions.) The first classification of scales is simply an enumeration, so that the terms ditonic, tritonic, tetratonic, pentatonic, hexatonic, and heptatonic simply indicate the number of tones in the scale. Octave duplications are normally omitted, although this may be a questionable procedure, since all cultures may not consider tones an octave apart to be so close in identity as do Western musicians.

Simple enumeration of tones tells us something about the music, but not really very much. Two scales containing five tones may be as different as g a-flat b-flat c d-flat and g a b d e. An indication of the intervals among the tones of the scale is important as well. Terms such as pentachordal, tetrachordal, and hexachordal indicate the number of tones as well as the fact that these scales are built out of successive seconds. We then proceed to a description of *mode*, another concept which has been used and defined in a number of different ways. For our purposes, mode is the way in which the tones of a scale are used in a composition. Thus, when we say that a song uses certain tones, we have given its scale; when we say that certain tones are important, certain ones appear only before or after particular others, and a specific one functions as the tonal center, we have given at least a partial description of mode. Scale and mode are usually presented on a staff, with the frequencies and the functions of the tones indicated by note-values—a practice started by von Hornbostel. The tonic is usually given by a whole note, other important tones are indicated by half notes, tones of average importance by quarters, rarely used or ornamental tones by eighths and sixteenths. Brackets and arrows can be used to indicate other distinctions, such as the tones used by each voice (see p. 162) in a polyphonic piece or the tones used in the individual phrases of a song.

Here we begin to approach the problem of tonality, which in ethnomusicology is a difficult one. (See, for example, Apel 1960:304.) That tonality also presents a difficult problem in Western music, with the exception perhaps of the music composed between 1700 and 1800, is evidenced by the large amount of literature composed of arguments about definitions. Nevertheless, in Western cultivated music one can talk about this elusive concept because the native composer and theorist is available as a source. For music in other styles, acoustic criteria based on the idea that certain intervallic relationships will bring about in man a feeling of tonal center, simply because of the inevitable effect of acoustical laws, have been postulated (see Hindemith 1945). While these may be valid, we cannot easily test the members of non-Western cultures for their reactions to descriptions of tonality based on acoustics. I do not wish to give the impression that I doubt the validity of the acoustic criteria of tonality; but I cannot find that they make a great contribution to the description of non-Western musical styles. If we are to talk about tonality at all, in ethnomusicological description, then we should use tonality as a concept directly descriptive of the music. And while counting the frequency of the tones in a song, and calculating the interrelationships of the tones in terms of their positions in the song, may produce results which violate the acoustical criteria of tonality, the information thus gained does tell something concrete about the song itself. To study tonality in any other way seems both risky and potentially meaningless; but at the time of writing, ethnomusicological descriptions of tonality which do more than simply enumerate the tones in the scale and indicate their relative frequency are rare.

Following are some methods which ethnomusicologists have used to identify tonal centers and to distinguish a hierarchy of tones in a piece: 1) Frequency of appearance is perhaps the most widely used criterion. 2) Duration of notes is sometimes used, that is, those tones which are long—whether they appear frequently or not—are considered tonal centers. 3) Appearance at the end of a composition or of its subdivisions is thought to give tonic weight to a tone. Initial position is also a criterion. 4) Appearance at the low end of the scale, or, again, at the center of the scale, may be a criterion. 5) Intervallic relationship to other tones—for example, appearance at two octave positions (while other tones appear only once), or appearance a fifth below a frequently used tone—is another criterion sometimes used. 6) Rhythmically stressed position is a further one. 7) We must never neglect the possibility that a musical style will contain a system of tonality which can only be identified by means other than those already known and used. An intimate acquaintance with the music of such a style would seem to be the best insurance against ignorance of such a system. Although the above criteria often conflict, most scholars, in their identification of tonal centers, seem to rely on a combination rather than a single one.

Other aspects of melody have been less formalized in description than scale and tonality. Melodic contour, for example, is usually described by very general terms, such as "arc," "pendulum," "gradual descent," etc. While a more comprehensive system of classification would be helpful here, the use of generally understood terms has advantages over specialized and rigid systems which—as in the case of scales—sometimes obscure rather than amplify the music to be described.

Rhythm. Since ethnomusicologists have paid less attention to rhythm than to melody, the methods for describing rhythm are much less well developed than those for movement in pitch. Sachs (1953) has attempted to provide some of the techniques which are required. But the concepts of intensity and stress in music have proved themselves so elusive that little real progress has been made. The study of length as rhythmic function is better understood, and length is easier to describe than stress patterns. Thus the best way to begin a description of rhythm is to count the various note values and describe their functions and environments, much as was done for the individual notes in the description of scales. Formulas and repeated patterns should be identified and noted.

Stress patterns, and ultimately meter, are more difficult to describe, and published transcriptions are not always reliable in this respect because of the desire of many transcribers to identify meter, and to show that their music has some regularity of meter. It is useful to distinguish among pieces which 1) have a single metric unit repeated throughout, 2) are dominated by a single metric unit but diverge from it occasionally, and 3) are not dominated by any single pattern. The terms "isometric" and "heterometric" have been used to distinguish the first from the other two kinds.

The definition of meter is bound to plague the ethnomusicologist, since it is a concept essentially confined to Western music and derived from special types of Western poetry. Rather than approach meter intuitively, the student is advised to identify it by using such objective criteria as stress and repeated patterns in note-length. It is true that he will sometimes turn out to describe something which is not exactly the same as the meter of Western classical music, but at least he will be describing an aspect of the music at hand rather than something which he only assumes to be present.

Tempo, a further aspect of rhythm, has usually not been described at all. It is usually indicated in transcriptions by an "M.M." marking, but this is only part of the notation, not of a description. Kolinski (1959) and Christensen (1957) have attempted to provide techniques for describing the speed of music. Their systems, essentially, express tempo in terms of the number of notes per minute (on the average), and this approach seems the best worked out so far.

It is possible to determine the average number of notes per minute from a transcription with a metronome (M.M.) marking. If, for example, the marking is ♩= 84 , one should count the number of quarter-note equivalents in the piece and divide by 84. This gives the number of minutes and fractions thereof which the piece took to perform. Then one should count the number of notes and divide by the number of minutes. The answer is the average number of notes per minute. This method of indicating tempo does not take into account changes of tempo; if these occur, and if each change of tempo is easily identified, each section with its own tempo should be treated separately in the way described above. Also, the aspect of tempo involving the length of beats, or the pulse, is neglected. But beats cannot easily be identified (or distinguished from half or double beats) unless the composer can identify them for you, or unless a percussion instrument performs them, or unless the notes of the melody are regularly the equivalent of beats.

Form. Form, with the specialized meaning as the interrelationship of sections, and the total structure of the piece including the interrelationship of melodic and rhythmic elements, has been classified in several ways. Unfortunately, labels such as "miniature sonata," "*reprisenbar,*" etc., taken from Western music and not descriptive but simply comparative in their function, have frequently been used and have obscured the form as it really appears. Two main problems face the describer of musical form:

1) the identification of thematic material, on which the rest of a piece is based, and 2) the identification of divisions in the music, that is, of sections, motifs, and phrases. The first of these, thematic material, tends to occur in longer pieces only, and for the ethnomusicologist it is primarily of interest in the study of Oriental cultivated music. The idea that there is a theme which is stated at the beginning, and on which the ensuing material—perhaps a whole piece—is based, applies mainly to European music composed after 1700. In the sonata form the distinction is very specific. But the notion that there is, somehow, a hierarchy of musical material in a longer piece, that there is primary material which is the composer's basic idea and on which other, secondary material is based, may be valid for other musics as well. No specific way of describing this phenomenon has been published, but the possibility of its presence should be kept in mind.

Dividing a piece into sections is necessary for describing its form. Criteria for division are repetition (i.e., a portion of music which reappears can be considered a unit); phrasing and rests (i.e., rests and dynamic movement such as a decrescendo may indicate endings of units); modified repetition such as a repeated rhythmic pattern or a transposition; units of the text in vocal music, such as words or lines.

The relationship among sections of a composition in which thematic and nonthematic materials are not distinguished is usually indicated by letters. Thus, a piece which has four different sections would be designated as A B C D. The length of each section, in terms of measures or note values, could be shown. Related but not completely identical sections are indicated by superscript numerals: A^1 and A^2 are variants of the same material; B^a is a new section which contains some material from section A. It is often convenient to indicate some other relationship of a specific nature. It is possible to indicate the interval of tranposition by figures in parentheses; thus, $A(5)$ is A transposed down a fifth. Devices of this sort are applicable to specific styles of music, and each style will suggest special ways of presenting its form.

Description of forms as a group is made by general statements of tendencies. Statements of this type might be made as to the number of different sections in a piece, the relationship among the lengths of the sections, the degree to which material presented at the beginning recurs, the extent to which special techniques such as transposition or variation are found, etc. All of these are properly part of a description of musical form, but no specific procedures or formulae for these statements have been evolved or generally accepted.

Other elements. Hardly any framework is available for the description of timbre and dynamics; but perhaps this is no great disadvantage, since preconceived systems of classification such as those found for scales and meters sometimes tend to obscure rather than facilitate understanding of the nature of the musical phenomena involved.

Harmony and polyphony do have some existing classifications into which these elements of music, as found in non-Western music, can be fitted for descriptive purposes. While these classifications certainly have their usefulness, they present the temptation of being made into procrustean beds. Moreover, we must not assume that a satisfactory description of harmony or polyphony has been arrived at simply because we have classified the music according to the criteria given below. It is quite likely that important aspects of the texture might thus pass unnoticed. But polyphony is such a complex aspect of music that some initial classification is probably even more useful here than in other aspects of music.

Western music makes rather sharp distinctions between polyphony, in which the interrelationship of two or more voices as melodies is paramount, and harmony, in which the succession of simultaneous intervals or chords is more important (but even in Western music all polyphony has harmonic aspects while in all harmony there is some interest in the melodic relationship among the voices). Distinguishing between harmony and polyphony, however, depends partly on the existence of music theory. In non-Western and folk music, we usually cannot make this distinction, since normally we can only view the material as outsiders without recourse to the composer's own point of view. We can't tell whether the non-Western musician conceives of the music as harmonic or contrapuntal, and to superimpose our own view is irrelevant. Perhaps we should assume that all music in which more than one pitch is heard is essentially contrapuntal, unless we know that the concept of chords is actually present, since such music is usually the result of several instruments or voices performing individual melodies, rather than of one musician performing chords. Whatever the case is, it seems best initially to class all non-Western music in which more than one pitch is heard at a time as one type of music, which we may for convenience call polyphony.

The two simplest approaches to description of polyphony are examination of the over-all relationship among the voices, and study of their note-by-note interrelationship. The over-all interrelationship can be described in terms of the relative importance of the voices, and of similarity or difference of their content. Two voices may be of equal importance or one may accompany the other. One may have a progressive form, without repetition, while the other has frequent or constant repetition. One may move through a large range and a scale of many tones while the other may be restricted. Again, the two or three voices may perform the same musical material at different times (imitation), at different pitches (parallelism), or in different variants or speeds (heterophony). The number of voices and the interrelationship of their tone colors—are all of the voices sung or are they performed on one kind of instrument? or is the music performed by a combination of instruments?—are relevant to a description of polyphony.

The harmonic aspects of polyphony are best studied through an exact accounting of the intervals found among the voices. If the progression is note by note, such calculations are relatively easy. It remains, after simply counting intervals, to indicate the kind of position which each occupies within its metric unit, phrase, or section, and which intervals are its neighbors. We may, by this kind of consideration, arrive at structural definitions of consonance and dissonance, based not on the acoustic properties of intervals but on the position which they occupy in the music. (See Kolinski 1962 for a lucid discussion of consonance and dissonance in world music.) If the progression is not note-by-note, more complex ways of stating the kinds of harmonic intervals must be devised. In the field of polyphony, the tendency to impose the standards of Western music theory on descriptions of non-Western music are perhaps the most tempting.

Manner of performance has been recognized since the early descriptions of non-Western music as an essential aspect of musical style, but it has not always been adequately defined. The assumption has been that a musical performance, as an event, consists of the music itself, which possesses a certain degree of permanence, and the way it is performed, which can be superimposed on the music itself. This idea, of course, stems from the Western cultivated music tradition, in which it is possible to separate what the composer has indicated in the notation and what is added by the performer. In traditional music this distinction exists only by conjecture, and while some of the phenomena usually covered in a description of manner of performance are important, the difference between them and the other elements of music should not be pushed too far. Ordinarily, timbre, vocal quality, and ornamentation are included here.

The idea that "manner of performance" is somehow not an essential part of music presents problems in musical analysis which can be illustrated in a consideration of ornamentation. In some periods in Western cultivated music history (the Baroque period, for instance), the insertion of trills, turns, and other ornaments was taken for granted and not specified by the composer. These ornaments could, in a sense, be considered nonessential, since their exact placement and nature were not specified, although their existence in the music at large was considered essential and is a hallmark of the style. But in non-Western music, it is not usually possible to distinguish between ornaments (trills, turns, etc.) which are essential to the music and others which are superimposed. Comparing different performances of one song may illuminate this matter, and informants may be able to make comments. But in a description of one piece of music, the only obvious difference between ornaments and non-ornaments is length: ornaments are made up of shorter notes than nonornaments. In view of this fact, while the term "ornament" may be admitted to indicate certain melodic features such as trills, because it may be descriptive to Western musicians, the concept of ornamentation as a special, nonessential or optional aspect of the music cannot be accepted without evidence from the music's cultural background.

Description of vocal technique lacks an adequate vocabulary. Designations such as "natural" or "unnatural" are meaningless, since all music is a cultural rather than a natural phenomenon. General terms such as "tense," indications of the use of falsetto and of the part of the vocal range employed, statements of comparison with other cultures are useful. Imitations of animal or instrument sounds can be noted. Obviously, ethnomusicologists have so far been delinquent in providing ways of measuring and describing various aspects of music. The "manner-of-performance" aspect can expect some help from the mechanical and electronic transcribing machines, when these are improved and more readily available. In several papers delivered orally, Alan Lomax has distinguished among about ten different kinds of vocal technique. These play a major role in his classification of the world's music into about ten areas (Lomax 1959). But there still looms the difficulty of communicating to the reader the character of a vocal style. Commonly used terms such as "tense," "relaxed," "pulsating," "pinched-voiced," etc., are very general and, moreover, seem to have meaning only to those already acquainted with different singing styles. One is tempted to follow the example of a student of South American Indians who stated that one singer, according to his compatriots, sounded like a cow, and added, "He did."

Other aspects of music remain, but the foregoing are the most obvious. Having commented on the customary ways of describing them, we may proceed to some sample minimum descriptions of individual musical compositions.

Examples of Analysis

It is not easy to teach musical description to the student of ethnomusicology. Much of what he may have learned in the theory of Western music may be useful, some of it will have to be modified, and nothing should be taken for granted. Description of individual pieces of folk and non-Western music, in ethnomusicology, must be more detailed than conventional analysis of Western music. A whole book could be written about each song; the samples here present only a decent minimum. In general, impressionistic statements should be avoided or labeled. And whether a whole piece, an excerpt, a variant of another piece, or an improvisation are being described depends, of course, on what has been done in the field and in transcription. Thus we see again how closely the various techniques of ethnomusicology are interrelated. While both listening and reading notation are necessary for description, the following paragraphs give samples of description of short pieces from notation only. (Figures 6 and 7 were transcribed by the writer, and thus the descriptions include material on vocal technique and timbre.)

No. 1. (Fig. 6) Arapaho song, not otherwise designated. Sung several times, but only one rendition in the transcription. Original pitch not given.

Scale, Mode, Tonality: Tones—g e c G E. This scale is considered tritonic, with two of the tones repeated at octave transpositions. The relationship of the tones is triadic, and the intervals between them are two minor thirds, a major third, and a perfect fourth. The frequency of the tones (in terms of quarter-notes—this is one way of stating frequency) is as follows: g-11, e-2, c-4, G-12, E-2. The fact that the two "G's" and the two

FIGURE 6. *Arapaho Peyote song.*

"E's" exhibit identical frequency is interesting. The note g appears slightly raised in the third measure, but there seems to be good reason for considering this pitch simply a variant of the tone g rather than an independent tone. The tonal center is G because this tone appears most frequently and constitutes the beginning and the end.

Range: minor tenth.

Melodic contour: Generally descending, with gradual lowering of the center of pitch. If the three-part form indicated below is accepted as the basic form of this piece, the first part centers about the tone g, the second begins on g and ends on G, while the third centers about the lower G.

Rhythm: One note value (quarter-note) dominates the song, appearing 29 times (counting eighths followed by eighth rests). Four eighth-notes and a dotted eighth-sixteenth figure are the only other note values. The grace-note in the last measure and the pulsations on the notes in the first three measures add to the rhythmic variety. This variety decreases between the first and second halves of the song.

Meter: Uneven, with units of four, five, and three quarters appearing. Stresses appear after bar lines.

Tempo: Quarter-note equals M.M. 120. Thus, according to the formula of Kolinski (1959) which designates tempo as the average number of notes per minute, the tempo of this song is 140. The duration of the song is slightly over 15 seconds.

Texture: Monophonic.

Form: Sections are not easy to separate. According to the points at which rests occur, there are three sections, which could be labeled A B^a C^b, indicating that the second section has material from the first, and the third, material from the second. According to the presence of repeated material, which indicates to some extent the length of independent units, there are five sections, marked by full bar-lines: A B A C D, which have the lengths, in terms of quarter-notes, of 5-4-5-7-11. Some of these sections could be subdivided, a new subdivision's beginning with each heavily stressed note, so that a third way of describing the form of the song (according to full and half bar lines), is a A B^1 A C

Figure 7. *"The Elfin Knight," collected in Indiana.*

B² D C B². Characteristic of this song is the presence of a closing formula for each of the three main sections, labeled B¹ or B², and the recurrence of certain formulae, such as c-G-E.

Timbre: Considerable tension on the vocal chords; falsetto on the high notes; pulsation on the longer notes in the first half.

Intensity: Quite loud, but diminishing in the lower and later portion.

No. 2 (Fig. 7) One stanza of a song in British-American folk tradition, "The Elfin Knight," collected in southern Indiana.

Scale and Mode: Hexatonic, with two octave duplications:

1   4   5   10   9   7   4   3   ] Number of occurrences
Final

The center of the range is used more than the extremes. The mode is related to the heptatonic Dorian and Aeolian modes.

Range: Major ninth.

Intervals: In scale, major seconds, one minor second, one minor third. In the melody, 23 unisons, 1 minor second, 8 major seconds, 3 minor thirds, 3 major thirds, 2 perfect fourths, 1 minor sixth, 1 major sixth.

Melodic contour: Generally undulating. Sections 1 and 2 have arcs, section 3 is ascending, section 4 an inverse arc.

Meter: Triple; the notation in 6/8 is probably no more justified than would be a notation in 3/8. One measure has an extra eighth; otherwise isometric.

Rhythm: Note values, counting each rest as part of the preceding note (this procedure may be justified here since the point at which a note stops and a rest begins varies from stanza to stanza):

eighth	35
fourth	4
dotted fourth	1
half	1
sixteenth	1
dotted eighth	1

The song is dominated by eighths, with longer notes appearing near the endings of sections.

Tempo: Average of 152 notes per minute.

Texture: Monophonic.

Timbre: No indication; no ornamentation.

Form: Four sections, coinciding with lines in the poetry. The sections are almost equal in length, and their interrelationship is expressed by A Bᵃ C D.

FIGURE 8. *Cheremis song.*

No. 3. (Fig. 8).

Scale, Mode, Tonality: Pentatonic, major seconds and minor

thirds among the tones. The tonality is difficult to establish, and may be described as changing with each line, because of the melodic material is transposed in each line. On the basis of note length and the importance of the cadence, the last tone of each line could be considered its tonal center. Possibly the repetition of rhythmic patterns and the basic identity of the four sections made the use of a strong tonal center (by the composer) unnecessary.

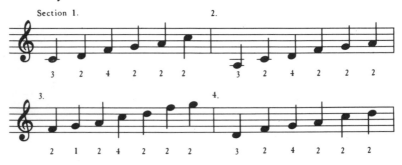

(Number of occurrences, section by section.)

Thus the tone of greatest prominence could be the final or the pre-final tone of each section.

Range: Minor fourteenth.

Melodic intervals: Unisons (8), major seconds (19), minor thirds (13), major thirds (1), perfect fourths (12), perfect fifths (6).

Melodic contour: Each section is an ascending and then descending arc; the over-all relationship of the four sections also describes an arc of sorts because of the considerably higher average range of the third section.

Meter: Duple, evidently with major stress every fourth quarter.

Rhythm: Note values—40 quarter-notes, 8 eighths, 8 dotted quarters, 4 halves. Halves appear only at section endings, dotted rhythms only in middle of section. The rhythmic arrangement is a repetition of a rhythmic pattern for each section, i.e., isorhythmic.

Tempo: Average of 153 notes per minute.

Texture: Monophonic.

Form: Four sections, of equal length and identical rhythmic pattern. Each section is a transposition, with some variation, of the first. Using superscript and subscript numerals to indicate approximate intervals of transposition upward or downward, the form can be expressed as A A_{2-3} A^5 A^{5-3}. If the interval of transposition is calculated according to the tones in the song's scale rather than the diatonic scale, the pentatonic intervals of transposition would be A A_2 A^3 A^2, with the third section a variant.

Polyphonic music requires the same kind of description of the individual voices as is done for monophonic music. This accomplished, a special description of the cumulative effects of the combined voices, and of the interrelationship of the voices, may be attempted. The samples of description below involve only the specifically polyphonic aspects of the musical examples examined. It is assumed that an analysis of the individual voices has already been made.

No. 4. (Fig. 9). There are three voices, the bottom one a repeated drone, the upper two moving in parallel thirds (major and minor, in a diatonic scale), each with a range of a perfect fourth. The middle voice occasionally reaches the pitch of the drone, but the upper one stays at least a major third above the drone. The rhythmic aspect of the polyphony is note-against-note. Since the drone provides the note of greatest frequency, it (the note C) can perhaps be considered the tonic. Since the interval C-E, sometimes with G added, appears most frequently at section endings (according to the transcriber's bar lines), it may be possible to assume even a tonic chord, C-E-G. There is evidently a hierarchy among the voices, the upper two a melody, the lowest an anchor.

No. 5. (Fig. 10). There are two voices, evidently of equal importance, with ranges which overlap on only one note. The rhythmic arrangement is note-against-note, with only occasional exceptions. The piece is presumably not complete; only an excerpt seems to be given in the transcription. The harmonic intervals have the following frequency: octave (6), major sixth (3), perfect fifth (9), major third (3), unison (1). At the beginnings of measures, which seem to be rhythmic as well as formal divi-

FIGURE 9. *Polyphonic song from the Caucasus.*

FIGRUE 10. *Polyphonic song from the Solomon Islands.*

sions, octaves or fifths appear. The two voices do not perform
the same thematic material, and tonality seems to be difficult
to define. Distribution of the tones between the voices is given
here:

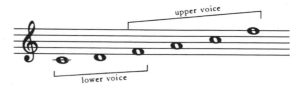

It is obvious, from the complex problems posed even by these very simple polyphonic pieces, that the description of polyphony is a complicated and detailed task. We need not wonder, perhaps, that most published descriptions of polyphony are relatively cursory and impressionistic, that statistical expressions of what transpires are rarely available, and that these descriptions are most frequently based on a single aspect of polyphony, such as the over-all relationship among the voices, or the intervals, or tonality.

Conclusion

The descriptions of musical styles of individual compositions presented here also indicate to how great a degree the student wishing to describe musical style from a written notation is dependent on the quality of the transcription and the information which is given with it. Notes on vocal technique are rarely given, tempo markings are often omitted, indications as to the portion of a piece transcribed are often not there. In polyphony, the number of performers, the kinds of voices used, reinforcement with instruments, the presence and specific rhythms of accompanying percussion instruments are often lacking. Thus, while the ethnomusicologist is frequently obliged to describe music which he knows only from paper, he is better off if he can have on hand recordings of the identical pieces, or at least of pieces in the same musical style.

Basic as the description of individual compositions is, it is of much less general interest than the description of bodies of music. The informed reader of ethnomusicological literature is usually able to provide, at a glance or within a few minutes, the kind of analysis which we have just given. Describing an individual piece of music is, then, only a moderate service to the informed reader. It is primarily done as a step toward describing a body of music, and for the benefit of the person who is doing the describing. Perhaps for this reason, descriptions of individual compositions are not common in the literature; and presumably such descriptions are much more readily available in an author's notes leading to publication than in manuscripts submitted for publication. Of course, the longer a composition, the more useful is a description of it; but curiously, the shorter and simpler a piece is, the more likely is a description of it to appear in print. Descriptions of the long musical forms of oriental cultivated music are sadly lacking, but they are not as rare for European folk tunes. In any case, the ethnomusicologist's greatest service in musical description is in the statistical or intuitive blending of individual descriptions into a description of bodies of musical creation—of musical styles as determined by composer, function, community, culture, or historical era.

Bibliography

Apel, Willi and Ralph T. Daniel (1960). *The Harvard Brief Dictionary of Music*. Cambridge: Harvard University Press.

Brandel, Rose (1962). *The Music of Central Africa; an Ethnomusicological Study*. The Hague: M. Nijhoff.

Bronson, Bertrand H. (1949). "Mechanical help in the study of folk song," *Journal of American Folklore* 62:81–90.

Christensen, Dieter (1957). *Die Musik der Kate und Sialum*. Berlin: author.

Flanders, Helen H. (1960). *Ancient Ballads Traditionally Sung in New England*, vol. 1. Philadelphia: University of Pennsylvania Press.

Hendren, Joseph W. (1936). *A Study of Ballad Rhythm*. Princeton: Princeton University Press).

Hindemith, Paul (1945). *The Craft of Musical Composition*, book 1. London: Schott.

Hood, Mantle (1954). *The Nuclear Theme as a Determinant of Patet in Javanese Music*. Groningen: J. B. Wolters.

*Kolinski, Mieczyslaw (1959). "The evaluation of tempo," *Ethnomusicology* 3:45-56.

*——— (1962). "Consonance and dissonance," *Ethnomusicology* 6:66–75.

Lomax, Alan (1959). "Folksong style," *American Anthropologist* 61: 927–954.

*Nettl, Bruno (1956). *Music in Primitive Culture.* Cambridge: Harvard University Press. Recommended reading, pp. 45–89.

———— (1960). *Cheremis Musical Styles.* Bloomington: Indiana University Press.

Peacock, Kenneth (1954). "Nine songs from Newfoundland," *"Journal of American Folklore* 67:123–136.

Roberts, Helen H. and Morris Swadesh (1955). *Songs of the Nootka Indians of Western Vancouver Island.* Philadelphia: Transactions of the American Philosophical Society, new series, vol. 45, part 3.

*Sachs, Curt (1953). *Rhythm and Tempo.* New York: Norton.

Schinhan, Jan Philip (1957). *The Music of the Ballads.* Durham, N. C.: Duke University Press. (The Frank C. Brown Collection of North Carolina Folklore, vol. 4).

*Seeger, Charles (1951). "Systematic musicology; viewpoints, orientations and methods," *Journal of the Amercan Musicological Society* 4:240–248.

———— (1953). "Preface to the description of a music," *Proceedings of the Fifth Congress of the International Musicological Society.* The Hague: Trio.

———— (1962). "Music as a tradition of communication," *Ethnomusicology* 6:156–163.

Sharp, Cecil J. (1932). *English Folk Songs from the Southern Appalachians.* London: Oxford University Press. Reprinted, Oxford University Press, 1952.

Chapter 6

THE NATURE AND DESCRIPTION
OF STYLE: SOME THEORIES
AND METHODS

THIS CHAPTER PRESENTS
problems but, on the whole, eschews solutions. For practical
purposes it is frequently impossible to describe a body of music
or a style of music except under the handicaps and disadvantages which are discussed. The ideal description of style may
be a completely unattainable goal, in view of the many questions
and problems which must be solved in the course of such work.
Ethnomusicologists must continue to work under these handicaps; to do otherwise would mean to abandon their work. But
they should constantly be aware of the conditions under which
they are working, and of the limitations which these conditions
place on their conclusions; thus they can at least evaluate these
conclusions and place them in their proper scholarly context.

There is no adequate survey of world music in ethnomusicological literature. There are a few works which indicate some
of the kinds of things found, and which divide the world into
broad, general areas of style. Nettl (1956) and Bose (1953)
indicate some of the tremendous variety, and Leydi (1961) goes
even into somewhat greater detail. All of these try to show that
all music can be described in the same general terms, that the
music of any culture can be recognized as music by any Western

student. On the other hand, List (1963) indicates several phenomena which may or may not be music, showing that even the broadest methods of musical description may not be adequate for all musical phenomena.

The ultimate purpose of description of musical style in ethnomusicology is comparison. It may be easy for a scholar to grasp the style of an individual composition by inspection, without having the elements of music which he sees or hears analyzed in writing; and it may not be too difficult for him to distill the essence of a homogeneous group of compositions But in comparing one body of music with another he must have some tools at his command so that he will be enabled to state verbally the similarities and the differences. And since he will wish to deal with any and perhaps all of the world's music, it is necessary for him to have a system of musical description available which can be used for all kinds of music.

We do not yet know the limits of the world's musical styles. To be sure, they are constantly changing, and certainly in Western civilization, the advent of the so-called electronic music and *musique concrete* heralds the need for radically new approaches to musical analysis. But we also don't know what the music of all of the world's other peoples is like. Descriptions of musical styles applying to whole cultures, tribes, or nations are still the exception. We have some idea of the kinds of phenomena which we may expect to find in the non-Western world, but we cannot be sure that completely unexpected things will not also be found. It is therefore necessary that the systems of musical description used contain as few as possible of the kinds of features which will lead to statements based on only one kind of music. Concepts such as tonality, meter, and specific kinds of form should be used with care so that they will facilitate rather than obscure the perception of musical styles in which similar but genetically unrelated phenomena are found.

One area of musical description in ethnomusicology is the particular province of the specialist in Oriental cultivated music. This is the analysis and description of the theoretical systems of

Oriental music, which may actually differ considerably from the music itself. The distinction between the statements of the musical theorist and the work of the composer and performer in Western civilization is quite evident. Whether such great distinctions exist in Oriental cultures cannot be said, but this possibility must certainly be faced. Thus, we read of tone systems which contain microtones—22 intervals *(srutis)* to the octave in the classical music of India. According to Bake (1957:206) these are important in Indian musical theory, but they do not occur in actual practice except in ornamentation, that is, two tones separated by one *sruti* do not occur successively.

This difference between a theoretical system and a practical one in the same culture also points up the difference between a musical system as found in the whole corpus of compositions and as manifested in the single composition. For example, the various scales and modes found in a group of compositions, when superimposed on each other, may yield a heptatonic scale, in spite of the fact that no single composition uses all seven tones. In the study of musical instruments of prehistoric cultures, false conclusions could be drawn if it were assumed that an instrument capable of producing, say, a diatonic scale (such as certain kinds of flutes) must actually have been used to perform melodies with diatonic scales

We have discussed in detail the problems of describing individual pieces of music, or perhaps more precisely, single renditions of individual pieces of music Such description, we have pointed out, is of use mainly in the compilation of a description of a body of these individual compositions. We have not even touched on the problems which result from the differences between the various renditions—by one or by several performers, between different stanzas sung successively and renditions given years apart—of the same piece, although the consideration of variants of one song would yield important information on what is significant and what is incidental. But description of musical style is most important when a group of musical compositions which have something in common are examined.

Musical Style and Musical Content

In musical terminology, distinction is sometimes made between content and style. Although these two aspects of music are logically inseparable, there are examples taken from observations of cultural dynamics which indicate that each may have a kind of life of its own, that each is capable of undergoing change by itself. By content we mean, of course, the individual musical idea—in Western terminology we might call it the theme—as manifested in the specific composition. By style we mean the aggregate of characteristics which a composition has, and which it shares with others in its cultural complex. When speaking of an individual culture or a single, unified corpus of music, we may have no particular occasion to distinguish between the composition and the style as a whole. Of course, a musical composition cannot exist without having certain characteristics of scale, melody, rhythm, and form. And these characteristics, again, are only abstractions which must ride, as it were, on the backs of the concrete musical items, of the musical content. It is when we study the musical relationship between two or more cultural groups that the distinction given here is especially useful, because it is possible for musical ideas to move from one culture to another and in so doing to change their character, and it is also possible for characteristics of a musical style to move without being accompanied by specific compositions or themes. Thus we may distinguish, in music, between content, the composition or its theme, and the stylistic superstructure, the nonthematic characteristics or traits. And the fact that this distincion is possible is of considerable value not only to the student of music but also to the student of culture at large. Let us examine the implications of this distinction in some cases involving acculturation.

The greatest problem in the study of the geographic movement and distribution of compositions and themes is the identification of genetic relationships among compositions and their variants. The study of such movement must usually, after all, be retroactive. Since we can rarely trace the family tree of a group of variants, we must begin by collecting musical items which we suspect of being related, that is, of coming from the same original form, and then demonstrating or disproving this relationship. And only when we have variants which can safely be considered related can we try to ascertain the effects of acculturation Finding genetic relationships in the vocal music of a single Western folk culture, i.e., the British, is relatively easy, for here there is a tendency for the verbal text to accompany the tune in its travels, and when text and tune types coincide in a geographic distribution, genetic relationship seems certain. But when a tune moves from one culture to another, as from a group speaking one language to another speaking a different language, there is rarely a similar transfer of verbal content.

A clarification of the term "genetic relationship" is necessary. After all, a man may take a song he knows or has heard and change it, creating what is usually called a variant. This presumably occurs when the style—not the content—is changed. Eventually, variants may become very, very different from their original or parent form. But a man may also make up a brand new song by copying, as it were, the stylistic traits—the superstructure, as I've called it—of songs he already knows. Now the two processes are obviously different: in one, the basic musical content remains constant and the stylistic traits change; in the other, the musical content is new but the style remains more or less the same. Yet when we find similar musical forms whose relationship is not clear, we can't tell whether this relationship is truly genetic or whether the forms are similar because of an identity of style. Mere similarity cannot be automatically taken as evidence of genetic relationship.

There seems to be greater variety in European folk music than in the music of a North American Indian cultural and musical area, such as the Great Plains. I say "seems" because this greater variety may be due to an objectively greater number of different phenomena in European folk music or it may be because I—a typical Western listener, perhaps—am more sensitive to distinctions in Western than in Indian music. In either case, the study of genetic relationships in the songs of an Indian tribe is more difficult than in a Western folk style because a large proportion of the repertory may exhibit similar or identical features, so that we would have to assume genetic relationship among all of these songs; we would have to assume that all of them stem from one original. Or we would have to explain the matter by assuming a practice of composition which is extremely imitative. There is no doubt, however, that both style and content are exchanged in North American Indian music. Willard Rhodes (1958) has shown the diffusion of a specific Peyote song among a group of tribes. George Herzog (1936), on the other hand, has indicated the acculturation of style elements in the geographic movement of the Ghost Dance religion. Here a type of form, which he calls the paired-phrase pattern, has by itself moved from its home, the Great Basin, into an area with a wholly different style, the Great Plains.

The style of the Peyote songs is also different from that of the other songs in the repertories of the various tribes which use Peyote (McAllester 1949). Most Peyote songs have some characteristics similar to those of the songs of the Apache, and it is presumed that the Peyote cult came to the Plains from the southwestern United States. But in the Great Plains, the Peyote songs have also taken on certain specific traits of many older Plains songs: they have the cascading melodic contour, the strophic form of which two long, similar descending sections form the basis. Nevertheless, they have the rhythm of Apache music. We may speculate about the reasons for the retention of certain Apache traits as against others which have given way to their Plains counterparts. The theory of syncretism, which Waterman derives from his belief that African musical features were retained by Negroes in the Americas because the Western musical styles which they encountered had certain similar features, does not seem to explain the Peyote situation. Is it possible that there are certain laws in the structure of the music itself according to which certain traits, by their own nature, tend to be more capable of being retained than others? Is there some element of cohesion or integrity in certain elements of musical style which enables them to remain intact under the strains of acculturation? Is it possible that the greater homogeneity of form and contour on the Plains made it necessary for the Peyote songs to take on Plains form and contour before they could be accepted on the Plains? And could it be that the smaller degree of homogeneity in rhythm on the Plains made possible the retention of Apache-like rhythm in the Peyote songs? In other words, could it be that the Plains Indians simply cared more about retaining their form and melodic contour than their rhythmic structure?

When a composition passes from one culture to another, and changes in the process, it must retain some characteristic, some spark or idea or motif which enables us to identify it and which testifies to its identity. No doubt various elements may be involved here. Sirvart Poladian (1942) believes that melodic contour, the over-all direction of the melody, remains constant more generally than other elements. Mode and scale, over-all form, and the presence of specific but minor earmarks such as a particular interval at a characteristic point, or a particular sequence of phrase endings—which Bartók considered the most reliable of constants—all of these could be the constant features around which revolve the changes which allow a composition to be greatly altered and yet to retain its identity. Among Peyote songs the rhythmic structure, which is related to the peculiar meaningless words of Peyote songs, is sometimes the key factor.

Moving to another side of our general topic, the matter of compatibility, described in publications by Waterman (1952) and Alan P. Merriam (1955), enters into our consideration. In order for acculturation to take place between two musical cultures, the musical corpora must in some way be stylistically compatible. Here the implication is that certain common features in the stylistic aspect of music must be present in both cultures before an exchange of material can take place. Presumably, then, once the stylistic and other cultural conditions warrant it, there will be a movement of musical content, i.e., songs, from one group to another. Following this speculation further, we should then observe greater approximation in style between the two groups. Thus we may find that musical acculturation may be an alternation of movement of style and content until the two cultures share a single musical culture. Needless to say, this hypothesis must be tested by observation.

We may ask, then, whether a law governing the existence or absence of acculturation in music could perhaps be discovered, or formulated, through quantitative approaches. We have stated that while a song can move from one culture to another and in the process take on characteristics of the second culture, it must retain some of its original characteristics. Would it be possible to break down a song into a number of traits—scale, melodic contour, mode, intervals, meter, etc.—and make a statement regarding the number of these characteristics which remain, and the number which are changed, when a song passes from one culture to another? Is it necessary, for example, to have a certain number of traits remain constant in order for a piece of music to retain its identity? Are certain aspects of music more likely to be these constants than others? Is there a hierarchy, as Poladian and Bartók imply? For example, let us imagine a song which moves from culture A to culture B; in making this move, it changes in a fundamental way its rhythm, scale, contour, etc., but retains the over-all form. Is it still the same song, or must it retain also a more specialized aspect of its style, such as a scale, in order to retain its identity?

A similarly quantiative approach could be followed in viewing the acculturation of stylistic features. It has been pointed out, for example, that certain features, such as the paired-phrase forms of the Great Basin area, have been adopted by the Plains tribes, whose music is generally quite different. Theoretically, it is possible for a stylistic feature to be passed from one cultural group to another without the simultaneous movement of specific compositions. Practically, this would seem highly unlikely in a culture without a written musical tradition. In the case of the Ghost Dance style, which is what the Great Basin style is called when found in the Plains, we know that certain songs were taught to the Plains Indians and that the Plains Indians then composed new songs in that style and adapted some of their old songs, especially those which already tended in the direction of the Ghost Dance style, to the paired-phrase form. Could we find out how much actual musical material must be passed from one culture to another before the second culture will begin producing its own material in the style of the first culture? I believe these are questions worthy of further study. Answers to them might help us to understand some of the specific musical phenomena which have resulted from acculturation.

Delimitation and Sampling

A body of music may be described at various levels. In the literature on the subject, the bodies of music are often not well defined, and the word "style" is frequently used to indicate a body of music which is described as having some homogeneity, without indications of exactly how this style is culturally delimited. In practice, descriptions of music strive toward statements of homogeneity, and the student taking upon himself the task of describing a body of music usually tries in advance to delimit it in such a way as to make possible an analysis which will yield a homogeneous picture. Frequently enough, a body of music as delimited by general cultural criteria exhibits a homogeneous musical style. But on the other hand, musicologists have occasionally picked, from a collection, those musical items which seemed to them to satisfy some ideas of musical style, and have neglected others. Such a procedure has, needless to say, limited value. A less reprehensible, but also limited, approach to describing a body of music is to accept a field collection as a unit, without questioning the degree to which it is representative of the cultural unit of which it is a sample. Of course it is often impossible to work with units other than the samples comprising field collections, but these should be taken as samples of cultural units, not as independent bodies of music with a validity of their own.

What kinds of bodies of music, then, are acceptable as units for musical description? There are many, and we can only give examples. Perhaps we can again make use of an analogy with language, which distinguishes between a language, a dialect—dialects of one language can be understood by speakers of the other dialects of that language—and an idiolect (the special character of the langauge as spoken by one person). Then linguists recognize the special characteristics of language as used for specific activities (e.g., scientific Russian is not very intelligible to ordinary Russians), of the language of individuals who are bilingual and whose manner of speech of each language is influenced by the other, and so on. Analogously, in music there is the over-all style, then regional substyles, village or tribal styles, and individual personal styles. Then there are styles used for special kinds of music, specific ceremonies, instruments, etc., and also styles which have developed under outside influences.

In contrast to language, which is most easily delimited at the highest level—linguists have an easier time distinguishing one language from another than one dialect from another—the greatest difficulty in musicology is deciding what is "*a* music." It is accepted that music is a form of communication, but unlike language, the listener does not know as readily whether he is or is not understanding a foreign music; thus the upper limits of musical style are usually defined arbitrarily so as to coincide with the boundaries of language, culture, or politics. Of these, language is perhaps the most reliable, since so much of musical performance includes, in vocal texts, linguistic performance as well.

In deciding, then, what is "a music," ethnomusicologists have most frequently used the music whose provenience is the same as that of a language as the unit of musical culture. This is essentially what the anthropologists have done in defining "a culture." These linguistic units in nonliterate cultures are often exactly equivalent to tribes which have a certain political organization—although the concept of tribe is a complex one, and although some so-called tribes consist of several very diverse units such as bands or villages. In the folk music of high cultures, the national boundary usually coincides with the unit of musical style, or at least it is assumed to do so. Ordinarily, then, the broadest musical style units in nonliterate cultures are smaller in area and population than are the analogous units in the folk music of a literate culture. Thus, consideration of the music of high cultures frequently appears in units larger than the linguistic ones. Descriptions of the oriental cultivated styles are usually in terms of national musics, but descriptions of Western cultivated styles usually take Western European culture as a unit despite its many nations and languages. Evidently musicologists tend to believe that "a music" at the simpler cultural levels is the music used by speakers of one language, and at more complex levels, the music used by a culture area.

The problem at the root of the difficulty in deciding what constitutes a unit of musical homogeneity is the absence of good measuring devices of musical homogeneity. We can tell whether two pieces of music are similar, whether they exhibit similar musical style, but we can only in very general terms indicate whether two pieces are more similar to each other than two other pieces. The tendency, in making such decisions, has been to use what was in Chapter 5 called the intuitive approach to description of music; certain striking features are weighed more heavily than others. Thus, Nettl (1956:141–2) divides the world into three main musical areas, largely on the basis of scales and polyphony, and without consideration of rhythm. The Orient and the Americas, because of their use of large intervals, are one area; the Near East, India, and Indonesia, because of the use of small intervals, are another. And Western Europe and Africa, because of their development of polyphony, constitute a third large area. This is an example of using special features of music to determine musical homogeneity without consideration of other features.

An alternative to using linguistic units as the upper levels of musical style description is the use of a concept called, after its general cultural model, the music area. Described in Chapter 8, it is more likely the *result* of musical description than the basis of it. Other units, similar to tribes and nations but smaller subdivisions of these, are villages, families, regions within a tribal area, bands. All of these bodies of music presumably give an indication of the *general* style of music in a culture; that is, a good sampling from each would indicate a style common to the entire population of the group involved.

Bodies of music exhibiting specialized styles may also be found. Styles of individual informants, for example, may not reflect the general style of a culture. This is also true of the styles of individual musical functions: ceremonies, work songs, love songs, ballads, etc. Music associated with individual instruments may also exhibit divergent styles, as may the music of professional musicians if contrasted to the music used by an unspecialized part of the population. Description of any of these specialized bodies of music is, of course, highly relevant to an understanding of the total musical culture. But frequently, music of a specialized nature has been erroneously believed (because other data was unavailable) to represent the total musical picture of a culture.

There was a time when it was assumed that members of nonliterate or folk cultures were unable to learn more than one kind of music. This has been disproved, especially through recognition of the fact that members of these cultures take part, in a creative sense, in the acculturation which many so-called underdeveloped nations have been undergoing. The fact that Plains Indians could learn, besides their own older musical style, also the styles of the Ghost Dance songs and of Peyote music and carry them on simultaneously, indicates that the learning ability of all peoples is about the same. The assumption that one can find out a great deal about the general style of the music of an ethnic group from one piece of music is obviously false. On the other hand, there is no doubt that all of the music used by one people must fall stylistically into one, or a few, groups, and that each of these groups of compositions has some homogeneity. There is no doubt that each song tells us something about a large group of songs in its culture. How many songs, then, do we need to describe the style of the whole group reliably? And what degree of homogeneity is required for us to classify a body of songs as belonging to one group? In other words, how can we proceed with the description of a body of music?

The statistical approach is the one most frequently encountered. Assuming that the musical compositions in question have some kind of common ground, be it that they are used by one group of people, or for one ceremony, or are played by one kind of instrument, it is possible to approximate a description of the whole body by describing a representative sample. How large should this sample be? Statistical theory has formulae by which the reliability of results based on a sample of the whole are measured. Stated simply, if the random sample is homogeneous, it will be reliable even though it comprises only a small proportion of the whole body; if it displays diversity, its chances of being representative are not as great, and a larger sample is required for reliability. In the study of traditional musics, the size of the total body is never known and, indeed, changes constantly; thus the relative size of the sample cannot be accurately estimated. In practice, ethnomusicologists should, and usually do, examine all of the material in a body of music which is available. Since they cannot know how much material was unavailable, they must evaluate the sample on the basis of its absolute, not relative, size. In practice, an analysis of about 100 compositions in a homogeneous style would usually be considered sufficiently large. If the sample turns out to be heterogeneous, a much larger sample should be found. This writer once analyzed over 1,000 songs from one culture and found that the description based on these was not really correct in the light of additional material found later.

But why should we even be concerned with the size of samples? Is it not enough to describe 100 songs without questioning the size of the body of music from which they are taken? The reason for these considerations, of course, is that we wish to know "how these or those people sing," or "what the music of that tribe is like." We wish to know the different musical types found in their repertory, and we assume that the information we gain from a description of their music will tell us something about other aspects of their culture. The orientation of the ethnomusicologist has almost always been directed toward a group of *people*, not toward musical compositions. Thus it is of relatively little interest to have the description of 50 songs unless we know just what, in cultural terms, these songs represent. This attitude is markedly different from that of some historians of Western music who have frequently used the description of music as an end in itself, and who sometimes analyze only in order to describe the aesthetic effect of a composition.

The ethnomusicologist usually works with elements of music, one by one, or with types of composition within one body of music. Both approaches are needed. Working with individual elements of music makes it possible to go into great detail, but it does not show the interrelationship of these elements. Typological study favors the striking, obvious musical features over the rest. The approach to a corpus of music by musical elements is essentially the same as that followed in the systematic description of an individual composition. The study of types of composition in one repertory is related to what we labeled as the intuitive approach, for the student proceeds by a cursory aural or visual examination of the material, dividing it intuitively into groups, and then checking his results by using a systematic approach within these groups.

The classification of musical compositions within ,a repertory or a body of music is related to typological description of a musical style. The presentation of large collections of transcriptions has frequently given rise to discussion of classification in order that the material can be presented in some sort of organized sequence. Thus, for example, Bartók in several of his collections uses the structure of the textual lines as the main criterion.

Classification of music itself is not a matter for discussion here. But the fact that musical criteria may be used simply as a basis for presenting material in a specific order is related to the intuitive approach of analysis in which certain elements of music are selected above others as the basis for description.

Authenticity

The theory that a culture or, for that matter, any group of people has its own pure musical style which is subject to contamination has played an important role in ethnomusicology. Authenticity is the word which designates the quality, distinguishing pure material from that which is not pure. Karpeles (1951) provides a good statement of the position. No doubt the assumption of authenticity is related to the theories which propose specific and predictable musical styles for various types of culture, or race. There are facets to this theory which make its application dangerous. The tendency on the part of the scholars interested in studying "authentic" styles is that they apply a double standard. They consider the music of an African tribe which has been influenced by another African tribe quite authentic, and the same holds true for French folk songs which have been influenced by Spanish folk songs. But they consider as unauthentic the English folk songs as sung by trained American singers, or the songs of an American Indian tribe if these are songs originally taught to the Indians by Western folk singers. This attitude seems curious in view of the fact that such a large proportion bears the unmistakable stamp of recent foreign influence. On the other hand, there is some value in regard for authenticity. The ethnomusicologist may be interested in musical utterances simply as events, without regard to their background, but he is more likely to be interested in music which is somehow representative of the musical culture and repertory of the singer and of the singer's cultural group. Thus, in studying the folk culture of the United States, a student will be served less by analyzing songs as they are sung by trained folk singers from American colleges than by studying those sung by Kentucky mountaineers. On the other hand, he will also perform a useful service by studying the songs sung by college folk singers. Only he should not confuse the two.

In considerations of musical style, we should mention the fact that some ethnomusicologists believe that authenticity can be detected through analysis of a musical style alone. They think that they can identify music which is authentic, and distinguish it from contaminated material without recourse to historical or cultural knowledge. Again, while it is possible that the so-called authentic styles of non-Western music share some traits, this is only a coincidence. The nonauthentic material today usually bears the characteristics of Western cultivated or popular music, and thus music which shows no or few Western traits is assumed to be authentic. But to take for granted that similarity to Western music is automatically a mark of nonauthenticity or contamination is to impose on ethnomusicology the very ethnocentric prejudices which it is one of our tasks to combat.

Is there a musical style and a body of music which is especially the property of each cultural group, and which can be distinguished from music which that group also knows, but which is of foreign origin? The interest in the "real" style of a people stems perhaps from the time, around 1900, when the idea of folk music was closely associated with nation and with nationalism, and when the students as well as the political directors of folklore were eager to cleanse their heritage of foreign elements. Another root of the interest in pure styles is the belief, formerly quite common among ethnomusicologists, that the music of a nonliterate culture does not change readily, and that the student, if he can only find a people's "true" or "pure" style, is assured of having material of great age. To a degree this point of view is certainly acceptable; but ethnomusicologists have no doubt that even in a relatively isolated culture, music does change, and even groups such as the American Indians and the Polynesians definitely have a music history. But the amount of change which these musical repertories have undergone in recent decades, under the stimulus of increased communication with each other, with Western civilization, and in certain cases with Oriental high cultures, must greatly exceed the amount of change previously experienced. Thus the student of a contemporary nonliterate culture may be confronted with a large amount of material which was acquired recently, and he may wish to separate this from the older material of the culture. Frequently he can do this on the basis of statements by informants, but often he must rely on his analysis of the musical style to make the distinction. Of course the thorough student of a musical culture must be interested also in the material recently acquired, and in the effect which this has had on the older music; to disregard the newer material because of its alleged "impurity" would be to make unsubstantiated judgments, and to neglect the obvious fact that the styles which now seem so ancient and pure would at one time have had the same impure character so far as an earlier investigator may have been concerned. And of course the study of musical change and of the interaction of musical styles on each other in a contemporary environment is in itself a fascinating one. Nevertheless, the description of the older styles of a culture, and to some extent the identification of older elements, is an important task. But we should, I believe, guard against an attitude which places greater value on the old, and which assumes the existence in the world of a group of pure musical styles whose change, in recent decades or centuries, is to be considered a contamination. Many collectors, especially those of Western folk music, have failed to describe some of the most interesting musical phenomena because they insisted on collecting only the old, "pure" songs.

Identification of the real, true musical style of a people assumes, moreover, that each culture has one main musical style, and a body of music which is basically homogeneous. This attitude is at the root of the many statements in ethnomusicological literature which give "the" style of a people on the basis of a few songs. It may be true that many nonliterate cultures exhibit a relatively homogeneous musical style. The need for keeping the music simple and for having it accepted by a large proportion of the tribe rather than by only a few avant-garde musicians is partly responsible, as is the fact that such cultures usually place little importance on artistic originality. But there are some cultures which have music in several styles, and roughly in equal proportion. The Shawnee Indians, for example, have songs in the style of the eastern United States Indians, in that of the Plains, and in that of the recently developed Peyote cult, as well as those of an archaic, simple layer present in children's songs and lullabies. It is possible, of course, to estimate the relative ages of these groups within the Shawnee repertory, but it cannot be said that any of them is more typically the property of the Shawnee than of the others, especially since none of them is the result of direct Western musical intrusion.

Still there can perhaps be said to exist some inherent thread of relationship between a group and the style of its music. Perhaps there is, after all, one kind of music which is particularly the property of a cultural group, in spite of the fact that we cannot assume an inherent relationship between the physical characteristics of a people and its musical style, and in spite of the fact that a culture's economic organization does not seem to have an inevitable effect on its choice of music. The reasons why a people use a particular musical style are varied, complex, and only very partially understood; some of them are explored in Chapters 8 and 9. In a consideration of description of musical style, we should, however, emphasize the interrelationship among the musical elements of a style as stabilizing forces. Thus the development of rhythm and responsorial performance in African music may have been responsible for the relatively lower development of melodic features and for the stability of meter, and also for the peculiarity of what Merriam (1962) calls the African idiom in music. While no culture can lay claim to exclusive possession of a musical trait, the structure of the musical traits themselves can create configurations of musical style which, because of the interaction of the elements of music, tend to achieve a degree of stability and a unique relationship to one group of people.

Examples of Descriptions

The following paragraphs discuss a selected group of descriptions of the style of bodies of music; while certainly not presenting a comprehensive picture of ethnomusicological procedure, the publications discussed here are a representative sample.

The analyses of Indian tribal music by Frances Densmore offer an example of a statistical approach carried out in a somewhat naïve and superficial manner; their very volume, and the fact that they are, in spite of their shortcomings, among the few descriptions comprising a large number of songs, justifies their discussion here. Densmore's *Teton Sioux Music* (1918) is the most detailed of this indefatigable worker's studies. She presents descriptions of the total Teton Dakota and Chippewa repertories as collected by her, as well as descriptions of individual song types within the Teton repertory. And she makes considerable use of graphs to aid the visual perception of the data. She classifies first the tonality of the songs (according to major, minor, and "irregular"), then the interval between the first note and the tonic of the song and between the last and the tonic. She indicates, for example, that the final tone is the lowest tone in 90 per cent of the songs. She gives statistics for the ranges of the songs, for the number of tones ("degrees") of the scale used in a song, and for the number of songs containing accidentals, and she classifies the songs according to the kinds of intervals used in the melody, labeling them as being "melodic," "melodic with harmonic framework," or "harmonic" in structure. She tabulates the number of upward and downward progressions in the meloldy, indicating that ca. 64 per cent of the tones are approached from higher tones, and she tabulates the melodic intervals (40 per cent are major seconds, 30 per cent minor thirds, etc.). She calculates that the mean average size of intervals in the repertory is slightly larger than a minor third. Rhythm is treated in terms of the number of songs beginning on accented and unaccented parts of the measure, the meter (duple or triple) of the first measure, and the number of songs (16 per cent) which have no change of meter. The drum accompaniments are similarly treated. The analyses of the individual Teton song groups (war songs, recent songs, etc.) and of the total Teton repertory are carried out similarly, not with graphs but with tables in which the songs tabulated are listed individually. The over-all form of the songs is not considered in Densmore's description of the style.

Evidently Densmore has done a thorough job of counting the phenomena of the songs in her collection. Nevertheless, her description of the style is in some ways meaningless, for it contains some things which need not have been done, while leaving others undone.

Among the relatively meaningless statements are those differentiating between major and minor tonalities. Here Densmore has indulged in a practice—which it is perhaps unnecessary to warn against at this date—of imposing the categories intended for one musical style on an unrelated one. The essential difference between major and minor, after all, is the difference between the kinds of third above the tonic note. In Western music between 1600 and 1900, composers, performers, and listeners agreed that this interval was of great importance so that it could justly serve as a criterion for classification of the tonality of an entire composition. But there is no evidence, in American Indian culture, that the distinction between major and minor thirds above the tonic is any more important than some other distinctions, for instance, that between the presence of the perfect fourth above the tonic in some songs and its absence in others. Moreover, Densmore's classification of songs as major or minor is intuitive in the sense that she had to classify many songs which did not have full diatonic scales, and thus had to decide what the missing tones would have to be. This approach, which is reflected also in the "gapped scale" analysis of Western folk songs with pentatonic scales published by some eminent European folk song scholars, has obvious dangers. Also among the less useful pieces of information in Densmore's study (1918:18) is a statement of the specific keys which were used—E minor, F major, etc. Again, these are concepts which mean something in Western civilization but not elsewhere. North American Indian culture does not have the concept of absolute pitch. A song is not to be sung beginning on a specific vibration rate. Nevertheless, Densmore might be giving us useful information if she simply stated on what tone a song begins. Studies involving pitch and vocal range, etc., could make use of this information. Similarly, we could make use of the information which emerges from statements classifying songs as major or minor. The professional ethnomusicologist can absorb what Densmore offers without accepting what is not useful. But there is danger in presenting a description of music in terms which imply relationship to other musical cultures. Thus, even a song which actually has all of the characteristics of the major mode should not—if it is not a European song—be classed as major, for such a statement would lead the reader to assume that the concept of major-minor was present in another culture, rather than to realize that—as is probably the case—the structure of the song is only by coincidence analogous to that of another culture's musical theory. From a consideration of Densmore's descriptions of style we may, then, learn the following: 1) It is useful to make exact counts of musical phenomena, and to present the results in statistical statements; 2) it is dangerous to take concepts from one musical culture and use them as the basis of description for another culture; 3) even when statements of this sort are technically correct, they may lead to false conclusions.

Densmore's analyses of her own transcription indicate that the quality and the approach taken in transcribing have a tremendous influence on the content of the description of these transcriptions. Especially in the description of rhythm is this influence felt, for there is much less standardization in the notation of rhythmic features than there is for melodic ones. Thus the placement of bar-lines, the identification of anacruses, or the length of measures in one piece as transcribed by several scholars could vary much more than the placement of the pitches. For this reason, statistics on the number of songs in a corpus which begin on an unstressed beat, or which do not show changes of meter, may or may not indicate something significant about its style.

The approach taken by Densmore is, then, a rather undiscriminating one. It is based on the assumption that anything one can say about a body of music is significant. Many students of musical style, especially those favoring a more intuitive approach to description, will take issue with such a point of view. The main purpose of describing bodies of music is, after all, to distinguish them from each other in ways which are significant in the sense that they reflect differences in cultural and historical tradition. Another purpose is to tell the listener what makes the music sound as it does, or what makes it have the particular effect on him which it has. Now it is quite likely that two styles as widely divergent as the Teton Dakota and a European folk music style have the same kinds of intervals, the same proportion of major seconds, minor thirds, etc., without having any basic similarity. Of course any two bodies of music will differ in some element of music. But could not the two musical styles which have identical proportions of intervals differ greatly so far as the actual use of the intervals is concerned? Does not the fact that certain intervals appear in a particular order, or that certain ones are followed by certain others, really constitute one of the essentials of the musical style? Such questions must be raised if we are to see a statistical approach to the description of music in its proper perspective. We may conclude that an interval count in a body of music can be significant for differentiating musical styles. The reason for the difference between two musical styles may indeed be the presence of many perfect fifths in one and their absence in the other. But if the latter style has fourths instead of fifths, the difference may be small or due to another aspect of music. Thus, in order to present a thorough description of a musical style with statistical means, many detailed studies of a sample must be undertaken. Densmore has made counts of a number of different elements of music in her Teton Sioux study, but there are many more which she might have undertaken; chiefly, these involve the relative positions of the musical phenomena. And a statistical description of a musical style which presents all imaginable aspects of the music has not yet been made.

Statistics in a more refined sense are used by Freeman and Merriam (1956) in a study not designed to describe musical style per se but to distinguish musical types on the basis of one feature or a group of related features. Specifically, their procedure was to tabulate the major seconds and minor thirds in the repertories of two cults in New World Negro music derived from Africa. The question posed by Freeman and Merriam (1956:466) is "whether or not certain groups of percentages in interval usage can be used as a criterion of identifying a body of song. In extension, if the measure proves valid, it should also be possible to trace musical influences which have played upon a specific group or tribe." The basic assumption of such a study is that the character of any body of music is unique, and that materials related to it or derived from it can be identified by measuring any aspect of that music if the sample is sufficiently large. This procedure is promising for differentiating and relating styles of music, but it does not tell what makes a particular style sound the way it does.

A number of special devices have been used to differentiate musical styles from each other in accordance with single elements of music, in ways similar to the use of interval counts by Freeman and Merriam. Among the most interesting are those describing scales and tempo devised by Mieczyslaw Kolinski. His method for describing the tempo of a single piece has already been mentioned. Kolinski (1959) also gives a method for describing, statistically, the tempo of a body of music, or rather, the average tempo of the pieces in that corpus. He shows that the music of various areas of the world can be distinguished by their average tempi, and, moreover, that the proportion of different speeds within the repertories also differentiates these musics. Thus, he indicates that the tempo structure of Dahomean Negro and North American Indian music is very similar, as indicated in Fig. 11. In the graph, songs are classified as belonging

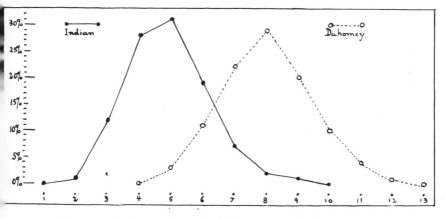

FIGURE 11. *Comparison of Dahomean and North American Indian tempo using Kolinski's method.*

to different speed groups. The figures along the bottom line indicate these speed groups, no. 4 representing songs with tempos of 91–120 notes per minute, no. 5, 121–150 notes per minute, etc. The importance of dividing the repertory into such speed groups must be stressed, for it is conceivable that a repertory having an average tempo of 150 has all of its music into the range of 140–160, while another repertory with the same average might have very few songs with a tempo of 150 but might instead divide its pieces between a slow 90 and a presto 200. Obviously, in statistical descriptions of musical phenomena safeguards must be found to guard against too superficial an approach. And of course it is of the utmost importance to have the units of the statistical scheme such that they do not conflict with the meaningful units of the style itself. An example of such a procedure would be to count intervals according to their Western names, lumping major and minor seconds together without accounting for the fact that the difference between a major and a minor second is as great as or greater than the difference between a major second and a minor third. In the case of tempo, a differentiation between significant and nonsignificant distinctions is not known. Thus Kolinski's approach is entirely "phonetic." He does not take into account the possibility that one culture may consider tempos of 150 and 120 identical, making it possible to sing one song either way, while another may feel them as radically different, one extremely slow, the other very fast.

Kolinski (1961) presents a scheme for classifying scales and tone systems. In Chapter 5 we discussed the description of scales of individual pieces. Here we are faced with a system of classifying and describing groups of scales, based on the circle of fifths. It is possible, of course, to classify single scales in this system, but its greatest use is for descriptions of entire corpora, and for comparative work. Kolinski presents each of the theoretically possible scales and then indicates, in detailed tables, which of them occur in Dahomean, Surinam, North American Indian, and British-American folk song.

The scheme proposed in Kolinski's classification of tonal structures provides for the placement within it of music according to three criteria: How far through the cycle of fifths does one have to go to obtain all the tones in the composition? How many tones of the resulting segment of the cycle of fifths are actually present in the specimen? And which tones are they? The scheme uses twelve basic "tint-complexes" (complete octave-equivalence is subsumed in this term), from Mono-type C to Hexa-type CGDAEB and from Hepta-type FCGDAEB to FCGDAEBF#C#G#D#A#. Within each tint-complex gamuts are classified according to the number of tints occurring, and listed systematically therein according to content. To prepare an observed scale for inclusion in the classification it is necessary that it be suitably transposed; and, at this stage, enharmonic and functional considerations are not taken into account. Finally, each possible tonal configuration is listed only at the earliest possible point of its occurrence in the scheme. Kolinski's illustration (1961:38) shows two scales, E#-F#-A and F-Gb-A, which belong to the three-tint group F-F#-A of the octa-type tint-complex FCGDAEBF# (no. 66 of a continuous enumeration from 0 to 348).

A fourth criterion moves away from the systematic to the analytical: "within each tint-complex several modes are to be distinguished according to the tint that constitutes the tonal center" (Kolinski 1961:42). There are several objections to Kolinski's method, among them the difficulty of identifying a tonic. Kolinski does not specify the criteria which he expects to have used in identifying his tonal center. Moreover, his scheme is only applicable to styles which have intervals no smaller than minor seconds. Nevertheless, it is an interesting exploration of new ways of providing descriptive and comparative data on scales and modes.

In the work of Densmore and of many other scholars who worked for relatively brief times with a large body of material, tabular, statistical presentation in which each song is accounted for is common. Perhaps a superior approach is that represented by the stylistic descriptions of George Herzog, who does not usually give detailed information on the features of each song but who presents a description of the kind of thing found most frequently, that which is found occasionally, and that which is rare. He almost always, like Densmore, presents a large number of transcriptions to supply evidence of his statements, and he cites some of the specific songs which contain the features which he describes, so that the reader can see them in the song itself, in addition to reading about it. Herzog's descriptions of style tend to be brief (as in Herzog 1928), and they function more as prefaces to the transcriptions than as the focal points of his publications.

In his works, Herzog stresses the aspect of music which he calls "manner of singing," and which includes descriptions of dynamics, vocal mannerisms, shouts, tempo. His descriptions of scale and tonality usually make use of the special features of the style rather than of a predetermined system used to classify the structures; the same is true of his discussions of rhythm, which are directly descriptive rather than classificatory. His discussions of form are more of a classificatory nature, for he distinguishes among progressive, iterative, and reverting forms, depending on the points at and degree to which they use material presented earlier in the song (see Herzog 1938:305). Probably his special treatment of form is due to the fact that while other elements of music could already be classified in terms of scale, contour, meter, the over-all structure of songs could not, except in so far as it corresponded to the established forms of Western cultivated music. A further feature of Herzog's descriptions of musical styles is his concern with song types. Having described the melody, rhythm, form, etc., of all of the songs in his corpus through thorough inspection, he tries to divide the material into smaller, more homogeneous groups (Herzog 1938: 306).

Herzog's method of describing style is largely based on that developed by E. M. von Hornbostel and Carl Stumpf, and has been used by his own students as well as by many other scholars. Its combination of detailed inspection with distillation is responsible for an especially satisfactory kind of presentation. Quite likely it requires a greater acquaintance with the material than does the approach based on detailed counts. These can, after all, be handled mechanically and worse yet, as we have pointed out, they include the risk of neglecting the important interrelationships among the elements of the music. Herzog's approach, then, contains some aspects of the intuitive approach to musical description described in Chapter 5.

A brief look at the methods from which Herzog's technique is derived may be in order here. Essentially, Hornbostel and Abraham, in a typical study (1906), divided music into the elements used also by students of Western music. Emphasis is placed on scales and intervals, which are measured in terms of cents. Rhythm, tempo, structure, and manner of singing are

treated in a cursory way. The approach is a mixture of the statistical and the intuitive, and there certainly is an attempt to
distill the essence of the style, to state what is typical, rather
than to give a detailed picture. Historically speaking, this method seems to have been tremendously effective, for it has been
maintained throughout the varied and the now not so brief history of ethnomusicology. As recent a work as Brandel's (1962),
which describes a complex and varied style in relatively few
pages, divides music into four main elements: melody, rhythm,
polyphony and form, and singing style. While melody still plays
the major role, the relatively greater emphasis on rhythm, form,
and vocal technique in Brandel's work is indicative of the trend
in musical description during this century. Those aspects of music
involving pitch were uppermost in the early scholars' minds, but
the others have now come to take their equally important place.
Brandel's description of Central African music is based on many
transcriptions, but except for occasional quantitative statements,
statistics do not play a role; rather, she presents examples of
what she considers essential to the style.

Densmore's statistical approach, refined and sophisticated by
the methods presented by Freeman and Merriam (1956), represents, then, one main type of the description of musical style;
the less rigid, more impressionistic, but possibly more empathic
method, represented by Herzog (1928), is another. These two
approaches dominate the serious ethnomusicological literature
to the extent that its purpose is simple description of style. A
third approach is represented by the work of Bartók and Kodaly.
It is perhaps motivated largely by the need for finding a system
for classifying melodies in order to place them in some sensible
kind of order in large collections. The most famous work by
Bartók (1925) may be used here as an example. The main criterion of classification is the number of lines per stanza, and the
number of syllables per line. Thus, the over-all structure of the
songs receives relatively more attention than the melodic characteristics. Within each category, Bartók describes also the
rhythm and the scale of the songs involved, and a summary of

each large group of songs consists of a broad characterization, in the Hornbostel-Herzog style, of presentation, melody, rhythm, ornamentation, etc. But considerably more emphasis is placed on form and rhythm than on the other aspects of music.

Some very respectable descriptions of musical style use terms and concepts which, rather than telling something about the music itself, describe it by indicating its effects on the Western listener. Thus Rose Brandel, in describing Central African melodic types, speaks of the "descending, motion-propelled octave melody" of the Watutsi (Brandel 1962a:83), and of a "quality of intensity and suspense" which "makes itself felt in a certain type of melody constructed on the tritone" (p. 80). Statements of this type actually abound in ethnomusicological literature. They have been criticized because they may cause the reader to misunderstand the author, who is—in most cases—trying to show the effect of the music on himself, and to use his own reaction as a way of communicating with his colleagues. Only the most naïve scholar would assume that a type of melody which, to him, sounds "emotion-propelled" must have the same effect on persons in the culture which produced the melody. Thus, Brandel (1962a:81) points out that chords in African music which have the structure of Western dominant-seventh chords enhance in the listener a feeling of unresolved harmony, but is quick to state that "there is danger in this kind of thinking, but it is mitigated by an awareness of the context with which we are concerned." No doubt the reader of Brandel's work, if he is sufficiently sophisticated not to confuse the author's reaction to African music with the African's own presumed reaction to his music, will get a better idea of the way the music sounds than he would from an aggregate of statistical tables. On the other hand, the trend in ethnomusicology is definitely away from such ethnocentric tools of description, for the world's music scholars are no longer exclusively Western, and there is no longer much use in sacrificing scientifically acceptable concepts and terms for easier communication.

Classification

The classification of compositions within a repertory is close-ly related to the problems of musical description. One purpose of classifying tunes, already stated, is to present them, in a col-lection, in a logical and rational order. Another is to find those musical items which are genetically related. Classification for the first purpose has been achieved in several successful ways. Bartók's classification of Hungarian folk songs according to the interrelationship of the musical lines is only one. Arrangement according to the range of the songs, or according to the kind of scale used, or according to nonmusical characteristics such as the function or age of a song, are all possible, and the char-acteristics of the style itself should determine which system is used. The kind of classification in question here has most fre-quently been applied to European folk music, for here is the area in which the largest collections have been made and pub-lished. During the first part of the twentieth century, a consid-erable amount of literature on this subject appeared. Herzog (1950:1048–49) provides a list of some of the more prominent publications.

Classification of music according to genetic relationship is much more difficult, and involves the fact that it is not really possible to present concrete proof that two tunes are actually derived from the same parent. Since music in oral tradition is easily changed, and since we usually know only contemporary versions of songs rather than their original forms, we must rely on external evidence, primarily that of simple similarity, to help us establish the genetic relationship. Here we should consider, again, the difference between the actual musical content of a piece, i.e., that part which distinguishes it from all other pieces even if these have similar or, perhaps, identical elements of music, and the style.

Classification of composition within a repertory may itself function as a kind of stylistic description. For example, George Herzog's descriptions usually end in a division of the corpus into "types." What he is doing in establishing them is something analogous to what the music historian does in describing pieces of music simply by classing them according to certain previously described types, e.g., sonata, rondo, fugue, etc. Herzog's procedure is to develop in each repertory a classification, based on his corpus of material, and to describe the style of each group systematically (see Herzog 1938:307–8). Of course all of the songs in a given group do not exhibit similarity in style in all elements of music, but they are identical in certain features. Selection of these features presupposes an intuitive approach on the part of the student. Having established his types, however, the ethnomusicologist hopes that he will be able to class future compositions in the repertory with which he is concerned within the typology. Classification, then, becomes a substitute for description.

Such a procedure is, of course, both acceptable and practical, but criticism of the classification itself is essential. Historians of Western music have sometimes fallen upon the error of overemphasizing the classification. Thus, they have classed rondos of the eighteenth century together and neglected the vast differences among individual forms of this genre. They have established a model for the form of the fugue, and without sufficient emphasis of the degree to which individual fugues diverge from this model, they have fruitlessly spent time trying to fit the fugues of various composers into their preconceived mold. Moreover, they have sometimes confused descriptive classification with the classification given to works of music by the composers of these works. And while it is, for instance, of great interest to find that certain works by Haydn and Hindemith carry the same title, "Sonata," this does not absolve the scholar from analyzing these works individually, and from noting that the forms of the two "sonatas" have very little in common. The lessons to the ethnomusicologist are obvious.

Lomax (1962) has devised a system which he calls "cantometrics," and which, by an elaborate system of classification, attempts to describe the chief traits of bodies of music, though it can also be used to describe individual pieces. By an elaborate coding system, using recordings—not transcriptions—Lomax assigns to spaces on a graph the manifestations of 37 different criteria. Out of these emerges a "profile," which he then uses to draw certain conclusions about the relationship between the musical style and the culture type of the performing group. For example, his first criterion is "organization of the vocal group"; this is rated "in terms of increasing group dominance and integration. The line asks the question: 'Is the performance a solo by a leader with a passive audience . . . or is the group in some way active in relation to the leader?'" If point 2 on the graph is checked, this means that the leader dominates completely. "Points 3 and 4 represent other solor singing situations. . . . Points 5 and 6 denote simple unison singing. . . . Points 10, 11, and 12 denote what we term interlocked relationship, i.e., when a part of a singing group overlaps another or performs a supportive function" (Lomax 1962:429). Intermediate numbers indicate intermediate stages in the degree of dominance of the leader. And in this manner various elements of musical performance—relation of orchestra to singer, tonal blend, melodic shape, type of polyphony and many others—are rated.

The main criticism levelled at Lomax's cantometrics is the subjectivity of the rating procedure, and this no doubt will prevent its general acceptance. The advantages of the system are that it can be used by individuals with little technical training in music, and that it stresses aspects of musical performance which do not usually emerge from transcriptions. But there is a question—since the judgments are admittedly "qualitative" (Lomax 1962:427)—whether the graphs tell us the same things which have in the past been expressed in prose, and whether they are a better form of communication.

Determinants of Musical Style

Perhaps the most fundamental questions which ethnomusicologists have tried to answer are "What makes the musical style of a people the way it is? Why do certain peoples sing in one style, others in a different style, etc.?" These are questions which involve not only description and study of the musical styles themselves, but also—and perhaps primarily—study of the cultural background and context of the music. Some of the theories which attempt to answer these questions rely primarily on the characteristics of musical style itself, and it is these which we should consider here.

One kind of theory is evolutionistic in orientation, assuming that all musical cultures pass, inevitably, through certain stages. The differences among the world's musical styles, according to this theory, are due to the fact that various cultures are found at various levels of evolution, but that all of these, if left alone and uninfluenced by each other, would pass through the same stages, including even the kinds of styles found in Western civilization. Few ethnomusicologists would claim adherence to this theory at its most blatant level, but traces of it are found in many studies. Even so distinguished a scholar as Curt Sachs, in his various works (e.g., Sachs 1962) seems to believe that different levels of culture produce different kinds of music, and that each musical style is bound to change into the next one. His division of music into earliest, later, and latest styles, mainly on the basis of the number of tones in the scales, indicates this. There are, no doubt, many cultures whose music history reflects an evolutionary scale. After all, the evolutionary schemes postulated usually assign the earliest spot to the least complex material and move on, from simple to complex; and no doubt the musical development of many cultures has moved in this direction. The objection to evolutionist theories is simply that there is no evidence that all cultures inevitably pass through a predetermined series of stages, and that the style of a music is determined by its position in the evolutionary scale. Moreover, there are instances of cultures moving from more to less complex music, for example, the change from complex counterpoint to homophony in eighteenth-century Europe. Also, we must not forget that our measuring devices for degrees of complexity in music are very poorly developed. Nevertheless, the idea that a people's musical style is determined by its level of development has had a tremendous impact on ethnomusicological research and writing.

Somewhat related is the type of theory according to which the kind of culture which a group possesses determines the style of its music. Surely there is much to be said for this theory, for the relationship between the musical experience and other aspects of life is so close that we must take for granted the possibility of such determination. Some of these theories, of course, go further, stating that all groups which have one type of culture will inevitably have one kind of musical style.

For example, some anthropologists (mainly of the early twentieth century) have divided the world's nonliterate cultures into three types, according to the bases of their economies—hunters, herders, and cultivators. Schneider (1957:13) gives a corresponding musical classification, saying that "among the hunters, musical performance is interspersed with much shouting," that among the cultivators, "an *arioso* style of performance prevails," while the pastoral peoples occupy a kind of middle ground between these two. Evolutionist overtones are found here as well, for the inevitable historical development, according to this theory, is from gathering to hunting and on to herding and farming, and so on to high urban civilization. The problem encountered by those who wish to make use of this theory is that it is on the one hand difficult to classify cultures and on the other hand difficult to classify the musical styles. And while many examples may show the kind of correlation shown by Schneider, there is still no proof that this correlation is inevitable.

A similar theory of Curt Sachs' has also played a prominent role in ethnomusicological literature. According to him, cultures are divided into matriarchal and patriarchal, according to the relative positions of men and women. Those cultures which are matriarchal, that is, in which women occupy a position of greater importance, have quieter singing styles, and use smaller intervals in melody and smaller steps in dancing, than do the patriarchal cultures. Again, this theory, while of great interest, does not seem to be borne out by a sufficient number of examples. Related to this approach is another viewpoint of Marius Schneider's (1957:13), according to which men play a greater role in hunting cultures while women play more of a part in agricultural groups. Correlated is the predominance of meter and of counterpoint among hunters (men), as opposed to the importance of melody and chordal harmony among cultivators (women). This theory cannot be properly evaluated without considerably more accurate descriptions of musical styles than are now available. But the difficulty of deciding whether a culture is mainly a hunting one, or whether men are actually more important, is exceeded only by the difficulty of deciding, in a piece of music, whether meter predominates over melody, and whether the harmonic or the contrapuntal aspects in a polyphonic piece are more important. Neverthless, we cannot abandon the notion that the type of culture will give us some indication as to the type of music. Most ethnomusicologists, for example, accept a very general correlation between complexity of culture at large and complexity of musical style. But they also take for granted the many exceptions to this correlation.

The relationship of musical style and race is one of the earliest theories in ethnomusicology. The idea that members of one racial group will inevitably sing in a certain way is not generally credited any more, and it is taken for granted that members of any race are able, if exposed to it, to learn any musical style. But the idea that each race has a musical style which is most natural to it is still accepted by some scholars. Thus, Schneider (1957:13) says, "race shows itself by timbre, by the general rhythm of movement, and by types of melody," and "racial characteristics in music are easily detected when one actually hears a singer, but they cannot be described in words." The similarity of music exhibited by cultures which share racial characteristics is usually explained by the geographical and cultural proximity of these groups. But since there are, indeed, physical characteristics which set off one racial group from another, we cannot reject the possibility that differences in musical style can come about through racial differences alone. Little conclusive research has been done because it is so difficult to remove cultural factors. Bose (1952) attempts to show that there are differences between the singing of Negroes and whites even when these are members of the same cultural group; but these differences are found in voice quality, not in the style of the music itself. Metfessel (1928), an early attempt to transcribe music photographically, is similarly inconclusive. Therefore we cannot, for the time being, accept the theory that race determines musical style.

Clearly we are not in a position to decide why musical styles have developed in certain directions and what makes them the way they are. We can identify a number of factors, but we can only speculate about laws and we certainly cannot predict musical behavior. Some of the attempts to formulate laws as the basis for such prediction are discussed in Chapter 8. We should mention here, however, the idea that musical factors themselves, in relationship to certain universals in the psychology of music, may determine the direction in which a style develops. For example, in cultures whose musical material must be passed on through oral tradition alone, it may be necessary for certain unifying devices to be maintained in order to serve as mnemonic aids. Music in such cultures can perhaps become complex in one or two of its elements, but not simultaneously in all of them, for complexity at too many levels might make it impossible for this material to live in the memories of people who cannot use notation as an aid to memory. This theory, however, like all of those involving the determinants of musical style, remains to be tested against the hard facts. We must conclude that ethnomusicology, so far as its understanding of the nature of musical style and its ability to describe style beyond that of the individual composition are concerned, is only scratching the surface of its ultimate task.

Bibliography

Bake, Arnold (1957). "The Music of India," in Egon Wellesz, ed., *Ancient and Oriental Music*. London: Oxford University Press, pp. 195–227. (The New Oxford History of Music, vol. 1.)

Bartók. Béla (1925). *Die ungarische Volksmusik*. Berlin. English translation: *Hungarian Folk Music*. London: Oxford University Press, 1931.

Bose, Fritz (1952). "Messbare Rassenunterschiede in der Musik," *Homo* 2, no. 4.

———— (1953). *Musikalische Völkerkunde*. Zürich: Atlantis.

Brandel, Rose (1962). *The Music of Central Africa; An Ethnomusicological Study*. The Hague: M. Nijhoff.

———— (1962a). "Types of melodic movement in central Africa," *Ethnomusicology* 6:75–87.

Densmore, Frances (1918). *Teton Sioux Music*. Washington: Smithsonian Institution. (Bulletin 61 of the Bureau of American Ethnology.)

*Freeman, Linton C., and Alan P. Merriam (1956). "Statistical classification in anthropology: an application to ethnomusicology," *American Anthropologist* 58:464–472.

*Herzog, George (1928). "The Yuman musical style," *Journal of American Folklore* 41:183–231.

———— (1936). *Research in Primitive and Folk Music in the United States*. Washington: American Council of Learned Societies, Bulletin 24.

———— (1938). "A comparison of Pueblo and Pima musical styles," *Journal of American Folklore* 49:283–417.

*———— (1950). "Song," in Funk and Wagnall's *Standard Dictionary of Folklore, Mythology, and Legend*, vol. 2. New York: Funk and Wagnall.

Hornbostel, Erich M. von, and Otto Abraham, (1906). "Phonographierte Indianermelodien aus Britisch Columbia," in *Boas Anniversary Volume*. New York: J. J. Augustin.

*Karpeles, Maud (1951). "Concerning authenticity," *Journal of the International Folk Music Council* 3:10–14.

*Kolinski, Mieczyslaw (1959). "The evaluation of tempo," *Ethnomusicology* 3:45–57.

———— (1961). "Classification of tonal structures," *Studies in Ethnomusicology* 1:38–76.

Leydi, Roberto (1961). *La musica dei primitivi*. Milano: Il Saggiatore.

*List, George (1963). "The boundaries of speech and song," *Ethnomusicology* 7:1–16.

Lomax, Alan (1962). "Song structure and social structure," *Ethnology* 1:425–451.

McAllester, David P. (1949). *Peyote Music*. New York: Viking Fund Publications in Anthropology, no. 14.

Merriam, Alan P. (1955). "Music in American culture," *American Anthropologist* 57:1173–1181.

———— (1962). "The African idiom in music," *Journal of American Folklore* 75:120–130.

Metfessel, Milton (1928). *Phonophotography in Folk Music*. Chapel Hill: University of North Carolina Press.

Nettl, Bruno (1956). *Music in Primitive Culture*. Cambridge: Harvard University Press.

Poladian, Sirvart (1942). "The problem of melodic variation in folk song," *Journal of American Folklore* 55:204–211.

Rhodes, Willard (1958). "A study of musical diffusion based on the wandering of the opening Peyote song," *Journal of the International Folk Music Council* 10:42–49.

Sachs, Curt (1962). *The Wellsprings of Music*. The Hague: M. Nijhoff.

Schneider, Marius (1957). "Primitive music," in Egon Wellesz, ed., *Ancient and Oriental Music*. London: Oxford University Press (The New Oxford History of Music, vol. 1), pp. 1–82.

Seeger, Charles (1953). "Preface to the description of a music," *Proceedings of the fifth Congress of the International Musicological Society*. The Hague: Trio.

Waterman, Richard A. (1952). "African influence on American Negro music," in Sol Tax, ed., *Acculturation in the Americas*. Chicago: University of Chicago Press.

Chapter 7

INSTRUMENTS

Most of what has been said about ethnomusicological theory and method in the past several chapters applies to all music, vocal and instrumental. Since the majority of the world's music is vocal, the methods of ethnomusicology are most frequently directed toward vocal music, and examples of analysis are songs. Instruments—and perhaps even more so, instrumental music—are frequently neglected. It is indeed true that singing is much more common than instrumental music. There are cultures which have no instruments, and there are others which have only instruments which provide rhythmic accompaniment to singing and are never used without song. While the Western urban man tends to think of music as primarily an instrumental undertaking, the student of folk and non-Western music sometimes forgets that non-Western peoples also play. And curiously, ethnomusicologists have paid much more attention to the structure and distribution of instruments themselves than to instrumental music. Of course it is often easier to collect vocal rather than instrumental music even in those cultures where instruments abound. Most individuals can sing and know some songs, but not everyone can play, and instruments are not always available. In recent decades, the individuals who could make native instruments have decreased in number. And of course it may not be easy to find the required players for an ensemble. Also, once instrumental music is collected it is, as a rule, much more difficult to transcribe than is song. A knowledge of the structure of the instrument and of the technique of the player is required, and this information may not be available from the notes accompanying a recording. This explains why instrumental music is not frequently transcribed or analyzed in the ethnomusicological literature. Instruments themselves, on the other hand, are frequently available for description even if their condition is such that they cannot be played, and even if no player is at hand. Thus descriptions of instruments are found in the ethnomusicological literature as well as in studies of other branches of culture.

Instruments are, indeed, of much more than ethnomusicological interest, and any student of culture should make himself competent to deal with them even if he must neglect other aspects of musical life. In the first place, instruments are one of our few clues to the history of traditional musical cultures. While recordings are almost entirely more or less contemporary, instruments or their pictorial representations are frequently found in archeological sites and may be excellent indications of musical life in bygone days.

In the world's cultures themselves, instruments usually have significance beyond the strictly musical. Thus, as indicated in many publications, especially by Sachs (1962:94–99), they frequently function as sex symbols—especially the flute and the drum for male and female respectively. Thus, Sachs states that "masculinity, in unimpaired purity, is the trumpet," and that "the flute seems to be a love charm everywhere." String instruments are considered by him to be feminine, as are drums, while some instruments have "conflicting characteristics of either sex." An example of the latter is a "trumpet made by cutting off the apex of a conch shell," which is masculine because of its "aggressive, frightening sound; but as it derives from a water animal and in its slit and lips reminds of a woman's sex organs, it is feminine as well" (p. 96). The obvious similarities between flutes, drumsticks, and male sex organs may lead the investigator to give more weight than is necessary to the symbolic connection. If we adopt a psychoanalytic view of the symbols, we would be in a position to say that the symbols exist in the minds of the peoples whether they acknowledge them or not. If the investigator confronts an informant with a symbolic interpretation of the instruments, he may find that the informant corroborates his theory. The question which is frequently neglected is whether the sexual symbolism of the instruments plays an important part in musical life, whether it is something to which informants give lip service, or whether it is more substantial. Thus, the fact that drums, played in pairs, may be called "female" and "male" may or may not indicate that these are sexual symbols, e.g., that they make the player or listener think of the appropriate sex or sexual activity when they are played. Terms such as "male" and "female" for two drums may be used simply for the sake of convenience. The way these terms are used, however, may give us insight into some of the values of a culture. Thus, as Sachs points out, Western culture would probably call the larger of two drums "male," and the smaller, "female." Some non-Western cultures reverse this, however, possibly because the higher tone of the smaller drum sounds aggressive, or because a matrilineal culture may consider women, as the carriers of descent more closely associated with the large things in life, or finally, perhaps, because drums—if they have a feminine connotation—should be classified according to the degree of femininity in them. Thus a large drum is "more of a woman" than a small one which, being "less of a woman," must be "more of a man." While there may certainly be some justification for assuming that some instrument symbols are world-wide or at least widespread, others are limited to individual culture areas or tribes.

But it is not only the nonliterate cultures which participate in this kind of symbolism. In contemporary American culture, for example, the possession of a spinet piano indicates a moderate degree of intellectual refinement, while the possession of bongo drums identifies the owner as a nonconformist, and a dulcimer hanging on the wall symbolizes the avant-garde intellectual. Possession of a Hammond organ, on the other hand, identifies the well-to-do business man who wishes to show a slight—but not too great—interest in "culture." Instruments (as well as vocal music) can be used to study cultural value systems and symbolism. In some cases, as perhaps in the example of the Hammond organ, the people who own and play the instruments are not aware of the symbolism. But in some cultures, the instruments are recognized and identified as symbols of things supernatural, natural, or cultural.

Especially in the world's simpler cultures, instruments are among man's most complex achievements of technology. We know that music occupies a position of high value in most cultures, especially in the simpler ones; thus it is not surprising to find that a high degree of technical and creative energy is lavished on their structure. To a great extent, this complexity does not involve only those features of the instruments which produce sound, for artistic work which has nothing to do with music is frequently included and may play a role in the instrument's symbolism. In Western civilization, of course, instruments as works of art or pieces of furniture have design and ornaments which go far beyond musical function. For this reason, study and description of instruments is important to the student of visual art, of material culture and technology, and again because instruments are sometimes preserved in archeological sites, to the historian of culture at large.

The fact that instruments are relatively so complex makes it possible to use them as indicators of cultural contact between peoples. If identical forms of instruments are found in separated areas, and if these forms are fairly complex, there is a strong possibility that they were brought from one area to the other, or to both from a third area. The simpler the instrument, the greater the chance that it was invented separately in each area. A famous attempt to connect two areas in this way was made by Hornbostel (1910), who found that the tuning of some panpipes in northwest Brazil and in Polynesia was identical, thus strengthening the theory of contact between Polynesia and South America.

In linguistics, too, instruments can play an important role. Since names of instruments are frequently diffused and borrowed along with the instruments themselves, studies of these names may be useful to the researcher in linguistic borrowing. And since the terminology of musical instruments, their parts, and their making is one of the rare instances of technical terminology in nonliterate societies, it offers the linguist an opportunity to explore this side of speech behavior. An example of research into musical instrument names and terms in one language is a study by Hause (1948), in which all words relating to instruments in the Haussa language are analyzed and their derivations explored. Curt Sachs, history's greatest expert on instruments, made much use of instrument names as historical evidence; thus the benefits are reciprocal: the student of instruments makes use of linguistic knowledge to learn about the origin and history of instruments; the linguist makes use of instrument names and techniques to study a particular side of language development.

But while the instrument of prehistorical times are of tremendous use to scholars in several fields, their importance to ethnomusicologists in finding out about the musical styles of the past should not be overstressed. The sounds—perhaps we should say scales—which can be produced on instruments indicate the limits within which a tonal structure must have been founded, but it is by no means certain that the owners of the instruments actually approached these limits. Thus, Mead (1924) gives detailed measurements of the pitches which can be produced by a number of flutes and reed pipes of the Inca, and includes several which have chromatic scales, but this, of course, does not prove that the pieces played on them used chromatic progressions. It must be remembered that instruments, since they are in many cultures important as pieces of visual art, may be constructed with visual designs in mind, and not necessarily in order to produce a particular kind of scale. For example, Wead (1902) has indicated that the distances between the finger-holes on flutes is frequently not determined so much by the pitches of the tones which they produced or by the need to accommodate the structure of the human hand, as by the visual effect of the spacing.

Instruments occupy a somewhat special place among the concerns of ethnomusicology. The various theories of the origin of music, and the motivations of musical behavior, such as the logogenic-pathogenic theory of Sachs in which music is the result of either speech or emotion, tend to stress vocal music. Sachs himself (1962:110) and also Bose (1953) stated the belief that instrumental music is of a different origin than vocal music, and that the instrumental music of a culture always differs greatly from its vocal music; moreover, that instrumental music throughout the world has certain common features. Instrumental music is believed to originate in magic and in the need for special objects of ritual which emit sounds. While we need not accept this theory as applying to all cultures, we must agree that the instrumental and vocal styles of a people often differ greatly. One reason, of course, is the structure of the instruments. The kinds of things which the human hands can do with an instrument, the kinds of things which random play will emit, may shape the style to a large extent. Bose (1953:215), however, considers a further reason, namely, that instruments travel from culture to culture more easily than vocal pieces, and that the instruments tend to carry with them, as it were, their musical styles. Thus, he cites the Tukano Indians of northwest Brazil, who use flutes and panpipes which probably originated with some of the more advanced South American Indian cultures such as the Chibcha; the Polynesians who use mouth organs which originated in East Asia; and the Africans whose presumably typical marimbas and xylophones came to them a few centuries ago from the East. In each case, Bose says, the instrumental styles differ greatly from the vocal styles because the instruments are not native to the cultures mentioned. He believes that these cultures have kept vocal styles of much greater antiquity but that they learned from the bearers of the instruments the music played on these instruments.

The essential unity of the world of instruments is emphasized by Sachs (1929). The similarity of forms, especially of those parts which are not essential to sound production, and the similarity of certain cultic functions of instruments the world over, led Sachs to believe that there were two main centers in which instruments originated and from which they diffused: the ancient Near East (Mesopotamia and Egypt) and China. In turn, these may have received their stimulus from an archaic central Asiatic source.

Related to the theory that instrumental music has a development separate from vocal music throughout the world is another view, stated by Sachs (1962:91–99), that instruments fulfill roughly the same functions in all of the world's cultures. The sexual symbolism of instruments is stressed by him and is assigned world-wide significance.

Classification

Among the theoretical preoccupations of ethnomusicologists has been the classification of musical instruments. Putting things in categories is perhaps a vice characteristic of most fields of research, but in the case of instruments there are some practical reasons for classification. Compartive work in organology depends on simple, accurate descriptions of instruments, for each culture has its own terminology, sometimes borrowed from other cultures, and frequently there is confusion in the native terminologies so that a particular name applies to one instrument here and to another one there. Thus, the one-stringed fiddle of the southern Slavs, the *gusle,* is only remotely related to the Russian *gusli,* a kind of psaltery. And the African *marimba* is not too similar to the North American one. Again, in Western culture, the jew's harp is not a harp at all, and the fiddle-like hurdygurdy is not like that hurdy-gurdy which is similar to a barrel organ. Moreover, instruments in non-Western and folk cultures do not have the degree of standardization which is found in the machine-made instruments of Western civilization, and indeed, the European instruments before *ca.* 1850 also exhibit a bewildering degree of variety. Thus it is not uncommon to find in museums instruments which have no proper designation, except perhaps the native name. A typical instrument of Negro Africa is called, in the literature and on museum labels, *mbira, sansa, zanza, kalimba,* finger xylophone, thumb piano, kaffir harp, etc. Lutes, mandolins, and guitars are confused, as are drums, log-drums without membranes, rattles, and scrapers.

Classifications of instruments are found in the early literature of China and India (see Kunst 1959:55–56). The Chinese classified the instruments according to the material of which they were made. The Indian system distinguished four groups: cymbals and rattles, drums and tambourines, stringed instruments, and wind instruments. Western European classifications are based on the musical style which is produced by an instrument, or on the way in which sound is produced on the instrument. The latter type of classification is like the Indian one, and curiously, the classification system which was finally accepted as standard is remarkably similar to that of ancient India.

Classifying instruments in accordance with their musical style cannot, of course, yield a system of universal validity. Grouping Western instruments as strings, wood-winds, brasses, and percussion reflects only the roles which these instruments played in orchestral music of the eighteenth and nineteenth centuries. But such classifications are of considerable value for understanding the cultural context of music

Nor should we disregard classifying instruments according to the way in which they are played. Sachs and Hornbostel (1961:8) question the propriety of this, saying that a violin remains a violin whether it is plucked, bowed, or struck, and a dulcimer remains one whether it is beaten or plucked. But future classifiers of instruments should consider this aspect of instruments along with the structure and sound-producing mechanisms.

The standard classification which we have mentioned is, of

course, that devised by Curt Sachs and E. M. von Hornbostel in 1914, based on the catalogue of a large instrument collection compiled by the Belgian, Victor Mahillon (1893) and translated into English (Hornbostel and Sachs 1961). The validity of this system is attested to by the large number of works which have used it, and by the fact that only very few attempts have been made to supplant it or to add to it. It has the advantage of using a decimal system, similar in structure to the Dewey decimal system used by librarians and inspired by Melvil Dewey, so that additional subdivisions can be made without difficulty. Kunst suggests adding a class of "electrophones" to the system.

Basically, the Sachs-Hornbostel classification divides the field into four groups: idiophones, membranophones, chordophones, and aerophones. These should not be considered as groupings which imply genetic relationship. Thus, the so-called earth drum, which consists of a membrane covering a hole in the ground, could, by the addition of a stick and a string, become a musical bow, which is a chordophone (the drum part now functions as resonator). No evolutionist ideas should be superimposed on the system. It is simply a descriptive one, which attempts to place, in logical order, the instruments of the world —along with some other instruments which have never yet been discovered but whose existence can be postulated as earlier forms of instruments which have been found. Museum exhibits now frequently use terms such as "aerophones," and the scholarly literature on the subject makes great use of them. Books on instruments usually proceed in the order used by Sachs and Hornbostel. But curiously, their numbering system has not been generally adopted. It would be of considerable value to have descriptions of instruments give the appropriate numbers from the Sachs-Hornbostel table. Thus, Merriam (1957) could indicate that the Bashi mulizi, an end-blown, open flute with finger holes, corresponds to number 421.111.12. The tables are detailed and will not be discussed here; a sample from that classifying chordophones is given below.

3   CHORDOPHONES   One or more strings are stretched between fixed points

31   Simple chordophones or zithers   The instrument consists solely of a string bearer, or of a string bearer with a resonator which is not integral and can be detached without destroying the sound-producing apparatus

311   Bar zithers   The string bearer is bar-shaped; it may be a board placed edgewise

311.1   Musical bows   The string bearer is flexible (and curved)

311.11   Idiochord musical bows   The string is cut from the bark of the cane, remaining attached at each end

311.111   Mono-idiochord musical bows   The bow has one idiochord string only   *New Guinea (Sepik R.), Togo*

311.112   Poly-idiochord musical bows or harp-bows   The bow has several idiochord strings which pass over a toothed stick or bridge   *W. Africa (Fan)*

311.12   Heterochord musical bows   The string is of separate material from the bearer

311.121   Mono-heterochord musical bows   The bow has one heterochord string only

311.121.1   Without resonator   NB If a separate, unattached resonator is used, the specimen belong to 311.121.21. The human mouth is not to be taken into account as a resonator

311.121.11   Without tuning noose   *Africa (ganza, samuius, to)*

311.121.12   With tuning noose   A fibre noose is passed round the string, dividing it into two sections
                    South-equatorial Africa (n'kungo, uta)

311.121.2   With resonator

311.121.21   With independent resonator   *Borneo (busoi)*

311.121.22   With resonator attached

311.121.221   Without tuning noose   *S. Africa (hade, thomo)*

311.121.222   With tuning noose
                    S. Africa, Madagascar (gubo, hungo, bobre)

311.122   Poly-heterochord musical bows   The bow has several heterochord strings

311.122.1   Without tuning noose   *Oceana (kalove)*

311.122.2   With tuning noose   *Oceania (pagolo)*

The subdivision of each of the four types is not made on the same basis. Idiophones and membranophones are divided according to the way in which they are played; chordophones, according to external features such as the shape of the body; and aerophones, according to the way in which air is made to act on the instrument. This inconsistency is based on the authors' desire to subdivide the classes in ways which are internally meaningful, but it is nevertheless a minor flaw in the classification. A second criticism could be leveled at the desire to distinguish between instruments which are "pure" and those which have undergone "contamination," i.e., been influenced by unrelated instrument types. If the classification is purely descriptive, the history of an instrument should play no part in determining its position.

In spite of the fact that the Sachs-Hornbostel classification was translated without changes after both authors had died, there is reason to believe that Sachs, especially, began to feel somewhat dissatisfied with it after it had been in use for some decades. I have a letter from Sachs, dated 1952, in which he discourages the idea of translating the classification, saying that a thorough revision was needed before any attempt at republication should be attempted. Complex as the Sachs-Hornbostel tables are, they are insufficient for certain types and areas, and have been expanded on several occasions. Thus, Hugh Tracey, in a handbook accompanying records of the *International Library of African Music,* provides additional categories for the great variety of African mbiras or finger xylophones. The number of manuals, position of the bass notes, and numbers of intervals in the scale are all indicated.

A system of even greater complexity was devised by Hans-Heinz Draeger (1948). Although it does not have the practical value of the Sachs-Hornbostel system, it provides a thorough examination of the theory of describing musical instruments, approaching them from the viewpoint of structure, manner of playing as it involves the player and the relationship of the parts of the instruments, as well as the rudiments of the musical style (monophony, polyphony, harmony, etc.) and the variety of sound types and tone colors which can be produced on it. Draeger's system cannot be used to order instruments in a museum or a catalog, but it provides a theoretical basis for ordering thoughts about an instrument, its music, and its cultural context.

Types of Studies of Instruments

A brief description of the most typical kinds of studies of musical instruments follows. Quite common is the study which attempts to describe all of the instruments of a tribe, nation, culture area, or continent. A model of these is Izikowitz (1936), which covers all of South American Indian culture in the order of the Sachs-Hornbostel classification. A detailed description of each instrument and a statement of its distribution (including its existence in North America) are included, and references to the instrument in the ethnographical literature are assembled in tabular form. Ways of playing the instruments, techniques of construction and of tuning are described. Occasional discussion of the cultural background is found, but the musical styles themselves are not included. Of special interest is the fact that both archeological and ethnographic materials are used to give a very comprehensive picture. Izikowitz's study has served as a model for other works of the same nature, for example, Söderberg's (1956), which proceeds essentially along the same lines as Izikowitz's for an area with a much richer corpus of instruments. Again, Fischer (1958) describes the instruments of Oceania in much the same way, but stressing more the geographical distribution and the role of the instruments in the culture. While Izikowitz and Söderberg use photographs, Fischer uses a large number of drawings to indicate the structure and method of playing.

Of course the study of instruments can—and should—be integrated with descriptions of musical culture and musical style at large. However, since the instruments can more easily be handled by scholars not trained in musicology than can the musical style, we find them appearing in a somewhat separate place in the literature, and the tendency has been to write descriptions of instruments without including their musical style while concentrating, in descriptions of music, on vocal music alone. An important exception to this is Malm's survey of Japanese music (1959) which is more than half devoted to musical instruments and their styles. Thus there are chapters on biwa, shakuhachi, koto, and shamisen music, and sections on instruments in the chapters on Noh and Gagaku. Malm approaches the instruments as producers of musical style, not so much as objects of material culture, and descriptions of the instruments themselves are given only for the purpose of understanding their music.

Of course the bulk of the literature on musical instruments involves individual forms as they are found in single or related groups of cultures. A classic of this sort is *Die Afrikanischen Trommeln* (1933) by Wieschoff, which describes and gives the distribution of African drums and of related forms in other continents. He is more concerned than Izikowitz with geographical distribution, for he adheres, in his theoretical approach, to the *Kulturkreis* theory, according to which distribution of culture traits indicates not only former cultural contacts but strata of cultural history. Wieschoff includes a number of maps of drum distribution; these indicate only the presence or absence of types in various tribal areas rather than function, musical style, or degree of prominence. Rather than following the Sachs-Hornbostel system, Wieschoff follows his own, discussing, in order, the material and types of drum heads, the manner of attaching them to the body of the drum, and the shape of that body.

A sample study of one instrument and its musical style is Merriam's description of the Bashi *mulizi* (1957); here Merriam is actually more concerned with the music performed and with the technique used in playing than with the distribution of the instrument. Another such study, by Camp and Nettl (1955), discusses the musical bow in southern Africa, giving the types, distribution, and manner of playing along with a brief analysis of the musical style of selected pieces, but the role of the instruments in the culture is not touched on. A useful feature is, however, a glossary of musical bow terms in some of the languages spoken in southern Africa. Here again we see the importance of understanding native terminologies for studying the inter-tribal and inter-cultural diffusions of instruments. It would be the ideal of organologists to have a complete glossary of musical instrument terms in all languages of the world. Considering that there are several thousand languages spoken by man, and that these are constantly changing, such a glossary will probably never be compiled. But the closest thing to it is Curt Sachs' *Real-Lexicon* (1913), which does give the names for instruments in many languages, to the degree to which they were available in the literature used by Sachs. This early work, a tremendous achievement, has never been superseded, and was reprinted almost fifty years after its first publication.

Unlike some of the other branches of ethnomusicology, organology has always provided a link between this field and the historical study of Western music. Nowhere is the historic contact between Europe and other continents, also between Western folk and urban music, more evident than in the instruments. And of course, in the major works of Curt Sachs, both areas are treated equally.

A "new approach to organology" is explored by Grame (1962), for here the importance of raw materials—bamboo in this case—for the development of instruments is stressed. The fact that the material of which instruments are made may be of great importance in the thinking of the world's peoples (as in the Chinese classification of instruments) and the symbolism of the various materials is well brought out.

Catalogs and Museums

Among the important publications in organology are the catalogs of musical instrument collections. Such catalogs are basic source material for the comparative study of instruments, for the student of this field cannot visit all collections which contain instruments of the type he is studying. The development of detailed catalogs of collections is, then, an important desideratum in ethnomusicology. Most of the catalogs now available are only moderately useful, for they tend to be directed to the layman alone and have publicity as their main raison d'etre. A comprehensive catalog should arrange the instruments according to some classification scheme—that of Hornbostel and Sachs, or geographically—and give, for each instrument, the exact place of collection or origin, the time it was collected, the size of the individual parts, the materials used, the tuning, if possible, and one or more detailed photographs. Notes on the cultural context of the instrument should be included as well. Mahillon (1893), the work on which Hornbostel and Sachs based theirs, is a detailed catalog which could serve as a model, as could that of the Crosby-Brown collection (Metropolitan Museum of Art 1902-14). Among the catalogs devoted to one instrument type, we should mention that of the Dayton C. Miller Collection (Gilliam and Lichtenwanger 1961). Here the arrangement is not classified, but a detailed index of types, trade names, and finger-hole arrangements makes it possible to locate the various kinds of flutes in the collection. But in recent decades few catalogs of great usefulness have been published.

A small booklet published by the Horniman Museum (1958) is interesting in so far as it combines the function of an introductory text on instruments and a catalog of the museum's collection. It does not go into great detail on the individual instruments, but it presents them in Sachs-Hornbostel order, explains their construction and the way they are played, and gives some information, including maps, on their distribution. Booklets of this sort could well be used by museums to direct the lay public; they are not, however, the detailed catalogs which the professional organologist would need. The kind of information which should be included in a catalog should also, of course, be made available to the viewer of a collection of instruments.

The care of instruments in a collection or a museum is a special field which we cannot discuss here. De Borhegyi (1960) gives a useful and moderately comprehensive bibliography of museology, including materials on the care of art objects. The restoration of instruments is also a field of great importance, especially since many instruments in collections are old, reach the museum in poor condition, and were collected by individuals who could not evaluate the condition of the instrument. Restorers of historical European musical instruments are highly paid specialists, and some of the more significant instrument collections, such as that in the Museum of Music History in Stockholm or the Musikwissenschaftliches Institut Berlin, employ full-time restorers. Restoring non-Western instruments has its own problems. The structure of the instruments themselves may be less complicated, but the restoring of parts which are to be tuned is most difficult. Adding strings to a Watutsi harp, or moving the tongues of a mbira so that the correct scale appears, is almost impossible. There are no theoretical foundations to guide the restorer, and all he can do is to use his intuition or copy similar instruments in his or other collections. Of course there are collections in which no attempt is made to keep instruments in playable condition. This is true of some of the ethnographical museums, such as the American Museum of Natural History in New York. Here instruments—especially of the North American Indians—are preserved in large numbers, but they are usually left in whatever condition they are brought. Such collections are, of course, still very useful, and there is no doubt that a collection which contains thousands of instruments would not be able to find the resources to restore all of them. Collections which keep instruments in playable condition are usually small; the Royal Tropical Institute in Amsterdam, which has a beautiful Javanese gamelan orchestra in excellent condition, is of this nature. But for the student of comparative forms, large collections are essential, and if these can be built only at the expense of keeping the instruments in playable condition, so be it.

Of course, the collector of instruments can play an important role in providing specimens which are in good condition and representative. No doubt many collectors have bought inferior or toy instruments from natives, and surely there are cases in which collectors have had their legs pulled. A. M. Veenstra of Johannesburg tells of an instrument in the British Museum which was labeled a flute but which, on closer examination, turned out to be a tobacco pipe. The admonitions given to collectors in Chapter 3 for music in general are applicable, of course, to instruments. The collector should get exhaustive information, he should find out not only what the informants tell him about an instrument, but he should, if possible, observe one being made, and make films of the techniques of playing. Instruments played in groups should, if possible, be acquired in groups. And once an instrument is acquired by a collector, he should play the notes which it produces onto a tape—especially if strings are involved. Then he should take care of the instrument, keep it in cool, dry places, if possible, and refrain from applying any wax, lanolin, or other preservatives unless he is well acquainted with their effects.

In addition to the collections of instruments in ethnographical, art, and musicological museums we should mention a unique way of preserving instruments and their culture, the so-called folk or outdoor museum. Such a museum consists of artifacts which illustrate the folk culture of a nation, and it usually has the structure of a village in which various kinds of buildings— farms, shops, dwellings, etc.—are displayed. In most of the buildings, crafts and methods of work are displayed through exhibits and by individuals who have learned, either through family tradition or from scholars, to do such work as pottery, weaving, basketry, and sometimes also instrument-making and playing, and who demonstrate these skills to the public. Although these museums are not primarily of musical interest, some of them do contain exhibits and demonstrations of instruments. The Scandinavian countries have pioneered in this field, and the museum at Skansen, outside Stockholm, and at Copenhagen are the most representative. In the United States, Greenfield Village and the

Edison Institute in Dearborn, Michigan, are worth seeing, among others.

It would hardly be possible to list and evaluate all of the collections which contain instruments of non-Western cultures and of folk music. Lists of such collections can be found in the large German encyclopedia *Die Musik in Geschichte und Gegenwart,* under "Instrumentensammlungen," and in *Grove's Dictionary of Music and Musicians,* 5th edition, under "Instruments, Collections of." Most nations of the world have collections which serve, primarily, to illustrate the native instruments of the region. General collections tend to concentrate on European instruments, and only incidentally to include others.

Among the collections worth seeing, the following are a selection: In the United States, Metropolitan Museum of Art, New York (world-wide collection including many oriental specimens); American Museum of Natural History, New York (best on North American Indian); Museum of Music, Scarsdale, New York (besides instruments, includes various artifacts relating to music, such as recording devices); National Museum, Washington, D. C. (huge collection of ethnographical material); University of California Museum, Berkeley; Commercial Museum, Philadelphia; Institute of Ethnomusicology, University of California, Los Angeles (oriental, particularly Indonesian); Chicago Museum of Natural History; Stearns Collection, University of Michigan, Ann Arbor.

In other nations: Musikhistoriska museet, Stockholm; Musikwissenschaftliches Institut, Berlin; Musikhistorisk museum, Copenhagen; Musée de l'homme, Paris; Horniman Museum, London; Gemeentemuseum, The Hague. And of course there are dozens of others. In conclusion, we may say that the work of collecting instruments has been well done. One task still before ethnomusicologists is the cataloging, photographing, and description of these instruments, and the publication of reliable information about them. Even more pressing is information on instrumental music and on the methods of playing, learning, and teaching the techniques used in performance.

Bibliography

Bose, Fritz (1953). "Instrumentalstile in primitiver Musik," in *Kongress-Bericht Bamberg 1953*, pp. 212–215. Kassel: Baerenreiter.

Camp, Charles M. and Bruno Nettl (1955). "The musical bow in Southern Africa," *Anthropos* 50:65–80.

Christensen, Edwin O. (1961). *Museums Directory of the United States and Canada*. Washington: American Association of Museums.

De Borhegyi, Stephen F. and Elba A. Dodson (1960). *A Bibliography of Museums and Museum Work, 1900–1960*. Milwaukee: Public Museum (Milwaukee Public Museum Publications in Museology, no. 1).

Draeger, Hans-Heinz (1948). *Prinzip einer Systematik der Musikinstrumente*. Kassel: Baerenreiter.

Fischer, Hans (1958). *Schallgeräte in Ozeanien*. Strassbourg: P. Heitz.

Gilliam, Laura E., and William Lichtenwanger (1961). *The Dayton C. Miller Flute Collection, a Checklist of the Instruments*. Washington: Library of Congress Music Division.

Grame, Theodore (1962). "Bamboo and music; a new approach to organology," *Ethnomusicology* 6:8–14.

Hause, Helen E. (1948). "Terms for musical instruments in Sudanic languages," Supplement 7 to the *Journal of the American Oriental Society* 68, no. 1, January–March 1948.

Horbostel, Erich M. von (1910). "Über einige Panpfeifen aus nordwest-Brasilien" in Theodor Koch-Gruenberg, *Zwei Jahre unter den Indianern*, vol. 2. Berlin: Wasmuth.

*Hornbostel, Erich M. von and Curt Sachs (1961). "Classification of musical instruments, translated from the original German by Anthony Baines and Klaus P. Wachsmann," *Galpin Society Journal* 14:3–29.

Horniman Museum (1958). *Musical Instruments*. London: London County Council.

*Izikowitz, Karl Gustav (1935). *Musical and Other Sound Instruments of the South American Indians*. Göteborg: Kungl. Vetenskaps-och Vitterhets-Samhälles Handlingar.

Kirby, Percival R. (1953). *The Musical Instruments of the Native Races of South Africa*. Johannesburg: Witwatersrand University Press.

Kunst, Jaap (1959). *Ethnomusicology*, 3d edition. The Hague: M. Nijhoff.

Mahillon, Victor (1893). *Catalogue descriptif et analytique du Musee instrumental du Conservatoire de Bruxelles.* 5 vols. Brussels, 1893–1922.

*Malm, William P. (1959). *Japanese Music and Musical Instruments.* Tokyo and Rutland, Vt.: C. Tuttle.

Mead, Charles W. (1924). *The Musical Instruments of the Incas.* New York: Anthropological Papers of the American Museum of Natural History 15, part 3.

*Merriam, Alan P. (1957). "The Bashi mulizi and its music: an end-blown flute from the Belgian Congo," *Journal of American Folklore* 70:143–156.

Metropolitan Museum of Art, New York (1902–14). *Catalogue of the Crosby Brown Collection of Musical Instruments of All Nations,* vol. 1–2. New York. (Handbook no. 13 of the Metropolitan Museum of Art.)

Sachs, Curt (1913). *Real-Lexikon der Musikinstrumente.* Berlin: J. Bard. Reprinted by Olms (Hildesheim), 1962.

———— (1929). *Geist und Werden der Musikinstrumente.* Berlin: J. Bard.

*———— (1940). *The History of Musical Instruments.* New York: Norton.

*———— (1962). *The Wellsprings of Music.* The Hague: M. Nijhoff. Recommended reading, pp. 91–110.

Söderberg, Bertil (1956). *Les instruments de musique du Bas-Congo et dans les regions avoisinantes.* Stockholm: The Ethnographic Museum of Sweden.

Wead, Charles K. (1902). "Contribution to the history of musical scales," *Report of the Smithsonian Institution for 1900,* pp. 417–423.

Wieschoff, Heinz (1933). *Die afrikanischen Trommeln und ihre ausserafrikanischen Beziehungen.* Stuttgart: Strecker und Schröder.

Chapter 8

MUSIC IN CULTURE – HISTORICAL
AND GEOGRAPHIC
APPROACHES

PERHAPS THE MOST IM-
portant task which ethnomusicology has set itself is the study
and discovery of the role which music plays in each of man's
cultures past and present, and the knowledge of what music
means to man. Although an interest in this task is professed by
most participants in our field, there is as yet little agreement
and little standardized theory regarding the procedures to be
followed in pursuing this interest. Ethnomusicology can not, of
course, claim credit for all scholarly interest in musical culture,
for the historians of Western music, the psychologists and sociologists of music, the folklorists and philosophers, and others, have
also explored it. But ethnomusicology brings to the study of
music in culture the points of view and the methods of anthropology, varied though these have been, and ethnomusicologists
are the only large group of scholars who claim an interest in all
aspects of musical life, in all cultures, individually and in groups.
Nevertheless, they are only at the beginning of their work, and
what they have accomplished so far cannot be summarized or
outlined. This chapter and the next, rather than attempting to
give a thorough exposition of all that has been done, present
a selection of the most influential and most promising theories

and studies. In these chapters we are interested in 1) the role which music plays in human culture and the ways in which this can be studied, and 2) the methods and theories by which music has been—and can be—approached in ways similar to the ways in which other aspects of culture are approached by anthropologists.

It seems to be most convenient to divide the study of music in culture into two broad areas: the study of the individual group, or person, or nation in one place and at one time; and the study of music in its spatial (i.e., geographic) and temporal (i.e., historical) environment. The first of these areas would seem to be a prerequisite to the second, but as is so often the case in a young discipline, the broader and more difficult questions have been broached before the narrower and perhaps less obviously fascinating ones. Thus there is much more theory and method available on the study of change in music, and on the geographic distribution of music, than there is on the study of music's role in one culture or in one person's life. Studying the geographical distribution of musical phenomena and the ways in which music changes, and participates in culture change, is important to an understanding of the role of music in culture. It may seem that representing the distribution of musical style traits on a map, for example, has nothing to do with other aspects of culture. But doing so might, for example, perhaps enable us to show how this distribution coincides with that of cultural or linguistic features, and how it is associated with them. It could tell us something of the way in which music was affected by the movement of peoples from country to country, and it might show something about the past associations of neighboring or distant peoples. By studying change in music we are approaching music as anthropologists would approach other aspects of culture, and in this way we are also learning about music as a phenomenon of culture. We shall devote ourselves, in this chapter, to a consideration of the historical aspects of the study of traditional musics (especially where no written records are available), and to the problems and significance of studying the geographic distribution of musical styles. These are two different matters with which we will deal separately, but which are in some ways closely related and interdependent.

Origin and Change

In spite of the variety of materials and aims, the historical aspects of ethnomusicology can be grouped into two principal classes—origin and change. Explanation of the origin of various phenomena has been at the root of many developments throughout our field, and until recently it predominated over the study of change. But while the study of origins has in a sense been exhausted or in many cases seems impossible to pursue further, the study of change promises to be of even greater interest when some methodological problems have been solved.

The problem of origin can be approached in a number of ways. For example, one may be interested in the manner of origin of a given phenomenon, or in its place of origin. The manner-of-origin approach has been one of the more speculative sides of ethnomusicology, and has provided considerable common ground between our field and historical musicology. The problem of the origin of music itself falls into this class, although ethnomusicological data can only corroborate or, more frequently, negate. Nevertheless, some theories of the origin of music which indicate the special function of music in nonliterate cultures and its close ties to religion are genuinely based on anthropological information (for a summary see Nadel 1930).

The search for the manner of origin of various generalized musical phenomena is also involved here. For example, the debate on the origin of polyphony carried through the decades (e.g., Adler 1908, Lachmann 1927, Schneider 1934), the arguments for single versus multiple origins of polyphony, the discussion on the possibility of various types of polyphony developing separately or together, would all be included in this category.

Slightly different is the treatment of specialized or localized musical phenomena. The origin of certain types of scales and meters is relevant here, insofar as the approach does not stress the development of one type from another; the latter should probably be covered in our "change" category. An example of this approach would be the investigation of the origin of the anhemitonic pentatonic scale: whether it was derived acoustically through the circle of fifths, through the repetition of a two-tone motif at different pitch levels, or through filling gaps in larger intervals. Another example is the origin of transposition or melodic sequence, which may be interpreted as variety introduced in a repetitive musical structure, or (since it is most frequently downward movement) as repetition modified by the prevailingly descending melodic contour of music (Kolinski 1957:3), or in still other ways. It would be difficult to exhaust the examples of the manner-of-origin quest in ethnomusicology, for it may be justly said that it has provided the impetus for a large proportion of the research in this field.

The search for the place of origin of musical phenomena, generalized and specialized, has pinpointed a number of problems in ethnomusicological method. The place of origin of medieval European polyphony (summarized by Reese 1940:249–58), of the styles of some Northwest Coast Indians (Barbeau 1934), of certain musical instruments, and even of individual compositions such as the folk songs in European traditions, to cite only a few examples, have produced a variety of studies and theories. The general problem of place of origin has been approached from the nonmusical side as well. Musical materials have been used to ascertain the possibility of cultural contact among widely separated peoples, and it is in this area that the historical orientation of ethnomusicology has made its greatest contribution to cultural anthropology.

The problem of change, although often related to and combined with the problem of origin, requires somewhat different approaches. We are interested in the reasons for change (or for lack of change), and in its nature, degree, and rate. This applies to various levels of musical organization. We can study the change in individual compositions or in larger bodies of music. We can try to trace the changes indicated by differences among the variants of a single song, and we can try to identify the reasons for them, whether these lie within the structure of the music or in its cultural context. We can try to measure, for comparative purposes, the amount of change that has taken place and try to determine how rapidly it has occurred. Similar matters can be studied—but with greater difficulty—in entire repertories, whether defined geographically or by their cultural milieus. If more than one composition is involved, statistical methods are usually drawn upon. Finally, investigations involving change are frequently associated with those concerning the place of origin of a musical phenomenon, for the obvious reason that if a musical item moves from one place to another, it is also subject to change, and it would be impossible to assess the change without considering the geographic movement.

It is useless to try within a short space to survey all of the studies in ethnomusicology involving historical perspective. However, the approaches of several of these studies are summarized in the following pages, and we will attempt to give examples of the general conclusions to which they have led, and to formulate some of the general tendencies which seem to prevail.

Problems of Origin

The origin of music, as well as of individual musical phenomena, has usually been explained by reference to three possible processes. It may be a coincidence based on the structure of a related phenomenon, it may be motivated by a nonmusical need, or it may be inevitable through some process of evolution—so say these theories, summarized by Kunst (1959:46–48). Thus, the origin of music in emotional speech (a theory not widely accepted) or in vocal signalling over a long distance (one more widely held) could be based on coincidence. A human need for music, and its resulting invention, are postulated in theories involving rhythmic work and religion as the cradles of this art. Music as a human version of mating calls, or as a specialized form which developed from a prelanguage and premusic generalized type of communication (Nettl 1956:136) are examples of evolutionist views.

Most origin theories involving smaller-scale phenomena are also based on one of these three approaches. For example, most forms of polyphony are attributed to discovery by coincidence or by faulty rendition of monophonic materials. This point of view does not explain why "faulty" rendition (e.g., singing of two variants of the same piece simultaneously, or overlap in antiphonal singing, or singing the same melody at different pitch levels) should in some cultures lead to the development of polyphonic music, while in others it is simply written off as error. The origin of some instruments is also attributed to coincidence—for example, the origin of the musical bow from the hunting bow.

It is also possible to postulate the development of musical features in some styles on the basis of aesthetic needs. The need for unifying factors in orally transmitted music may bring unity in one element in order to balance the elaboration or heterogeneity in another. It is possible, for example, that a style in which tonal material is being expanded (over a period of years or centuries) will also introduce the melodic sequence in order to offset the diversification. Or a style based largely on repetition of short melodic formulae may introduce and encourage improvisation and variation in order to offset the large degree of unity. This view is supported by the complementary distribution of the unifying elements in some styles of music.

The evolutionist view is represented by such hypotheses as that the direction of musical change remains constant; so, pentatonic scales naturally develop from tetratonic scales if the latter have in turn developed from tritonic scales. The opinion that there are stages through which all musical cultures inevitably pass is, of course, also pertinent here.

The problem of single versus multiple origin has occupied ethnomusicologists on many occasions. On the whole, they have adhered to the generally accepted anthropological viewpoint, using geographic distributions and assuming that the likelihood of multiple origin decreases with the complexity of the cultural feature whose origin is being sought. They have also used data from acoustics (Hornbostel 1910) to explain the presence of the same phenomenon in widely separated areas. The main problem faced here by ethnomusicologists is the measurement of degree of complexity and similarity. The problem is shared with cultural anthropologists, but it is somehow more specialized here because of the peculiar structure of music. It is possible, after all, that musical material, being in structure relatively independent of other cultural elements and being easier than other features to describe and analyze, is better suited to measuring than are some other cultural phenomena (Merriam 1956: 465).

Problems of Change

Why, how, and under what conditions does music change? Although these questions have not been answered with scientifically predictable results for any one type of music, they have considerable significance even for material outside the scope of ethnomusicology, as have the converse questions regarding the identification of stability and of stabilizing factors in music.

It is first necessary to define musical change. In traditional music, change seems to be a phenomenon substantially different from change in a high culture. While changes through substitution in a repertory occur in both kinds of culture, it is only in those cultures which make use of oral tradition that established compositions are altered. (Of course, changes in performance practice of written music also must be considered in high cultures.) Thus, change in a fine art tradition tends to be cumulative, new material simply being added to the old, while the old remains at least to a degree part of the heritage. In an oral tradition it may be change in a more profound sense, old material being eliminated as new material is introduced.

Changes in a repertory, or beyond the simple alteration of the individual compositions, occur in various ways. Individual elements of music may undergo change, while others remain the same. New songs may be introduced into a repertory, causing the older material to change by assimilation; or the new material may gradually change to accommodate the style of the old. Changes in a repertory, if not caused by the substitution of new compositions for older ones, are of course determined by the changes wrought in individual compositions. But when change in a repertory is evident, it is often impossible to determine what has happened to individual compositions. Thus the two levels of change must usually be approached in contrastive ways.

There are many reasons for musical change, and the following discussion is limited to those involving music in oral tradition. However, the same reasons, and perhaps others, may be relevant to cultivated music. We are not in a position to assert under what conditions, how fast, and how much music changes, and which aspects are most subject to change. It is possible to divide the approaches of scholars to change into two main classes: those which make use of strictly musical (or aesthetic) criteria and concern themselves with the characteristics of the musical material itself; and those which make use of nonmusical criteria, including cultural and racial ones. Of course, these approaches are not mutually exclusive; both must be used, and which one is finally preferred depends on the individual case.

The first to be generally accepted were racial criteria. These were partially subscribed to by such men as Carl Stumpf, E. M. von Hornbostel, and Marius Schneider (1946). Today they are not generally accepted; but they have been the subject of technical investigation by Metfessel (1928) and Bose (1952). On the whole, racial approaches tend to concentrate more on musical stability than on change. The musical relationships among members of different racial groups are of course intertwined with cultural relationships, and to separate the racial factors is a difficult and sometimes impossible task. Nevertheless, statements have been made (e.g. Schneider 1938:290; Schneider 1957) that the style of music is determined by the culture, but the manner of performance, vocal techniques, and so forth, are determined by the racial background, and there have been attempts to associate specific musical traits with certain racially defined groups — cascading melodic contours with American Indians, for example. Since members of a race have normally lived in close cultural contact, the existence of common musical traits hardly proves racial or physically inherited traits. Even when the characteristics of a racial group, such as the African Negroes, are brought from one place to another, such as from Africa to the New World, we have no convincing case for racially inherited musical characteristics. The notion that members of a racial group tend to accept materials from physically similar groups more readily than from different ones seems too speculative. Moreover, it is negated by such cases as the distribution of individual songs through the various physical types of Europe, the influence of Arabic music on East African Negro music, and the relatively similar musical styles of Africa and Europe (viewed on a broad scale) as compared to the musical contrast between African Negroes and the physically similar Melanesians. The accompaniment of cultural influences by racial ones in many cases obscures the problem, and we must conclude that the racial approaches to musical change have not contributed much to ethnomusicology.

Among the many things which cause musical styles to change is the contact among peoples and cultures, and the movement of populations which is one cause of such contact. It is probable that most documented cases of changing repertories are due to culture contacts. Peoples living side-by-side influence each other, and where there is movement of populations the greater number of contacts increases the possibility of musical change. One might conclude from this that a tribe which moves about experiences greater or more rapid musical change than does one which remains among the same set of neighbors. The former tribe might also have a high rate of elimination of musical material; or, holding on to old styles as new ones are introduced, it might increase the total number of styles in its repertory. Thus we conclude that a tribe with many outside contacts may have more variety in its music than one with a stable and limited set of contacts. This approach is illustrated by a study of Shawnee music, in which we see that Shawnee contacts with other Indian tribes resulted in the introduction of new styles. The Shawnee around 1950 had music which could be traced back to their contacts with the northern Algonquins, the southeastern United States, and the Plains Indians. On the other hand, we find that the Pueblos have a rich and complex but rather unified musical style, perhaps because (at least in recent centuries) their contacts with other tribes have been limited. The generally conservative nature of Pueblo culture may also be involved here.

Another problem involving musical change through cultural contact is the direction of influence. This can generally be answered with some degree of certainty: the more complex style tends to influence the simpler one. This does not necessarily mean that the music of the more complex culture is introduced into the simpler one, for occasionally the (generally) simpler culture may have the more complex music. A variety of stylistic combinations may also occur, as indicated below in our discussion of acculturation. In these combinations, however, it seems likely that each culture contributes the elements which it has developed best or to the greatest degree of specialization. For example, the mixture of African and European styles found in Haitian music consists essentially of African rhythm, antiphonal singing, and drum accompaniment but European melodic structure, perhaps because the melodic aspects of music are more highly developed in European folk music than in African Negro music.

A musical style may move from one tribe to another without the accompanying movement of a tribe or people itself. This can happen when songs are taught by one culture to a neighboring one, or when individuals move from one tribe to another, or from one country to another. The musical style which is thus moving is likely to change the repertories of the tribes or nations through which it passes, but it may itself also undergo change, influenced by the tribal styles with which it has made contact. For example, the Peyote style, as defined by McAllester (1949), presumably moved from the Apache and Navaho to the Plains Indians. It retained a feature of Apache music, the use of a restricted number of note values (only quarter and eighth notes are usually found), but in the Plains it evidently acquired the cascadingly descending, terrace-shaped melodic contour. Possibly the forces described above operated here: the melodic contour of the Plains, a specialized and well-developed type, was strong enough to encroach on the Peyote style, but the more generalized rhythmic structure of the Plains was not strong enough to alter the specialized rhythmic organization derived from the Apache. Thus it may be justified to assume (although there are few documented examples) that specialized features in music are less easily changed than generalized ones, and from this to proceed to the hypothesis that generalized features are constantly undergoing change in the direction of becoming specialized. A specialized feature may be defined as one having a striking, overriding characteristic which allows little flexibility for the composer's imagination to provide original effects.

Movement of musical material occurs not only in large bodies of music but also at the level of the individual composition, where the same forces seem to operate. In European folk music it is possible to identify tunes which have moved through large areas. They seem rarely to have influenced the music of these areas to any great extent, but they themselves have changed for reasons discussed below ("The Role of the Individual Composition"). It might be possible to infer that the larger a moving body of music, the greater is its influence on the repertories through which it passes, and the less it is itself subject to change.

Another force toward change may be called assimilation, the tendency of neighboring styles to become similar. While musical material which moves from one place to another influences the styles in its environment, there is also a force of attraction among the styles which are in constant contact. Thus, an area in which there is little contact among groups is likely to have diverse styles, but one in which the mutual contact is great is likely to have a more unified style. An obstacle to testing this hypothesis is the lack of measuring devices for degree of musical similarity. Yet it is possible to compare an area with much internal communication, such as Europe, with one in which communication is inhibited, such as Oceania, and find the hypothesis substantially borne out. Of course, the presence of other factors must also be considered here.

It is not possible to make decisions about musical change, its causes and directions, on the basis of strictly musical information. It is likely that certain directions of change do predominate and that one can in some cases, and with the corroboration of other kinds of information, decide such matters as the relative age of musical styles on the basis of structural features in the music. In most cases, music seems to move from simplicity to greater complexity (but not always!), so it is assumed by most scholars that the simplest styles are also the oldest. As indicated above, there may be movement from generalized to specialized elements—if it is possible to classify music in this way. Once a specific direction has been established, there may be a tendency to continue it for centuries. For example, if the tones in the scale of a song have been increased from three to four, further increases will follow, or at least a decrease will not ensue. These tendencies are speculative, and beyond the obvious simple-to-complex movement, they have not been used in specific investigations.

Other changes for which there are musical causes are related to oral tradition. Because there are mnemonic problems present in the oral transmission of music, the material must adhere to certain specifications in order to be retained. The music must be simple, and there must be unifying devices such as repetition, a drone or parallelism in polyphony, isorhythmic structure, repetition of a metric unit, a definitely established tonality, melodic sequence, the predominance of a single tone, etc. The necessity for the presence of such features tends to inhibit change, or to channel it in specific directions. Thus, perhaps a melody with a rigidly isometric structure is free to become heterometric after having become isorhythmic. A melody with a hierarchical arrangement of tones, in which important and secondary ones are easily distinguished, may lose this arrangement after the introduction of sequences, since there is less need for the unifying function of the tonal structure. Again, these forces have not been studied in many examples; they are presented here as a possibility for future research. They can be observed in some European folk songs which have undergone change while passing from one ethnic group to another, but whether these changes are due strictly to assimilation is an open question.

Measurement of the rate of change in music, and the amount of change in a given instance, awaits the discovery of proper methods. On the basis of impressionistic observation, particularly in the field of cultivated music, we may assume that change takes place irregularly; sometimes it is rapid or sudden, sometimes almost absent. In European music history there seem to be intervals during which musical style changes rapidly, while between them it changes only slightly over long periods of time. Sachs (1947) believes that this is connected with the length of a person's productive life, and in effect blames it on the reaction of each human generation against its predecessor. It is often stated that the music of nonliterate cultures must be somewhat closer to the beginnings of music than is Western cultivated music, and that "primitive" music must therefore have changed more slowly. It is also possible that the rate of change is proportional to the complexity of the music. This may be due to the fact that where there are more features, more are subject to change. Or it may be caused by the more generally dynamic nature of complex cultures. Of course, the fundamental value system of a culture is also involved.

There is evidence that at least in some cases, music changes less rapidly than do other aspects of culture. Thus, most nonliterate cultures which have had close contact with the West have taken on more European material culture, economic organization, and religion than music. Although reconstruction is difficult, there may be similar examples among the nonliterate cultures which lack Western influence. The Apache and Navaho have possibly retained more of the northern Athabascan musical heritage than of certain other aspects of that culture. The Hungarians have retained some of the musical features shared by other Finno-Ugric peoples such as the Cheremis (Kodaly 1956: 23–59), but otherwise their culture has become Westernized. The reasons for this slow rate of change probably vary with the example, and comparison of music with other cultural features is methodologically difficult.

There are two ways of studying individual cases of historical change in folk and nonliterate cultures and their music. One can try to reconstruct events of the past, or one can observe the changes occurring at the time at hand. The latter approach has been used in a number of cases involving acculturation (for example, Merriam 1955). The former has been used less often in cases involving individual repertories or styles (Nettl 1953, 1955b), but more often in general questions such as those involving the relative age of musical features. For example, it has been used to reconstruct the history of European folk songs by comparison of variants. There are definite limitations to both approaches. The reconstruction method is limited by inadequate material and by too great reliance on speculation. The study of change in the present limits the amount of time during which change may take place, and involves specialized situations in which the cultures being studied are usually feeling the influence of Western civilization (Wachsmann 1961).

The Role of the Individual Composition

The individual composition must be especially considered in historical research in ethnomusicology. Its is a problematic role, for there is no clear-cut definition of what constitutes "a composition" in folk and primitive music, and this very lack accentuates the importance of historical orientation. Should one consider a group of variants with proved genetic relationship a single unit of musical creation? Most scholars would prefer this to a working definition of the single variant or rendition as "the composition," but they are then faced with the problem of proving the relationship. At the other extreme, one could devise melodic types which may or may not have internal genetic relationship, as has been done by Wiora (1953), and call these individual compositions without even considering the question of actual common origin. This would have the advantage of grouping similar materials and thus simplifying the picture. There are other possibilities, all of which show that isolation of the unit of musical creation is much more difficult in traditional than in Western cultivated music.

The problem of measuring degrees of similarity among different musical items has already been mentioned. It would appear that in some styles, all or most of the pieces are so similar as to be comparable to related variants of single compositions in other styles. For example, most songs of the Plains Indians appear, by virtue of their specialized melodic contour (terrace-shaped) and form (A^1 A^2, with A^2 an abbreviated form of A^1) and by use of similar scales, as closely related to each other as the variants of a single English folk song found in several

English-speaking countries. Thus the criteria used for one culture do not hold for others. Informants' statements may be of help in some cases, and they have on occasion differed considerably from my own calculations.

Another problem is the identification or classification of musical items which, although composed at separate times, are based on each other or on a common model. In many cultures, the emphasis on originality (however one defines this term) is probably not as great as in Western civilization since about 1750, and there may be cases in which new songs are created simply by copying an already existing song with only slight changes. For descriptive purposes in all of these situations it is probably advisable to accept the informant's classification, but in comparative work this is usually not feasible.

The very existence of the problem of identifying individual units of composition points up some of the essential differences in historical change between cultivated and traditional material. In some non-literate cultures it seems that entire complexes of musical material are built up from a single composition. This process, described by Roberts (1933) and called by her the "pattern phenomenon," may occur, for example, when a ceremony unites a body of music which tends to become homogeneous by the process of intensifying the specialized elements of its style. In some cultures (Nettl 1954a:89), new material is consciously created from the old, either by elaborating songs already in existence or by combining material from several songs to form new units. The extent to which these products are individual compositions may also be questioned. To be sure, a similar problem occasionally appears in cultivated music, as when the ultimate source of a composition is investigated. Thus music historians may try to trace a musical theme through the various "borrowings" by composer from earlier composer until the real originator of the theme is found. In traditional music the problem becomes substantially greater in cultures which encourage improvisation and where music may be performed with considerable change in each rendition. One must also consider the problems of defining the compositional unit if each rendition or stanza is different, and of dealing with entirely improvised material. These examples show why the history of individual pieces has rarely been studied, especially in non-literate cultures.

Some Methods of Investigating Change

Among the various approaches to historical problems in ethnomusicology and the interpretation of descriptive data in a diachronic manner, two are selected for brief discussion here: evolutionary and geographic. We label an approach evolutionary if it recognizes a generally valid series of stages of musical style, into which the data are then fitted. The schemes arranging musical material into a time sequence may apply to generalized concepts or to more specific local ones. For example, it is believed by some that each culture goes through a stage of monophonic music, after which polyphony is developed. Cultures which have a great deal of polyphony, such as many in Negro Africa, are thus assumed to be higher in the musico-evolutionary process than those which have very little polyphony, such as the North American Indian. The difficulty with this view is that the results might be reversed if some other element of music were the criterion. It could be postulated, for example, that there is an evolutionary process from short, repetitious forms to longer, strophic ones; in this case the Indians would be ahead of the African Negroes, assuming that typical rather than exceptional examples are used. In a classification of the music of the Finno-Ugric tribes in Russia, Lach (1929:17) states that the simple forms of the Mordvin, which are usually repetitious, place that tribe in a lower evolutionary category than the Chuvash, who have many strophic songs with four different phrases per song. The Cheremis, who have many forms which begin in a typically strophic manner and then go on to repeat one phrase several times, are placed in an intermediate category. The same data could be interpreted differently, and without the use of evolutionist schemes. One of the problems faced by the classifier of tribes according to evolutionary principles is the selection of representative material. There would be different results if one used the average and most common, or the simplest, or again the most complex material within a repertory as a basis for comparison. Furthermore, the assumption that all cultures ultimately pass through the same set of musical stages is even superficially only valid if one makes the grossest sort of distinctions. Evolutionary schemes must thus be limited, if they are to serve any useful purpose at all, to restricted areas and phenomena, and the existence of other factors must always be admitted.

Universally applicable stages for elements of music other than form have also been postulated. They are usually quite logical and would be accepted as valid for most cases even by opponents of evolutionist approaches. For example, the development of scales from two or three to finally four tones probably took place in many cultures, although a development of tetratonic from ditonic without the intermediate tritonic is also possible. Similarly, most strophic styles probably developed from simple repetitive forms, but this does not necessarily indicate the future development of strophic forms in all styles which now have only simple repetition of single phrases.

There has been special confusion in the case of rhythm. Some students believe that metric chaos, or the absence of metric organization, precedes unification into metric patterns. On the other hand, it might be assumed that metric simplicity, repetition of a simple metric unit such as 4/4 or 3/4, precedes heterometric structure which, to the listener, may appear confusing and unorganized. A given piece may be analyzed as metrically unorganized or metrically complex, and many evolutionist statements in ethnomusicology have been made on the basis of such subjective distinctions.

Evolutionary stages have also been hypothesized for the

development of repertories. Bartók (1931:12) postulates three stages in the development of folk music. First the repertory is homogeneous; all songs are in the same style. Then special substyles are developed for certain categories of songs, such as Christmas songs, weddings songs, and music for other ceremonies. In the third stage these ceremonies disappear, and with them the correlation between song functions and musical styles. This scheme seems applicable in some cases, if we take the music of some non-literate cultures as examples of the first stage. It is not known whether Bartók also allows for the appearance of intermediate stages caused by the impoverishment of repertories, whether he believes the third stage to be attainable in all cultures, and whether the disappearing ceremonies and the submerging of their peculiar styles are not replaced by other, similar categories.

Other such schemes have been advanced; some have been mentioned in Chapter 1. Characteristically, they divide music history into three stages (is this a commentary on Western cultural values?). Evolutionary schemes perhaps have their greatest value in their contribution to arrangement and classification of musical material. And while they frequently help to explain individual cases of development, they have never become generally acceptable. We can say categorically that there is no evidence to support the notion that music passes through predetermined and predictable stages.

The geographical approaches to historical questions have been more valuable. They are used because anthropological theory has developed hypotheses to the effect that certain kinds of geographic distribution indicate the likelihood of certain past conditions or events. For example, the distribution of a cultural trait (an instrument, for example) in noncontiguous, scattered areas may mean that this trait was once widespread and has remai. el only in isolated pockets. The fact that certain musical features have the same geographic distribution as those of another facet of culture may mean, possibly, that they have been associated for some time. Again, the fact that a trait is found in a highly developed state in one spot on the map, and less well developed in the surrounding area, may mean that it originated in the center. At times too much has been made of the importance of geographic data in ethnomusicology, especially so far as their interpretation along the lines of historical perspective is concerned. But while their importance is probably greater for simply classifying and presenting information, their value to the study of musical prehistory must not be underestimated. We must, then, turn for several pages to a discussion of some of the problems of studying the distribution of music. Our historical and geographic considerations are then combined in our discussion of musical areas, below.

Studying the Distribution of Music

There are two main uses which ethnomusicologists make of geographic concepts: 1) They plot the distributions of musical phenomena, entire styles, individual compositions, but most frequently of individual traits abstracted from their styles which can be present in various stylistic environments. An example of the latter is a scale type found with various kinds of meter or form, so that its distribution is not affected by the other elements in the same composition. 2) They classify the world in terms of musical areas which exhibit some degree of internal unity and contrast with neighboring areas.

During the late 1950's, several publications have mentioned the desirability of mapping the distribution of music in the world. Paul Collaer (1958) indicates that mapping the distribution of individual traits or features of music would yield historical insight in various ways. Later, Collaer (1960) began publishing such maps in earnest. Fritz Bose (1959) goes so far as to postulate specific steps in making distributional studies and setting their results down on maps. He suggests 1) making individual maps of single elements of music and musical instruments; 2) mapping the use and function of each of these: 3) preparing comparative maps; 4) making maps comparing musical features with other aspects of culture and language. Bose's scheme is obviously predicated on work primarily based on instruments and does not go far toward solving the problems inherent in the preparation of maps for music per se. He is desirous, evidently, of using those aspects of music which correspond most closely in their nature to those elements of culture already treated cartographically, that is, instruments. The problems we will investigate in this section are primarily those, however, which do not have analogous features in other fields of culture frequently described with the help of maps.

Certainly statements of the distribution of music, that is, statements which indicate the geographic location of musical phenomena, have been made in hundreds of publications. In the field of musical instruments, maps have been made by many, especially Sachs (1929), Roberts (1936), and Izikowitz (1935). Maps of musical styles have been less common, but do appear in some publications—for example those of Collaer (1960) and Jones (1959). However, the over-all problem of the distribution of musical phenomena in the world has not been laid out in theoretical terms. The purpose of this section is to outline the kinds of things in music which can be studied in terms of their distribution, and to indicate some of the kinds of musical distribution which can be found in the world's cultures.

Studying the geographic distribution of musical phenomena is, generally, a more complex matter than the typical distributional study in anthropology. Anthropological statements of distribution have usually (but not always) restricted themselves to saying that a given trait is present—or absent—in the culture discussed. To ask whether music is present or not in each of the world's cultures would not yield a variety of answers, since cultures without music of some sort (using the broadest definition possible) are unknown. What we want to know is what kind of music is found in the various parts of the world, and how the world's peoples are related musically. Ethnological studies of distribution, with their breakdown of traits into units which simply are or are not present in a given place, are most easily approximated by musical instrument studies. Thus, we could state that the banjo is found in a certain group of cultures, nations, tribes, or other kinds of units, and not found in the rest of the world. Taking the places in which the banjo exists, one could map the distribution of the number of strings, the material from which the instrument is made, and so on. Such a study would tell us a good deal about the qualities of the banjo around the world. But a similar sort of study for musical style would be less productive, mainly because music itself cannot be broken down into easily circumscribed components. The problem of mapping musical distribution is primarily one of identifying relationships among forms which are not identical or similar, and of rejecting as unrelated others which may seem, on the surface, to be related. For example, one might wish to decide which of various similar tunes are actually variants of one basic type. Or, one could try to find out whether two slightly different pentatonic scales are really sub-types of one form.

There is, moreover, the problem of deciding on geographic units to be used as a basis for stating distributions. Should we use units determined by political affiliation, by language, or by physical geography? (Fortunately, these would often coincide.) Should smaller units, such as villages, be taken into consideration? Or perhaps families, which are often the units of musical distribution which can most conveniently and accurately be studied? And let us not forget that, as in speech, each individual has his own musical peculiarities and should perhaps be considered as the basic unit of musical style. But at that point, the problem becomes academic: world-wide distribution of musical phenomena could only be plotted by reference to a combination of linguistic and political units, if we limit ourselves to the present state of musicological information. On the basis of these units, let us proceed to a presentation, in outline form, of the alternative approaches to distributional studies in music:

1) Approach by element of music, such as type of scale, kind of rhythm, polyphony, etc.

a) *General.* This would include, for example, a statement on the distribution of pentatonic scales in general, or of general (nonspecific) types of pentatonic scales such as the scales without half-tones, or of rhythmic aspects of music such as heterometric structure, or the isorhythmic stanza, or of broad types of polyphony such as imitation.

b) *Special.* Here would come statements of the distribution of specific patterns, or of melodic types such as the well-known terrace type of cascading melody used by the Plains Indians. There is, of course, a large area of overlap among these "general" and "special" elements of music. The special elements would seem to be much harder to handle, being harder to define and to identify.

A set of maps giving the distribution of these elements of music would yield, by itself, a sort of picture of the world of music at a given point in time. But it would be, in some ways, misleading because it would ignore relationships which exist at other levels of distribution discussed below.

A refinement of the technique of plotting musical elements by themselves is the quantification of material. This is an approach which has hardly been used as yet—and which, in the present state of knowledge of the world's music, cannot be considered all too reliable. Nevertheless, it deserves mention because of its potential importance.

In saying that the mere presence or absence of music would make no good basis for study because music exists in every culture, we neglected to point out the quantitative aspects of musical culture. Immediately, we would find differences in the amount of music existing in each culture. The number of compositions in a repertory, the amount of time spent in musical activity, the amount of music known to an individual (including the songs or pieces he recognizes, and the number he can perform) could be studied and mapped for comparative purposes. The counting of compositions would itself be problematic because of the difficulty, in some cultures, of identifying a compositional unit and distinguishing it from its own variants and unrelated but similar units. Finally, the number of styles or distinguishable bodies of music in a repertory could be counted. In some cultures—especially the simplest ones—there may be only one such style, while other repertories (such as that of the Shawnee) have several distinct styles. High cultures of Europe and the Far East may have many more, depending on the time of origin of each composition, the instruments in their variety, the function of music (a church music style, a dance music style, etc.) and the segment of the population using it (popular vs. "classical" music). A comparative study of the numbers of styles in cultural units would indeed yield interesting results; but first we would have to define "style" in this sense of the word.

Besides counting compositions or styles, quantification of musical data in a technical sense could play a major role in distributional studies of individual elements of music, beyond indicating simple presence or absence. There are few elements of music (such as pentatonic scale, strophic form, etc.) which are not found practically everywhere. When Collaer (1958:67) indicates the desirability of mapping the distribution of the anhemitonic scale, he must mean some sort of quantitative approach, for some compositions using such a scale are found in practically every culture. Most useful for various sorts of studies utilizing distribution would be an indication of the strength of this scale in each repertory: is it found in every song, or in the vast majority (as in Cheremis songs), in half of the songs (as in some Plains tribes), or only occasionally (as, perhaps, in nineteenth-century Western cultivated music)? Of course, such statements would have to be based on large samples of material from each repertory, samples which are really representative, for many cultures are represented in the ethnomusicological literature by large, exhaustive collections from single ceremonies which might still not give accurate pictures of the entire musical cultures.

Since studies of the percentage of compositions in a repertory which contain a given trait are not common, an example of such a study is briefly presented here. It is, unfortunately, based on small samples of varying reliability, and should be viewed as a

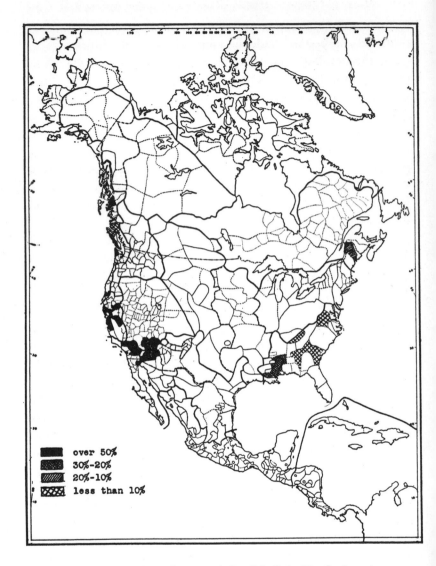

FIGURE 12. *Distribution of the "rise" in North American Indian music.*

sample of method rather than as a statement of musicological fact. It concerns the phenomenon of North American Indian music known as the "rise" identified and so designated by George Herzog (1928): In a song with a nonstrophic structure, a short section is repeated at least twice, then followed by another bit of music at a slightly higher average pitch, which in turn, is followed by the lower part. This alternation can continue for an unspecified period of time, but the lower section tends to appear more than once at a time, while the higher or "rise" section is sung only once each time it appears.

The rise occurs in the music of a fairly large number of tribes along both coasts of the United States and Canada. Figure 12 gives the distribution among those tribes which have been studied, and the approximate percentage of songs of each tribe in which the rise is found. It is strongest (occurring in over 50 per cent of the songs) among the Yuman tribes of the Southwest, and among the Miwok, Pomo, Maidu, and Patwin of central California. In the repertories of the Northwest Coast Tsimshian and the Southeastern Choctaw it occurs in 20–30 per cent of the songs; among the northeastern Penobscot and the northwestern Nootka, it occurs in 10–20 per cent of the songs; and in the songs of the Kwakiutl of the Northwest Coast and Vancouver Island as well as the Southeastern Creek, Yuchi, and Tutelo, in less than 10 per cent. Considering that most of the other tribes of the coasts are musically not well known, it is probable (provided the samples used are reliable) that the rise has a center of distribution in the southwestern United States, and a thinning-out strength across the southern part of the United States and up both coasts. This information can be interpreted in several ways, but at any rate it is more valuable than a simple statement that these tribes have the rise in their repertories.

Some work along similar lines in North American Indian music has been done by Frances Densmore (1929). Her comparative tables usually include the tribe or tribes which the study at hand contains (Pawnee in the case of our reference) and compares them only with figures representing the entire group of tribes whose music she had previously studied. Nevertheless, if her analyses were reliable, it would be possible to make cartographic representations of her figures which would, then, indicate the distribution, in quantitative terms, of certain special and general elements of music in North America.

A. M. Jones (1959, vol. 1) has made a map of types of harmony in Negro Africa, using as a basis the main interval between the voices (unison, thirds, fourths-fifths). No indication is given on the map of the amount of such harmonic music in each repertory, and of overlapping distributions (if any).

Marius Schneider (1957:13–14) would evidently be opposed to the approaches outlined in the last three paragraphs, for he believes that certain types of music are inevitably linked to certain types of economy, such as hunting, sheep herding, and farming. If a hunting culture has in its repertory music which is of a style different from the main body of its music, Schneider would presumably consider it nonauthentic. It is evident that if we were to make a musical map of the world—based on elements of music or even on the distribution of individual compositions —according to Schneider's view, we would have to distinguish between the music which could be said to belong properly to a culture, and that which has infiltrated it from the outside, and we would have to base our distribution somehow on this distinction, rather than on quantitative considerations. This would throw us again into the knotty question of what is "the real" music of a culture, a question discussed in Chapter 6.

2) Distribution of compositions. While we could follow certain kinds of scales and rhythms throughout the world and get one kind of picture or map, we might approach the entire problem of musical cartography from the point of view of the individual compositions—pieces or songs. Our first problem would be to find out what the unit of musical creativity actually is; for although in Western cultivated music we might have no difficulty identifying a piece, this is more difficult even in Western folk music. In nonliterate cultures we are sometimes baffled by the way in which informants will insist that two musical items

which seem identical to use are really independent pieces, and how, in other cases, two seemingly very dissimilar songs will be called alike by the informant.

Assuming that we can come to a decision on what constitutes a composition, we must then identify a) similar forms which are genetically related, and b) similar forms which are similar only because the style (the scale, rhythm, form, etc.) in their repertory makes the independent creation of similar forms likely. We are concerned (as we were in Chapter 6) with distinguishing musical content from musical style. Plotting the distribution of songs and their variants has hardly been attempted. An approach (in which genetic relationship is not necessarily assumed) has been made by Wiora, who gives similar tunes from many parts of Europe in order to show the stylistic homogeneity of European folk music (Wiora 1957:50–53). Here it becomes evident that distribution of elements of music may be quite contrary to distribution of compositions, at least within certain limits. The variants of a tune as sung in Hungary, Spain, and Ireland are very different, perhaps because the styles of these three cultures, as determined by the elements of music, are so different. On the other hand, the three styles are relatively alike when compared to African or Chinese music, and perhaps as a result, the composition in question is limited to Europe and does not appear in Africa or China.

Again, Marius Schneider (1957:24) offers an interesting sidelight, saying that a melodic type (i.e., a group of melodies similar enough so that genetic relationship could be inferred, or a type of music the various forms of which have some inner relationship which cannot always be identified by analysis)

is revealed above all in performance and in the peculiar way in which metre and melodic line coalesce in the rhythm. On paper it can be grasped only incompletely, but the ear detects it immediately. The same melodic idea, appearing simultaneously in the music of two different peoples, can be used by each of them in a different type. On the other hand, the same type may appear in two different melodies although the actual notes may have little in common.

Recent work by Alan Lomax also emphasizes the importance

of the manner of performance rather than the melodic, rhythmic, and formal aspects of music when it comes to deciding upon the world map of music.

We must, then, distinguish among three kinds of phenomena when considering the distribution of compositions: the variants —definitely established as such—of a piece; similar melodies without definite genetic relationship, such as the "wandering melodies" which are of long standing as musicological curiosities; and melodic types, which are somehow intermediate between pieces and specialized elements of music, such as the "rise."

The distribution of compositions in nonliterate cultures has not been studied thoroughly. Rhodes (1958) has published a rare exception, a study of the distribution of one Peyote song. But detailed investigations of this kind would presumably show whether songs coincide in their distributions and form "areas," or whether each song has an area of its own which is different from the distribution of every other song. Quantification of such data would involve the number of variants of a song found in each culture or sub-culture, the number of individuals knowing the song, and the amount of use to which the song is put.

3) The distribution of musical styles, or the identification of musical areas in the world, has been attempted by various scholars. A musical area is one which exhibits a degree of homogeneity in its music but is larger than the tribe, village, or language group. As such it is similar to the culture area used by American anthropologists (for definition of which see Kroeber 1947:3–7). The concept of the musical area is beset by some of the same problems faced by users of the culture area concept; among them are the difficulty of formulating criteria for identifying the area, and the lack of measuring devices for degrees of musical similarity or stylistic unity. Like the culture area, the musical area is primarily a tool for musical classification, and further conclusions about it as a unit of historical development may be drawn only with great caution. Ethnomusicologists began constructing musical areas in order to systematize the vast amount of stylistic data which is available about the hundreds

of tribes and ethnic groups in each continent. The fact that these areas may be functional in other ways was not foreseen at first and still does not ordinarily play a part in their construction.

Musical Areas in Ethnomusicological Literature

Although sometimes approached consciously and systematically, musical areas have also appeared in ways only incidental to the research which produced them. It has usually been assumed that musical distributions would coincide with other anthropologically defined areas. Thus, E. M. von Hornbostel believed that some racial areas, for biological reasons, were also musical units. He assumed, for example, that the American Indians shared a single main style, now known to be common only to some of the tribes in North and South America, and that the manner of performance, especially the voice timbre, was the main criterion of identification (Hornbostel 1923). Accordingly, he at times stated that the performance practices in singing were determined racially, but the other aspects of the style were learned (or determined culturally). This theory was also supported by Bose's experiments (Bose 1952). The notion of racially determined musical areas is otherwise widespread and can be accounted for by the tendency of a racial group to be located in one area of the world, and incidentally to constitute a cultural unit of some sort. This tendency was exploited by myself in an attempt to divide the world into three large areas (Nettl 1956: 142–43). The Americas and the Far East make up one of these areas, and it could be called the Mongoloid area, although it is evident that the cultural influences of Asia on America may be responsible for the similarities between Far Eastern and American Indian music, rather than any biologically inherited style preference. In other words, although racially defined areas may coincide with musical areas, the notion that biological inheritance is the cause need by no means be accepted as the explanation.

The areas defined by culture in general have in several investigations been assumed to be related to musical areas. Using the culture area concept, Helen Roberts' (1936) description of North American Indian music, one of the classical attempts to construct musical areas, was really a description of musical style in each culture area. Nevertheless, Roberts also subdivides some culture areas, such as the southwestern United States, where she identifies a Hokan, a Shoshonean, and a Navaho style—although these subdivisions are not found in the divisions of the continent into culture areas which are generally accepted. Similarly, cultural units are the basis of musical distribution in Merriam's division of Negro Africa into the Guinea Coast, the Congo, and the Eastern areas (Merriam 1953; 1958). The use of both style traits and instrument distributions for constructing areas is a feature of Merriam's study (while Roberts constructs separate instrument areas), and it is important to note here that instruments often serve as important criteria for culture areas themselves. But since the presence of an instrument does not really give information about the style of the music performed on it, instrument distributions do not have an essential place in this discussion. Needless to say, however, a culture whose musical repertory is dominated by instruments, such as Negro Africa, may have its styles determined to a large degree by these instruments and the kind of music they are capable of producing. In other areas, however, the distribution of a particular instrument may have no relationship at all to the distribution of vocal styles. This is true, for example, in the case of panpipes, which are found in spots throughout the world in combination with many different vocal styles; the similarity of panpipes in Oceania and South America does not have a close parallel in vocal music.

Quite different from the use of areas in a classificatory sense (in both music and culture) is the *Kulturkreis,* a concept devised for culture at large which cannot easily be transferred to a single aspect of culture such as music. The theoretical differences between a *Kulturkreis* and a culture area include the following characteristics of the former: 1) it need not be contiguous on the map, 2) it is usually based on a few key traits, and 3) it may overlap with others since it is not only an area but also a historic era (see Lowie 1937:177–94). The difficulty of transferring such a concept to music alone is obvious. But it has nevertheless been done by a number of scholars, particularly with reference to musical instruments (for example, in Sachs 1929), but also with musical style as a whole (for example, in Danckert 1939), and with individual elements of music. Schneider (1934), although he does not label his attempt as relevant to *Kulturkreis* theory, is clearly under its influence in establishing areas for polyphony (south Asia and South America; Micronesia; Polynesia; Africa). In uniting south Asia with South America, for example, he postulates a noncontiguous area and, characteristically for the *Kulturkreis* school, he gives these areas the significance of historic units—they indicate a particular stage and time of development—even though he does not pretend that other traits will have the same distribution.

Identification of Musical Areas

Assuming that musical areas exist as functional units, their very identification poses methodological problems, and a number of alternative methods are possible and may produce differing results. The student has the choice, for example, of using clusters of traits, single important traits or what we may call "specialized" or particularly distinctive traits as the main criteria, or he may make a strictly inclusive, statistical statement which treats equally all described traits of a given style or corpus of music. The basis for constructing a musical area is usually a group of descriptions of tribal and regional styles which must then be either lumped or separated. Statistical differences among such styles can easily be found, as can be seen in a study by

Merriam (1956); but statistics of this sort can also be misleading if not properly used, for they do not separate significant from insignificant distinctions.

Using North America as an example, we find that musical. areas would differ depending on the criteria used, but the different constructions would tend to have something in common. This is perhaps evidence for the hypothesis—discussed below— that musical areas are actually functioning units in culture. If single traits or elements of music are used as criteria, large areas tend to emerge. For example, if melodic contour is the only criterion, two areas could be identified, one occupying the central portion of the continent, with heavily descending melodies, and one occupying the coasts and the northern and southern extremes, with undulating contours. But in each area the diversity would otherwise still be great.

The use of specialized musical traits, that is, of traits which have been developed to some degree of complexity and intricacy, and which are, on the whole, restricted to single regions, is another possible approach. Of course it is necessary to distinguish between the greater or smaller degree of presence of a trait and between the simple presence of a trait in one repertory compared with its complete absence in another. In the latter circumstance we would have an example of a specialized trait; but there are few musical traits which are completely absent in any culture. Applying this criterion to North America, the isorhythmic structure coupled with descending, cascading melodies would make possible the identification of a musical area around Lake Superior, an area quite small compared to the culture areas. Again, the use of only two rhythmic values in the songs of the Apache and Navaho would make these tribes the sole inhabitants of a musical area, even though they do share other musical traits with some of their neighbors.

A cluster of musical traits seems to be the most common and successful criterion of a musical area, especially if some of these traits are "specialized" while others are shared with some, but not all, neighbors. This method is illustrated in the diagram in Figure 13, in which trait clusters and a specialized trait are found in a hypothetical continent. The fact that areas 1 and 2 share traits A and C, while areas 2 and 3 share traits B and D, makes area 2 the only one with all four traits, and this information could be sufficient to call the three areas genuine musical areas. But it would be possible also to interpret this entire "continent" as a single musical area, with area 2 a kind of center of development or distributional nucleus. Since area 2 also possesses a specialized trait, E, however, which its neighbors lack, this interpretation seems less useful than our first one.

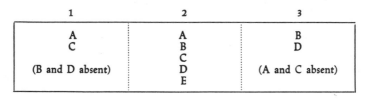

1	2	3
A C (B and D absent)	A B C D E	B D (A and C absent)

FIGURE 13. *Diagram of distribution of traits in musical areas.*

This method of combining trait clusters with specialized traits was used by myself in the identification of North American Indian musical areas. The division of Negro Africa by Merriam (1953) is similar, for it postulates three areas, the center one of which shares with both neighboring areas certain traits and develops some of them to a specialized degree. The implied construction of a musical area by Picken (1937) in Southeast Asia, on the other hand, illustrates the use of a single, specialized trait as a criterion.

The identification of borders and their nature is a problem which logically follows these considerations. For while the borders of a musical area are at times clear-cut, they may also be so vague in other cases that the areas are clearly marked only by their centers. Thus the Plains area of North America is characterized at its center (Arapaho and Dakota tribes) by sharply cascading, terrace-shaped melody, large range, great vocal tension, scales of four or five tones, large intervals, and melodic

fourths at key points. At the eastern boundary of the Plains, the
so-called "wild rice" (Menomini and Winnebago) and Prairie
(Pawnee) districts, the cascading melodies are smaller in number and are replaced by a more generalized contour which happens to be similar to that of the Eastern tribes, and the tetratonic
scales subside in favor of five- and six-tone ones (as in the
eastern United States). On the other hand, the eastern characteristic of responsorial singing does not extend to the Prairie and
"wild rice" tribes, which makes these something of a no-man's
land between the Plains and the East. On the western border of
the Plains, the Plains traits do not, however, extend to the neighboring Great Basin area (or did not, until recently)—or vice
versa—except among the Ute Indians. This can perhaps be due
to the natural barrier of the Rocky Mountains. The difficulty
of identifying musical areas and their boundaries is even greater
in the Old World, where influences between high and nonliterate
cultures and the more rapid cultural changes have produced
combinations of styles whose distribution has changed more
rapidly in recent centuries than has the more stable North
American Indian music.

Musical Areas and other Distributions

The fact that musical styles influence each other is obvious,
and that style combinations should emerge at musical area boundaries is inevitable. What is perhaps surprising is the fact that
the borders can be identified at all, and that some are relatively
sharp. There are at least two possible reasons for this situation:
1) the musical areas coincide with other areas, natural, cultural,
and linguistic; and 2) the style elements in a musical area complement each other to such an extent that for structural reasons
they coincide in their distribution. But in separating a style or
repertory into its components, we must be careful to distinguish
between the elements of a style (rhythm, melody, form, etc.)
and the song types (based on functions of the songs).

Natural areas evidently coincide with musical areas in some cases, and natural barriers may also be effective musical barriers. Very obvious is the Himalaya chain, which draws a rather sharp line between two main types of oriental music. Islands and island groups may be musical areas, although water is at times an ineffective barrier. Micronesia and Melanesia could be construed as musical areas (based on small intervals and parallel polyphony in the former case, and the development of more complex forms of polyphony in the latter), but Indonesia seems to have been subject to more influence from several Asian styles than these mainland styles have been influenced by each other. In the style of its folk music, Great Britain seems to be aloof from the neighboring European countries whose musics are, by comparison, more strongly interrelated.

Areas determined by vegetation and fauna seem to be the bases of musical areas in Africa, for here the boundaries coincide approximately with those limiting cattle breeding. In North America, the island- and shore-dwelling Eskimo and Northwest Coast tribes belong together musically, as do the inhabitants of the Great Basin desert area. The possibility that a natural environment itself determines a musical style must not be rejected outright, although it cannot carry great weight. The development of instruments and of functions of music is no doubt affected by such conditions. Finally, however, some musical areas do not coincide with gross natural areas at all, and where they do, direct influence of the natural environment on musical creativity can hardly be assumed.

The possibility of racial distribution coinciding with musical areas has already been mentioned, and the direct influence of racial (physical) factors in music seems unlikely or at least unproved except in a cultural context. The relationship of cultural area to musical area is generally close, even though the two rarely coincide exactly. Thus, in North America, the tribes of the eastern United States form a cultural and musical unit; the Plains tribes, although they are linked to the Pueblos in musical character, constitute an area in both respects, as do the Northwest

Coast tribes and those of the Great Basin area. The cultural contrast between East and West Africa is reflected in music, as is
that between Negro and North Africa. Europe is, on the whole,
a cultural unit as well as a musical one, in both folk and cultivated music.

The points at which cultural and musical areas do not coincide are also of interest. In the southwestern Unitel States, for
example, a single Indian culture area contains tribes belonging
to three musical areas (Pueblo, Yuman, Navaho-Apache), perhaps indicating that in this case the musical traits of an earlier
period remained at least partially intact while the other aspects
of culture changed more rapidly and amalgamated into a more
unified pattern. In Europe, the cultural entity formed by Ger-
man-speaking peoples does not find reflection in the relatively
great differences between north German and Alpine folk music.
The great cultural differences between Japan and China are con-
tradicted by a relative similarity of musical style (but again:
how can we measure degrees of similarity?), which may also be
a relic of earlier times. Even in these cases, however, the relationship between musical and cultural distributions seems complicated only by what may be a tendency of music to change (in
the cases mentioned) at rates different from other cultural elements. The hypothesis that certain culture types (determined by
way of reckoning descent, subsistence, etc.) coincide with or
determine certain types of musical style need not be accepted,
for the actual connection, in human life, between music and
other activities, ceremonies, dance, etc., is sufficient to explain
the congruent distribution of music and such activities.

The quasi-linguistic nature of music points to the possibility
of musical areas which coincide with areas occupied by speakers
of a language, or a language family, or other linguistically determined groups. Here also there is conflicting evidence. In North
America there is little correlation between language and music;
indeed, one of the most closely knit musical areas, the Plains,
is divided among five language families (Algonquian, Siouxan,
Kiowa, Uto-Aztecan, and Athabascan), while only one musical

area, the Athabascan, comprising Apache and Navaho, coincides approximately with a language family. The Indo-European language family does not share one musical style, although a large portion of its speakers, located in Europe, share a broad sort of homogeneity. Several of the Finno-Ugric peoples, along with some Turkic-speaking ones, share some musical traits, such as melodic sequences at the fifth, even though their areas of habitation are not contiguous. The music of the Semitic-speaking peoples can be described as possessing a single style, but it is shared with some neighbors speaking unrelated languages, including Persians, Turks, and to some extent, Spaniards. These examples show that there is only occasional congruency among musical and linguistic areas. In the case of individual languages, the correspondence is much closer, for the obvious reason of simple communication within a language area. But the theory that the origin of musical styles can be traced through language relationships cannot be generally accepted, for musical styles seem to cross language barriers and to be more prone to change and annihilation than basic language relationships.

As we implied earlier, musical areas may tell us something about the prehistory of music, especially if we compare them to culture and language areas. A musical area with a sharp boundary coinciding with a culture area with a sharp boundary may be one which has a long history of stability. Another one which does not coincide with language or culture units may be a layer of material recently introduced—or an exceedingly archaic stratum. An area with much stylistic variety may be one which has undergone frequent contact with other cultures, and constant change. One with a unified style may have existed in relative isolation. Of course we do not know precisely what historical conclusions we can draw in each case, but there is no doubt that these musical areas can eventually be used to gather important information about the world's musical past, and about the relationship of musical events to events in the history of language and culture.

Musical Areas as Independent Units

It is evident that musical areas are sometimes closely related to natural, cultural, and linguistic areas, but we have seen that they are sometimes quite independent of them, and that they sometimes retain their individuality through periods of stylistic change. One important reason for this kind of cohesion, and one which has perhaps not been sufficiently explored, is the functionality of the individual elements in the total style. Some musical styles are made up of musical elements (rhythm, melody, etc.) which complement each other or which are interdependent to such an extent that a change in one stimulates changes in particular directions in other elements. Thus, a change from isorhythmic to freely moving rhythm may be accompanied by a change from heterometric to isometric structure, a tendency which can be observed in African and New World Negro music. These complementary changes may be based on the need, in orally transmitted music, for the presence of certain unifying elements as mnemonic aids, and on a desire for a certain degree of unity-bringing simplicity. They are also evident in some cultivated traditions, such as European organum, whose increased complexity seems to have been accompanied by a gradual simplification of meter.

Some musical areas have perhaps achieved stylistic integration, as indicated by interdependence of musical elements, to a greater degree than others, and it is those that have which are probably genuine musical areas. On a large scale, African Negro music, although considerably influenced by outside styles, is a unit whose identity is rather clear. In North America, the Plains and the neighboring Great Basin are stylistically integrated units to a greater extent than, for instance, the Navaho-Apache area, which is not clearly distinguished from its neighbors and whose songs exhibit more variety in style. The number of sub-styles in an area is also a criterion of the degree of integrity in a musical area. An area with a single style or a few overriding traits seems destined to remain intact longer than one with great variety. A heterogeneous area would appear to be particularly receptive to outside influences, and perhaps it could be interpreted as one whose musical traits have not complemented each other in a satisfactory way, and whose inhabitants are, as it were, searching for the proper degree of specialization in musical style. Accepting these factors, we could consider the possibility of musical areas gradually being formed by the tendency of musical elements to combine in complementary fashion until the proper style has been found, and being, in turn or simultaneously, dissolved by the disrupting influence of outside cultures. At a given time, the world's musical areas may be at various stages of this development: the North American Plains in the perfected stage of integration, but being influenced and diversified in the late nineteenth century by the Ghost Dance and Peyote styles as well as by European music. The area of European cultivated music, on the other hand, may be consolidating itself into a stylistic unit (comparable perhaps to its state during the Baroque period) after a multitude of influences and innovations during the past century—some from the outside, from folk and oriental music—have borne upon it. Needless to say, these statements are highly speculative, but they may help to solve some of the problems connected with geographic distributions in music, and with the phenomenon of musical areas in particular.

Conclusions

Quite aside from the musical area approach, it would also be useful to plot the distribution of stylistic types—such as the North American Indian Peyote songs and the Ghost Dance style, which were superimposed on older tribal repertories, the peculiar style of singing epics in the Balkans, etc. There are some cultures which have several different styles each of which is accommodated more or less equally with the rest, and this is in itself worthy of cartographic and historical investigation. The fact that a kind of combination of musical elements can develop considerable homegeneity and then spread, as a unit, from culture to culture, without necessarily bringing it the individual compositions, is somewhat analogous to the picture of compositions spreading across stylistic lines. In other words, a composition can move—and change its style—to an area with a different style; and a style can move—assuming that new compositions are created with it as a basis—across the lines of distribution of individual compositions.

We have combined the discussion of change and of geographic distribution because these are the broad, comparative, and potentially world-wide ways in which music can be studied as a phenomenon of culture, and in which the theories of anthropology as a comparative science can be applied to music. The possibilities of distributional and historical studies mentioned here indicate that the music of the world is indeed a complex phenomenon, inexplicable in terms of any single theory or dogma. The beginnings of musical cartography could proceed along any one of the lines mentioned, but it would hardly be complete if all of the components of musical distribution discussed here were not included. And the study of the world's musical cultures would hardly be complete without detailed consideration of the manner in which music changes, and the way in which musical phenomena come about.

It remains for us to make some suggestions for independent study on the part of the student. Broad theoretical study in the field of change in music is not well suited to short-term work, nor, as we have seen, is it as free of the unproved assumptions and the theoretical biases as one would hope to have it in projects for the beginning student. The most promising approach is perhaps the study of distribution of musical compositions and of stylistic features. Thorough study of certain features whose distribution has already been stated impressionistically, especially for European folk, African, and North American Indian music, should be pursued. The areas mentioned are best because their music has been published in greatest quantity. Types of scales and rhythms as well as form patterns should be used. In all cases, the student should be careful to go beyond statements of the mere presence or absence of a trait, to weigh his findings carefully against the reliability and size of the sample which is used, and to take into account the cultural and linguistic context of the music.

Other projects which need to be pursued involve the study of musical change as it occurs. Finding informants who have made recordings in the past and asking them to re-record is one approach. Observing the change in the repertory of a community or an ethnic organization over a period of months might be useful, and studying the differences in repertory and style between older and younger individuals of a community could be of great interest. Adding concrete data to an area of ethnomusicology which has so far been dependent mainly on unproved or unprovable speculation would appear to be a tremendous service.

Bibliography

Adler, Guido (1908). "Über Heterophonie," *Jahrbuch der Musik-bibliothek Peters* 15:17–27.

Barbeau, Marius (1934). "Songs of the northwest," *Musical Quarterly* 20:107–116.

Bartók, Béla (1931). *Hungarian Folk Music*. London: Oxford University Press.

Bose, Fritz (1952). "Messbare Rassenunterschiede in der Musik," *Homo* 2, no. 4.

——— (1959). Remarks made at symposium on musical cartography of Africa, in International Musicological Society, *Bericht über den 7. internationalen musikwissenschaftlichen Kongress, Köln 1958*. Kassel: Baerenreiter, p. 337.

Collaer, Paul (1958). "Cartography and ethnomusicology," *Ethnomusicology* 2:66–68.

——— and Albert van der Linden (1960). *Atlas historique de la musique*. Paris: Elsevier.

Danckert, Werner (1939). *Das europäische Volkslied*. Berlin: J. Bard.

Densmore, Frances (1929). *Pawnee Music.* Washington: Smithsonian Institution (Bulletin 93 of the Bureau of American Ethnology).

Herzog, George (1928). "The Yuman musical style," *Journal of American Folklore* 41:183–231.

Hornbostel, Erich M. von (1910). Über einige Panpfeifen aus Nordwest Brasilien" in Theodor Koch-Gruenberg, *Zwei Jahre unter den Indianern,* vol. 2. Berlin: E. Wasmuth.

——— (1923). "Musik der Makuschi, Taulipang und Yekuana" in Theodor Koch Gruenberg, *Vom Roroima zum Orinoko,* vol. 3. Berlin: E. Wasmuth.

Idelsohn, A. Z. (1921). "Parallelen zwischen gregorianischen und hebräischorientalischen Gesangsweisen," *Zeitschrift für Musikwissenschaft* 4:515–524.

Izikowitz, Karl Gustav (1935). *Musical and Other Sound Instruments of the South American Indians.* Göteborg: Kungl. Vetenskaps–och Vitterhets-Samhälles Handlingar.

Jones, A. M. (1959). *Studies in African music.* London: Oxford University Press.

Kodaly, Zoltan (1956). *Die ungarische Volksmusik.* Budapest: Corvina. English translation, same publisher, 1960.

Kolinski, Mieczyslaw (1936). "Suriname folk music," in M. Herskovits, ed., *Suriname Folklore.* New York: American Folklore Society.

——— (1957). "Ethnomusicology, its problems and methods," *Ethnomusicology Newsletter* 10:1–7.

Kroeber, A. L. (1947). *Cultural and Natural Areas of Native North America.* Berkeley: University of California Press.

Kunst, Jaap (1959). *Ethnomusicology,* 3rd edition. The Hague: M. Nijhoff.

Lach, Robert (1924). *Die vergleichende Musikwissenschaft, ihre Methoden und Probleme.* Vienna: Akademie der Wissenschaften.

——— (1929). *Tscheremissische Gesaenge.* Vienna: Akademie der Wissenschaften.

Lachmann, Robert (1927). "Zur aussereuropäischen Mehrstimmigkeit" in *Kongressbericht der Beethoven-Zentenarfeier.* Vienna: Otto Maass.

*Lowie, Robert Harry (1937). *The History of Ethnological Theory.* New York: Farrar and Rinehart. (Excellent for general anthropological background.)

McAllester, David P. (1949). *Peyote Music.* New York: Viking Fund Publications in Anthropology, no. 13.

Merriam, Alan P. (1953). "African music reexamined in the light of new material from the Belgian Congo and Ruanda Urundi," *Zaire* 7:245–253.

———— (1955). "The use of music in the study of a problem of acculturation," *American Anthropologist* 57:28–34.

*———— (1958). "African music," in Bascom and Herskovits, ed., *Continuity and Change in African Cultures,* p. 49–86. Chicago: University of Chicago Press.

Metfessel, Milton (1928). *Phonophotography in Folk Music.* Chapel Hill: University of North Carolina Press.

Nadel, Siegfried (1930). "The origins of music," *Musical Quarterly* 16:531–546.

Nettl, Bruno (1953). "The Shawnee musical style," *Southwestern Journal of Anthropology* 9:160–168.

———— (1954a). "Notes on musical composition in primitive culture," *Anthropological Quarterly* 27:81–90.

*———— (1954b). *North American Indian Musical Styles.* Philadelphia: American Folklore Society.

———— (1955a). "Change in folk and primitive music: a survey of problems and methods," *Journal of the American Musicological Society* 8:101–109.

———— (1955b). "Musical culture of the Arapaho," *Musical Quarterly* 41:335–341.

———— (1956). *Music in Primitive Culture.* Cambridge: Harvard University Press.

Picken, Lawrence (1957). "Music of Southeast Asia," in Egon Wellesz, ed., *Ancient and Oriental music.* London: Oxford University Press (New Oxford History of Music, vol. 1).

Reese, Gustave (1940). *Music in the Middle Ages.* New York: Norton.

Rhodes, Willard (1958). "A study of musical diffusion based on the wandering of the opening Peyote song," *Journal of the International Folk Music Council* 10:42–49.

Roberts, Helen H. (1933). "The pattern phenomenon in primitive music," *Zeitschrift für vergleichende Musikwissenschaft* 1:49–52.

*———— (1936). *Musical Areas in Aboriginal North America.* New Haven: Yale University Publications in Anthropology, no. 12.

Sachs, Curt (1929). *Geist und Werden der Musikinstrumente.* Berlin: J. Bard.

*———— (1947). *The Commonwealth of Art.* New York: Norton.

Schneider, Marius (1934). *Geschichte der Mehrstimmigkeit,* vol. 1. Berlin: J. Bard.

———— (1938). "Die musikalischen Beziehungen zwischen Urkulturen, Altpflanzern und Hirtenvölkern," *Zeitschrift fur Ethnologie* 70:287–302.

———— (1946). *El origen musical de los animalos-simbolos*. Barcelona. Instituto Espanol de Musicología.

———— (1957). "Primitive music," in Egon Wellesz, ed. *Ancient and Oriental music*. London: Oxford University Press (New Oxford History of Music, vol. 1).

*Wachsmann, Klaus P. (1961). "Criteria for acculturation," in International Musicological Society, *Report of the Eighth Congress New York 1961*, pp. 139–149. Kassel: Baerenreiter.

Wiora, Walter (1953). *Europäischer Volksgesang*. Köln: Arno Volk (Das Musikwerk, vol. 4).

Chapter 9

MUSIC IN CULTURE — CONTEXT

AND COMMUNICATION

THE ROLE OF MUSIC IN
culture itself, that is, in the lives of individuals and groups as
it can be observed directly, has been approached by ethnomusicologists in various ways. To classify these does not seem possible at present, nor can we extract from them much in the way
of theory, for they have involved essentially the simple description of musical types, uses, values, and activities. Most of the
work done in this area of ethnomusicology so far remains in the
notes of field investigators; relatively little of it has been published. And the reader is urged to regard much of the material
in our Chapter 3 as particularly relevant to our present concern,
for in most ways the method of studying music in the culture of
individual peoples is field work.

It certainly seems best for an ethnomusicologist to be equally
interested in music as a part of culture and in the structure of
music. In practice it has not always been possible to maintain
this combination of interests, for much information on musical
life comes from nonmusical anthropologists. Ethnomusicologists
have always encouraged anthropologists to pay heed to music
and to note data of musical interest even if nothing could be
said about the music itself. Certainly the desire of the ethnomusicologist to say to the cultural anthropologist, "Never mind, even
if you are tone-deaf you can still find out about the meaning of

music in the lives of your informants," has produced important field research.

But the structure of music may also shed light on the role it plays in the culture. For example, the fact that Plains Indian women sing along with the men in most songs but usually do not begin until the men have sung the first phrase may be a significant clue to the relationship between the sexes. For example, perhaps information on the musical thought of Plains Indian culture can be gained from the fact that the Arapaho Indians evidently recognize the difference in structure between Peyote and older songs, but not between Ghost Dance and older songs, even though the three groups of music would seem quite different from each other. Thus the structure of the music should not be completely neglected in a study of music as a part of culture.

We can perhaps divide the material in this chapter into three areas: music as something to be understood through culture and cultural values; music as an aid to understanding culture and cultural values; and music in its relationship to other communicatory phenomena in culture, such as dance, language, and poetry.

Music and Its Cultural Context

Ethnomusicologists are certainly not the first to argue that music can best be understood through a knowledge of its cultural context. Historians of European Baroque music have long spoken of the analogy of symmetrical musical forms and symmetrical stage sets and gardens, and of the similarity between heavily and artificially ornamented paintings and architecture on the one hand and embellished music on the other (Bukofzer 1947:2–3). In ethnomusicology this idea was also felt early, for the notion that race, type of economy, and type of descent determine musical style is certainly a result of the feeling that music is closely related to other aspects of culture. The methods of studying culture and cultural values as they bear upon music are, on the other hand, poorly developed. Directions to and exhortations of field workers abound, but there seems to be no clear-cut pattern to follow.

The most generally useful type of study on cultural context of music would seem to be the presentation of a total picture of one culture, tribe, or community. There are no such studies available, and of course the presentation of a group's musical life literally *in toto* would seem impossible of attainment. But there are some examples in which a broad view of the musical culture of one tribe or culture is given.

Perhaps the closest to an ideal is reached in some of the early publications of the Bureau of American Ethnology of the Smithsonian Institution. Shortly after 1900, the Bureau was in a position to publish several extremely detailed accounts of North American Indian tribes, their cultures and ceremonies, which fortunately included descriptions of singing and musical life as well as transcriptions of melodies. One of these, by Fletcher and LaFlesche (1911), describes the Omaha tribe in a monograph of some 650 pages. Included are accounts of ceremonies in exact detail, with transcriptions of the songs at the points at which they were sung. The transcriptions are perhaps not of high quality, and some of them are needlessly furnished with piano accompaniments by the composer J. C. Fillmore. Analysis and interpretation of musical life is also absent, and techniques of eliciting information about music which would normally not be verbalized were not used. But the kind of step-by-step description used by Fletcher and LaFlesche (who was himself a member of the Omaha tribe) is extremely useful as primary source material and gives a reasonably reliable overview of music in the life of one tribe. Even more detail of description is found in another publication by Fletcher (1904), an account of the Hako, a Pawnee ceremony, in which dozens of songs, transcribed by Edwin S. Tracy, are included. Here the entire song texts are transcribed and translated, and the choreography is approximately indicated. An "analytical recapitulation" is included. Unfortunately this type of detailed description is only too rare in ethnomusicological publication. Few institutions have had the resources and the inclination to publish such exact accounts as has the Bureau of American Ethnology, and no doubt many descriptions of ceremonies and of musical culture at large are lying unpublished in the drawers of ethnomusicological field workers. Old-fashioned in a musicological sense and naïve-sounding as the works of Alice Fletcher may be, they are monuments of research. And the fact that they failed to place the raw material in theoretical perspective makes them, today, more rather than less valuable compared to the many publications of the same period which abound in stimulating but unprovable speculation.

In more recent years, the Bureau of American Ethnology has attempted some less detailed but more theoretical monographs on Indian ceremonies which are similar in spirit and value to the old *Annual Reports*. Fenton (1953) gives a description of the Iroquois Eagle Dance with transcriptions and analysis of the dances and songs by Gertrude P. Kurath. Again, this kind of description gives a step-by-step account of the role of music in one segment of Iroquois life.

Less detailed but more inclusive accounts of musical culture are rare. The studies discussed above approach their subject from the broad cultural view, and include music only as it is a part of the whole culture. Occasionally we find accounts of musical culture which are approached from the musicologist's sphere of interest. Burrows, in a study of Uvea and Futuna music (1945), begins with a large section on "songs in native life," discussing the various uses to which music is put and the types of songs. Transcriptions of songs are included, but analysis of the music is reserved for a special section of the book.

There are some descriptions of musical life as it involves one phase of culture. For example, Waterman (1956) describes music of the natives of Yirkalla, Australia, emphasizing the musical life of children. In addition to enumerating the uses of music and describing musical activities, Waterman is able to synthesize his findings in a way which has rarely been possible for most investigators, for he indicates just what single main purpose is accomplished by music. Thus he says that "music functions at Yirkalla as an enculturative mechanism, a means of learning Yirkalla culture. Throughout his life, the aboriginal is surrounded by musical events that instruct him about his natural environment and its utilization by man, that teach him his world-view and shape his system of values" (Waterman 1956:41).

Merriam (1962) also devotes himself to one aspect of music in a culture; in this case, it is the activity surrounding the *epudi*, an ocarina of the Basongye of the Republic of the Congo. This instrument is used as a signal for hunting, and Merriam considers it important for an understanding of the instrument to know something about the habits and techniques of Basongye hunting. In this study, Merriam describes also the structure of the instrument, the role it plays in native classification of sounds, and the style of music produced.

It is one thing to describe the uses and functions of music in their cultural context, and another to abstract from these a system of musical values or aesthetics. Herzog (1938) gives a short survey of the role which music plays in the thinking of various North American Indian tribes. Attempting generalizations of the kind made by Waterman, above, it gives us a rather cursory glance at a field which was later studied in more detail (with one tribe, the Navaho) by McAllester (1954); but it points the way toward one of the most interesting areas of ethnomusicology.

Finally, we should mention a type of description of musical culture which covers an area broader than the tribe or community. Brandel (1962) discusses, for all of Central Africa, the various kinds of music used by all or most of the tribes in the area: ceremonies, work songs, entertainment, litigation, dance, and signalling. Although all of these publications—from Fletcher's (1904) to Brandel's (1962)—presume to present the cultural context of music on the assumption that we will understand culture better through inclusion of music, and music better in its cultural context, there is obviously a great difference between the rather plodding, step-by-step account of Fletcher and the sweeping general statements of Brandel. Both types of publication are needed.

The musical values or aesthetics of a culture are also an important area for studying music through its cultural role and context. The members of most non-Western cultures, especially the nonliterate and folk societies, have difficulty in verbalizing about music. Asking them what good or bad music may be, or what constitutes good or bad singing, and the reasons for the answers, may not produce results. Studying the aesthetic values of a tribe involves more than simple questioning of informants, although this is also a possible avenue of approach. Correlating answers with actually observed musical behavior is a way of getting at the answers, as is the analysis of music and of statements about music appearing in ordinary conversation or in folklore texts. Few studies have been made, and as so frequently is the case, the North American Indians provide material of a pioneering nature. McAllester (1954), whose study through a questionnaire of Navaho values and of musical thinking has been discussed in Chapter 3, provides a model. Although much of what he discovers about Navaho musical values and their relationship to their culture is hardly surprising, his work at least attempts to formulate a method. Herzog (1938) gives samples of various Indian informants' statements about music and backs these with analyses of folkloristic texts, but a tribal aesthetic does not emerge. Again, we are only on the threshold of a broad area yet to be discovered.

A further approach to music as a cultural phenomenon is the concept of musical performance as an event. Although few readers will be surprised to hear that a musical performance involves attitudes on the part of composer, performer, and listener, and that the relationship between listener and performer is an important one, the study of this particular relationship and of the events leading up to and following a performance—and of course their effect on the performance—has not been widely pursued. Lomax (1959) is particularly concerned with the "music-as-behavior" approach to ethnomusicology. He believes that performers' gestures, the cooperation among performers and between them and the audience, the presence or absence of an audience, and related matters must be understood before what he considers the purely formal elements of music—scale, rhythm, structure—should be approached. His basic tenet is that certain aspects of culture (and not others) determine musical style to a great extent. Here Lomax is comparable to those scholars who consider the form of economic life (Schneider), or the type of descent (Sachs), or even the racial characteristics as the determinants of musical style. Lomax (1959:950) says that "sexual code, positions of women, and treatment of children seem to be the social patterns most clearly identified with musical style." For example, he believes that "high-pitched, strident singing" is "a symbol of the burning pain of sexual starvation." Like all theories which ascribe musical style to a single variable in culture, the sex theory of Lomax is difficult to prove, and even in the convincing cases which Lomax cites (i.e., the tense singing of the Puritanical whites of the eastern United States versus the relaxed singing of the sexually more relaxed southern Negroes), other causes should also be considered. But the interest of Lomax's view for this chapter is the fact that in his approach to musical style classification, he considers the non-formal elements, i.e., the vocal mannerisms, the singing style, and the conditions surrounding the musical event, as more germane than the scale, rhythm, and form. Musicologists before Lomax have considered these elements important, but usually subsidiary to the scales and rhythms. Lomax's classification of styles according to vocal technique is an important step toward developing a methodology for studying music as an event in human life, rather than simply as an independent work of art.

It is evident, then, that ethnomusicologists have done three kinds of things in relating music to its cultural environment. They have furnished a few descriptions of musical life without interpretation of the findings; they have occasionally approached the cultural values and musical aesthetics of a culture; and they have classified musical styles in accordance with and as related to specific types of culture, basing their cultural classification on economy, type of descent, and sexual attitudes.

Classification of Music As an Indicator

Relatively little work has been done in the area of native classification of music. Although it is definitely a part of the aesthetics of a group and although it is perhaps one of the easier aspects of music for members of nonliterate cultures to verbalize about, this area has barely been approached, in spite of occasional exhortations (Merriam 1960:110) to include it in research. Native classifications of music may furnish material for the study of cultural values through music. It may even be possible to shed light on the cultural values of Western civilization by analyzing the various ways in which music is classified by urban Americans, and the student wishing to apply ethnomusicological method to Western musical culture may find here an area for making a start.

It is typical, of course, of our civilization that individuals do not agree on the types and kinds of music which exist. There is at least a chance that members of nonliterate tribes would agree on the kinds of music which their tribes use, i.e., that you would get roughly the same answer to the question "What kinds of music are there, or what kinds of songs do you have?" from most members of a tribe. The more complex the culture, the less likely we are to find such unanimity. In approaching about sixty informants who were college students (in the course of a survey conducted in Detroit in 1962), we found many different answers to such a simple question as "What kinds of music are there?" The most common answer reflects the educated American's preoccupation with the time of origin of a work of art, for classifications such as medieval, baroque, classical, romantic abounded. Geographic classifications were also found; a number of students classified music as "Western," "foreign," and "folk," or as classical, popular, and folk. A number of individuals who distinguished between classical and popular music added jazz as a separate category. Quite possibly, the social level of performer and audience plays a role in the classifications of music by Westerners. A few of the students who were questioned distinguished between good and bad music, but they were not asked to define these terms. Surprisingly few, however, based their answers on criteria of musical style. For example, distinctions such as polyphonic and monophonic, or instrumental and vocal, did not appear. No one classed music as solo, chamber, or symphonic. Only one distinguished between contemporary and older music, which might indicate a classification on the basis of musical styles. The uses of music also seemed to play a small role in the classifications presented by college students. Thus, no one classified music as consisting of concert, dance, church, marching music, etc.

This small sample and the preliminary kind of method used could hardly provide statistical validity, and no attempt to draw definite conclusions can be made. The project was carried out only to see in what directions further work could be done. If we used the results for drawing conclusions, we could possibly say that these students stressed the historical criterion and indicated the importance of time and place of origin in our thinking about works of art. They also indicated an influence on the part of ethnomusicological thinking when they gave classical, folk, and non-Western as categories, thinking which may have been influenced by the current interest in under-developed nations. Their neglect of classes based on musical style may reflect the current tendency to accept all musical styles, to be relativistic, and as such to have or exhibit no strong preferences or feelings; and their neglect of classes based on the uses of music may indicate the relatively small role which any musical activity other than listening plays in our culture, and the resulting tendency to consider music as having a strictly passive value in our society.

There is also the possibility of examining written or traditional statements made by members of a culture regarding musical content, and of interpreting these statements in the light of—and for shedding light on—cultural values. Among the materials of this sort in nonliterate societies is folklore. Tales, legends, myths frequently mention music, and there are myths dealing with the origin of song, with the way songs are taught and learned by culture heroes, with the role that songs play in the mythological development of a tribe. In cultures with written traditions, writings on music, especially those of a theoretical and critical nature, are excellent material for the sort of study we have in mind. Much of what we have found out about the history of music in Oriental nations comes from the theoretical writings of the past. Of course the relevance of theoretical writings to actual musical practice cannot be taken completely for granted, and statements made by the writers must be checked, wherever possible, against known musical facts. But it would also be useful to examine the writings on music by themselves, for their own sake, in order to see whether any information about cultural and aesthetic values emerges from them. It would be useful, for example, to examine Western music criticism in newspapers in order to see what the criteria of judgment are, and what the musical values of the critics— and presumably to some extent of the readers—turns out to be; and also, to what extent these values are actually reflected in musical trends. There are many approaches to musical culture besides the direct one to the informant. For example, the way in which American libraries treat and classify music in their catalogs may give us insight into the value structure of our culture.

The fact that musical compositions are first classed and referred to according to composer—something we take for granted, but to which there are actually several alternatives—indicates **the importance to us of the person who created a work of art, and perhaps also of the time and place of its origin. The historical orientation of the Western-educated public is a special** feature in our value structure; this was also shown in the typical classification of music among college students.

The intensely personal nature of compositions is also stressed in our library classification. Then, libraries distinguish between cultivated music, which they consider the best and most important music, and which is called, in the subject headings, simply "music," on the one hand, and other types: folk music, popular music, and jazz, omitting now the consideration of non-Western music. The large category of just plain "music," i.e., cultivated music, is, in the subject classification, subdivided according to time of origin, into two broad classes separated by the year 1800. For example, there is a subject heading "Symphonies" and another, "Symphonies—To 1800." Could this reflect our basic assumption that the origin (the composer) and the time of origin of a composition are among the most important things about it? Normally, libraries do not classify according to nation of the composer, according to the first performer, the sex of the composer, etc., but according to time of composition. The choice of the year 1800 might also be significant, though it may not reflect classifications used by musicians who have no contact with libraries. There seems to be no more justification for using 1800 as a cut-off point than 1750, 1775, 1600, or 1900. These other dates would probably reflect more exactly some fundamental differences in musical style. Although certain eighteenth-century composers are assuredly very dear to the hearts of many music lovers, library classifiers and users, on the whole, presumably consider music written after 1800 as "ours," considering the music of the nineteenth century as reflecting their own culture as much as does music written after 1900, while music before 1800—Haydn, Mozart, and earlier—is in a separate class. The imperfection of using such indices to our own culture as library classification is evident; yet a study of the various seemingly arbitrary ways of classifying music in our lives may give us some information about our value systems as reflected in music. In the case of American libraries, these would be the importance of origin, of the composer, and the desire to divide things into two groups—based on the "ours–not ours" criterion which has built into it an overtone of "good–less good."

No doubt the conclusions here tentatively stated could be argued. The important things to be noted, however, are the possibility of using methods derived from ethnomusicology for learning something about the aesthetic biases and values of a complex culture such as ours, and the utility of using classification systems—traditional ones as well as published ones, such as those of libraries—to provide an approach to these values.

Music and other Systems of Communication

Music is, among other things, a way of communicating, and it bears close relationships to other such systems, especially dance and language. Music as a system of communication is the subject of many writings, among which those of Seeger (1962) provide theoretical underpinnings and terminology which, however, have not been widely adopted. The relationship between music and dance has not been studied as widely as one might suppose, considering the fact that in many cultures much of the music is accompanied by dancing. The two scholars who have contributed most to this field are Curt Sachs and Gertrude P. Kurath. Sachs, the author of the most widely accepted history of the dance (Sachs 1938), traces the genesis of musical and dance behavior to the same roots of rational and emotional expression, and tries to show that certain cultures have similar characteristics in their dances and their songs. Thus he indicates (1937:188-89) that the size of intervals and of dance steps is correlated, and cites specific examples some of which, it must be said, seem to be based more on Sachs' own interpretation than on provable facts. Thus, his statement that there is something "soft, yielding, swinging about the Semang (Malacca) melody—just as the dance of the Semang is soft and swinging" (1937:190) remains to be repeated in more descriptive terms. But since no accepted terminology or measuring device for correlation between dance and music is available, we must accept Sachs' statements as at least possibly correct, and as signposts for future work.

Gertrude Kurath has worked in more specific and less broadly theoretical problems than Sachs, having described the music and dance of specific ceremonies and shown the interaction of musical and choreographic form. Fenton (1953) includes an essay illustrating Kurath's approach, and her own survey (Kurath 1960) shows what has been accomplished in this area.

The relationship between language and music has been studied to a considerably greater extent than that between music and dance, and we should like here to present a fairly detailed discussion of this area as a sample for developing research in the relationship of other types of communication to music. Among the surveys of this field, that published by Bright (1963) is most to be recommended because it presents a linguist's view of an area usually reserved for the musicologist.

Interest in language-music interrelations ranges from the very detailed and specific relationship between the words and the music of a song to philosophical speculation about the symbolic significance of musical elements and the primordial connection between music and language at large. In the field of traditional music these connections are especially close because a great deal of the music is vocal, and because to members of simpler cultures the tunes and texts are sometimes inseparable concepts. This makes the comparison of the structures of words and music in folk song an essential aspect of folklore research. Thus, study of the specific interrelationships as found in one song is especially proper to ethnomusicology. But other phases of the music-language relationship can also profitably be studied with the use of folk and non-literate material. Cultures with tone languages offer interesting problems. Songs with meaningless syllable texts may show something about the perception and interpretation of musical structure in other cultures. Occasional examples of the musical representation of extra-musical

concepts or ideas are fascinating. The homogeneity of function-
ally similar songs in some cultures could be traced to the structure of the texts. Indeed, a chapter such as this, which attempts
to give a brief survey of a broad field, has as its first task the
establishment of some system of organization of the various
kinds of problems which can be encountered and studied. Thus
the following classification.

First, it is possible to divide types of language-music relationships into two classes: I) that in which the relationship is
of a general nature and is not necessarily found in specific items
of music, and II) specific relationships between the words and
the music of individual compositions or bodies of music. Class II
can be divided into two areas, A) relationship between music
and the meaning of the words, and B) structural relationships
between music and text. Area B can be divided into two groups,
1) the relationship between music and linguistic features such as
lines, rhyme, stanza which are present only in poetry, and 2)
relationship between music and linguistic features found in
language at large, such as stress, length, tone, intonation. The
purpose of the next paragraphs is to discuss some of these relationships with the use of examples, and to indicate some ways
in which they could be studied. Our purpose is not, however, to
present conclusions on the frequency and geographic distribution of these relationships, or concerning the relative strength
or importance of music and language in any individual body of
music, or similar questions of a general nature.

I. *General Relationships between Language and Music.* We are
first confronted by the fact that language and music have much
in common. Primary among these common features are movement in time (rhythm) and pitch (melody). It is this basic
similarity which has caused some scholars (e.g., Nadel 1930)
to assume that music and language had a common origin, and
in some cases, that music arose out of speech. But whereas this
kind of speculation can lead to no concrete conclusion, it is of
great interest to study similarities in the organization of pitch,

stress, and length in specific languages and their accompanying musical styles. For instance, it is noteworthy that in the Czech language strong accents appear at the beginning of all words of more than one syllable. In the folk music we find a corresponding development: musical phrases or sections usually begin on stressed notes, and the stresses are vigorous. This occurs not only in songs, where this phenomenon could be the direct result of melodies with appropriate stresses being assigned to poems, but also in instrumental music, where there is no such direct relationship. Thus it could be the result of a deeply-rooted tendency common to both music and speech.

A similar type of relationship is found between the English language and much of English folk music. In both, the melodic contour tends to descend at the end of a section, phrase, sentence, or song. Other examples can be found throughout the world, but their cause has not been agreed upon. It may be argued that similar tendencies in the language and music of a culture are based on deep-seated aesthetic preferences, and that they may even be inherent or racially determind. On the other hand, it could also be assumed that structural relationships between a given language and its musical style are due simply to the fact that one was modeled after the other. This relationship and the exceptions to it are among the most intriguing aspects of ethnomusicology.

II. *Specific Relations between the Text and Music of Individual Compositions.* This type of study has been carried forward in many publications (see the chapter bibliography), but only rarely have studies been made which indicate all of the many relationships between a tune and its words. Various aspects of this problem are outlined below.

A. *Relationships Involving the Meaning of the Words.* This type of relationship poses problems faced also by the student of representative or "program" music in Western culture. It must be assumed that nonmusical material is portrayed in some way in a great deal of music. This is done by the composer either consciously or unconsciously, and he may or may not indicate what the music is intended to portray or what the listener is supposed to feel or think. The identification of the existence of such nonmusical material is difficult even in Western music (historians have for decades argued about the existence of "programs" in Beethoven's major works); but it is even more difficult to trace in traditional music, in which the composer's word is rarely available. Informants are not usually articulate on such matters, and there is a great temptation for the student to superimpose his own ideas of what the music may represent, ideas which often have no place in the culture he is studying.

One kind of representative music which is usually recognized by informants is the use of animal cries in songs. For example, these appear in many American Indian songs, and are treated in two distinct ways: as realistic animal cries before, during, or after a song; and as part of the musical structure in rhythm and melody, in which case they are less realistic. The latter treatment could be classified as true representative music. It is found in Fig. 14, in which the last three notes ("tak-tak-tak") are said to represent the call of the turkey, but still fit into the musical structure.

FIGURE 14. *Shawnee Indian song.*

In the music of some nonliterate and folk cultures, songs which serve a particular function tend to exhibit musical similarities. Although this could sometimes be interpreted as musical representation, it is rarely recognized as such by informants, judging from the reports in the literature. This stylistic unity may be due to a number of cultural and musical factors, and it may have something to do with the nature of the function. The fact that in European folk music, marching songs are vigorous, children's songs are simple, and dance songs correspond to the tempo and rhythm of the dance cannot be considered evidence of "program music." But it is that to a small degree nevertheless, for the association of a particular kind of music with an activity or idea in the culture is a kind of musical representation, and perhaps this kind of association is at the basis of the Western tradition of program music.

B. *Structural Relationships*. These form the largest body of problems studied in ethnomusicological literature, and they are

FIGURE 15. *"The Gypsy Laddie," collected in Indiana.*

perhaps easiest to approach. Again, we subdivide into two main areas.

1. *Text-Music Relations in the Over-All Form of a Composition.* This can be studied by dividing both music and text into shorter elements such as phrases, lines, measures, and feet, and comparing them. In European folk song, according to Herzog (1950), there tends to be a close tie between musical and textual lines; they usually coincide. Thus, in Fig. 15, we can superimpose analyses of the two structures, plus the rhyme scheme, with the following results:

> Text content: A B^a C^a D
> Rhyme scheme: A   B   C   B
> Music: A B^1 A B^2

This song reveals considerable contrast between musical and textual structure, even though the main units coincide in length. Fig. 16 stresses repetitive elements:

Figure 16. *Czech folk song, "Ach synku, synku."*

Text content: A   A   B   B
Rhyme scheme: A   A   A   A
Music: A¹   A²   A³   A¹

In Fig. 16, contrastive to Fig. 15, the musical and textual elements show similar tendencies in the interrelationships of their lines.

In some cultures, poetry is not organized in terms of lines, nor is the music. For example, among the North American Plains Indians we find songs whose structure is in two sections, the second one a variation of the first. The first section is accompanied entirely by meaningless syllables. The second section, which is usually shorter and at a lower average pitch, contains some meaningless syllables but also the meaningful text, which has a prose-like structure. Fig. 17 illustrates this kind of form. The meaningful text is underlined, and only the text of the second section is given. This kind of interaction of text and tune evidently has dramatic value; the first section, with its meaningless

FIGURE 17. *Arapaho song.*

text, serves to prepare the listener for the climax, which arrives with the meaningful text and the repetition (with variations) of the melody.

The examples offered here illustrate only a handful of the many kinds of over-all formal relationship between music and text in traditional song. However, they should show the value of this kind of study and the relative ease with which it can be attacked. This kind of study should lead, aside from immediate conclusions, to a better understanding of aesthetic values in nonliterate and folk cultures.

2. *Relationship between Phonetic Features in Language and Their Musical Analogues.* Music and language have in common at least three important features at the phonetic level: stress, length, and pitch. In music, individual tones tend to be stressed, long, or high compared to their neighbors, just as in language individual syllables may be significantly differentiated by these features. It is useful to study the interaction of these features in song, in order to determine the fate of words when they are set to music and the extent to which musical structure accommodates the text. No general conclusions are available, although a number of studies of this problem have been made; we are sure, however, that no single principle is universally observed, and that very complex relationships, subject to all sorts of rules and exceptions, are sometimes found. The following examples show some of the things which can happen.

In most Western European poetry the division of the line into feet coincides with the division of music into measures, defined as repeated stress patterns. There is a strong tendency for the stressed syllable in a foot of poetry to coincide with a stressed beat in the measure. In Fig. 15 all of the stressed syllables coincide with the stressed tones, as indicated by the markings in the text. But singers and listeners in English-speaking folk cultures are sometimes willing to accept gross violations of this principle.

In some Eastern European folk music, the poetic line is not subdivided into feet. The number of stressed syllables is not constant, as it is in Western European poetry, but the total number of syllables per line is. Thus in many songs one would expect little correlation between musical and linguistic stress. The music does operate with metric principles, but the text does not. In spite of this, there may be considerable correlation between the two kinds of stress in Czech folk songs. Fig. 18 (with stressed syllables underlined) has ten out of fourteen stressed syllables occurring on stressed notes. In the same song, an examination of the correlation between long syllables (marked with accents) and long notes (quarter and half notes) shows that out of twelve long syllables, six occur on long tones. This is significant since only eight out of 28 tones are long ones. Such a study must take into consideration the question of the significance of stress and length in the language involved. Thus, in a language such as Czech, in which stress is mechanically placed on the first syllable of each word, it is less important than in some other languages, such as English, where the misplacement of stress could occasionally even change the meaning of a word.

FIGURE 18. *Czech folk song, "Černé oči jdéte spát."*

Correlation of linguistic and musical pitch patterns is of great interest in the so-called tone languages—those languages in which the intonation pattern of a word is significant so far as the meaning is concerned, and in which a change in pitch pattern could actually change the meaning. These languages, spoken in Africa, the Americas, the Orient, and elsewhere, actually differ greatly in their treatment of the pitch element. But in all of them it could be assumed that the pitch movement of the music must be the same as that of the text when it is spoken; otherwise words would be misunderstood. Actually this assumption is unfounded, for several students of African cultures (Schneider 1943-44, Jones 1959, King 1961) have found a very complex interaction between musical and linguistic tone. Words may be understood from their context even when their pitch pattern is violated. Special rules govern the setting of words to music—and so on.

Fig. 19 shows what may happen in a very simple song in the Owerri dialect of the Ibo of Nigeria, a people whose language has two main tones, high and low. The tone of each syllable as it would be spoken is indicated above that syllable (acute accent indicates the high speech tone). Examination of the relationship between the pitch movement of the text and that of the music reveals that in this song, although the musical pitch movement does not always reflect that of the language, it is never the opposite. In other words, in this song, a change from low to high in the text can be accompanied by upward movement in the music, or by level movement, but not by downward movement; and the converse applies to downward movement in pitch.

FIGURE 19. *Ibo war song.*

Much more detailed studies of the interaction between speech tones and musical pitch are now available. Schneider (1943-44) presents a detailed study for the West African Ewe, while Jones (1959) gives a general theory which is presumed to apply to many African tribes and languages. King (1961:38–42) explores the relationship among the Yoruba, while Herzog (1934) gives tentative conclusions for the Jabo of Liberia and for the Navaho Indians—the latter a rare case of attention given to a non-African tone language. Nettl (1954) explores the function of tone, stress, and length in Arapaho.

Some additional problems in music-language relations which fall outside the outline used above should be indicated in closing. In some cultures there is a difference between the ways of speaking and singing various words and sounds. In Pima (Arizona), the sound "t" in the spoken language is (according to Dr. Herzog) sung as "n." In French songs, the final "e," silent in speech, often is sung as a separate syllable and occupies a musical tone. A different kind of problem is that studied by Bartók (1951), Bronson (1944, 1952), and others; it concerns the degree to which a tune and a song-text form a unit historically, and to what degree they tend to be interchanged. This problem has been approached in European folk repertories but hardly at all in nonliterate cultures. Furthermore, the influence of language on instrumental music is important. For example, Herzog (1945) has shown the use of language pitch patterns in African drum and horn signalling, and he has indicated that much of the xylophone music of the Jabo in Liberia is based on the tone patterns of spoken utterances and is recognized as such.

Of interest also, in the area of music-language relations, are certain forms of communication which cannot easily be classed as either speech or music, but which seem to occupy a sort of middle ground, containing elements of both. List (1963) provides a classification of this phenomenon, which in the past would probably have been called simply wailing, shouting, and grunting, according to the degree of stability in pitch, the degree to which intonation is relevant, and to which scaler structure of intonation is used. As we move from speech, which has indefinite intonation in the sense of using fixed pitches and intervals, in the direction of fixed intonation, we arrive, by way of the so-called "*Sprechstimme*," a sort of artificial speech form in which the direction of pitch is important and even exaggerated, at true song. In another direction, if speech, which usually has considerable variety of pitch, moves away from this variety, we arrive at monotonic expression, which has a fixed pitch, by virtue of its negation of pitch variety. This fixed pitch provides the first tone of a fixed-pitch scale, which is the essence of song. Thus the area which is at the boundary of speech and song extends from the monotonic chant to the "*Sprechstimme*," and List (1963:9) provides a diagram for classification.

The best way for students to begin work in the music-language area is to study individual songs, in reliable transcription, somewhat in the manner in which the examples in the above paragraphs were treated. There are, so far, too few studies of individual songs, and too many broad statements not sufficiently documented. List (1957) is a detailed study of the broad interactions of words and music in the variants of a single British ballad, and it could be used as a model for certain kinds of projects.

Conclusion

If we have succeeded in demonstrating anything in this volume, it should be that ethnomusicology is a field that has only begun to scratch the surfaces of its possibilities. From an adjunct of historical musicology, a science dealing with a distinctly Western phenomenon, it has emerged as an area of importance in its own right. It has developed a great deal of theory which exists, somewhat unorganized, under a still too small body of documentation. The scholars in our field have not rallied to a single battle cry or dogma (which is good), and they frequently have been unable to communicate with each other because of the divergence in their backgrounds (which is bad). Yet their achievements are impressive. More than in the other arts, in music it has been taken for granted that strange and seemingly irrational forms exist, and that these can be understood through analysis of their structure and of their cultural context. The educated public and, to a degree, the public at large in America and Europe have become aware of the aesthetic values of non-Western musics. The historian of Western music takes for granted that some knowledge of non-Western music is essential to him—something not as frequently recognized by historians of Western art and literature. And ethnomusicology has begun to show that music the world over is more than artifact, but that it is—even in the simplest cultures—an essential part of human life.

Bibliography

Bartók, Béla, and Albert P. Lord (1951). *Serbo-Croatian Folk Songs.* New York: Columbia University Press.

Brandel, Rose (1962). *The Music of Central Africa.* The Hague: M. Nijhoff.

*Bright, William (1963). "Language and music: areas for cooperation," *Ethnomusicology* 7:26–32.

Bronson, Bertrand H. (1944). "The interdependence of ballad tunes and texts," *Western Folklore* 3:185–207.

———— (1952). "On the union of words and music in the Child ballads," *Western Folklore* 11:233–249.

Bukofzer, Manfred (1947). *Music in the Baroque Era.* New York: Norton.

Burrows, Edwin G. (1945). *Songs of Uvea and Futuna.* Honolulu: Bernice P. Bishop Museum.

Fenton, William N. (1953). *The Iroquois Eagle Dance,* with analysis of the Iroquois Eagle Dance and songs by Gertrude Prokosch Kurath. Washington: Smithsonian Institution. Bulletin 156 of the Bureau of American Ethnology.)

Fletcher, Alice C. (1904). *The Hako; a Pawnee Ceremony.* Washington: Twenty-second Annual Report of the Bureau of American Ethnology, part 2.

Fletcher, Alice C. and Francis LaFlesche (1911). *The Omaha tribe.* Washington: Twenty-seventh Annual Report of the Bureau of American Ethnology.

*Herzog, George (1934). "Speech-melody and primitive music," *Musical Quarterly* 20:452–466.

—— (1938). "Music in the thinking of the American Indian," *Peabody Bulletin*, May 1938, pp. 1-5.

—— (1945). "Drum signalling in a West African tribe," *Word* 1:217–238.

*—— (1950). "Song," in Funk and Wagnall's *Standard Dictionary of Folklore, Mythology, and Legend*, vol. 2. New York: Funk and Wagnall. Suggested reading, pp. 1038–1041.

Jones, A. M. (1959). *Studies in African Music*. London: Oxford University Press.

King, Anthony (1961). *Yoruba Sacred Music from Ekiti*. Ibadan, Nigeria: Ibadan University Press.

*Kurath, Gertrude P. (1960). "Panorama of dance ethnology," *Current Anthropology* 1:233–241.

*List, George (1957). "An ideal marriage of ballad text and tune," *Midwest Folklore* 7:95–107.

—— (1963). "The boundaries of speech and song," *Ethnomusicology* 7:1–16.

Lomax, Alan (1959). "Folk song style," *American Anthropologist* 61:927–954.

—— (1962). "Song structure and social structure," *Ethnology* 1:425–451.

McAllester, David P. (1954). *Enemy Way Music*. Cambridge: Peabody Museum Papers, vol. 41, no. 3.

Merriam, Alan P. (1960). "Ethnomusicology, discussion and definition of the field," *Ethnomusicology* 4:107–114.

—— (1962). "The epudi—a Basongye ocarina," *Ethnomusicology* 6:175–180.

Nadel, Siegfried S. (1930). "The origins of music," *Musical Quarterly* 16:531–546.

*Nettl, Bruno (1954). "Text-music relations in Arapaho songs," *Southwestern Journal of Anthropology* 10:192–199.

Sachs, Curt (1938). *World History of the Dance*. New York: Norton.

Schneider, Marius (1943–44). "Phonetische und metrische Korrelationen bei gesprochenen und gesungenen Ewe-Texten," *Archiv für vergleichende Phonetik* 7:1–6.

Seeger, Charles (1962). "Music as a tradition of communication, discipline, and play, Part I," *Ethnomusicology* 6:156–163.

Waterman, Richard A. (1956). "Music in Australian aboriginal culture—some sociological and psychological implications," *Music Therapy* 1955: 40–50.

SOME PRELIMINARY AND
PREPARATORY EXERCISES
AND PROBLEMS

THE FOLLOWING LIST OF
assignments may be helpful to the student who is interested in
preparing himself for research in ethnomusicology. On the whole
the assignments can be carried out in an American or European
city in an institutional environment. They could serve as projects
for class work. Most of them are not ethnomusicological per se;
but they are intended to help the student to see more clearly
some of the problems of ethnomusicological field, laboratory, and
desk work, to give him practice in some of the techniques of the
field, and to illustrate some of the points in the body of this
book. Suggested techniques for the researcher are given in several of the chapters (particularly Chapters 3–7). The assignments given here will require, in some cases, the use of those
techniques.

Chapter 3

(a) Practice recording the singing and playing of acquaintances
with a tape recorder. Try various kinds of microphone placement in a room, outdoors, for different combinations of voices
and instruments. Also practice taking photographs of perform-

ers, performing groups, and instruments; if possible, make a motion picture of a performer or a group, or of dancing.

(b) Make a collection of songs which a friend or relative remembers and can sing. Make recordings and write down relevant background information.

(c) Make tape recordings (with permission, of course) of the performance of a group of musicians at a folk festival or the picnic of an ethnic group.

(d) Find a person with whom you can spend a good deal of time, and ask him to describe his entire musical life—what songs he knows, what his musical values are, what music he listens to, etc., and write a report of it.

(e) Find a piece of music (classical or popular) of which two different recordings are available, and study the differences. Try to describe these objectively.

(f) Learn to play a simple folk or non-Western instrument, possibly from a member of a foreign culture who is visiting your community.

Chapter 4

(a) Listen to some of the simple songs of a non-literate culture (Australian, North American Indian, or Oceanian may be good ones to start with) on a reliable recording (Folkways, Columbia World Library of Folk and Primitive Music are good possibilities). Practice thinking through the melodies or singing them after listening.

(b) Transcribe some of these songs according to the methods outlined in this chapter. Transcription can also be a group exercise; one person can transcribe at a blackboard while others offer constructive criticism.

(c) Record some of your own singing, or that of a friend, and make transcriptions.

(d) Several days apart, make separate transcriptions of one piece and compare the results.

(e) Make a hand-graph from the notation of a simple song.

(f) Using a Kunst monochord (or another stretched string), practice identifying intervals plucked at random in terms of quarter-tones or smaller units.

Chapters 5 and 6

(a) Read some descriptions of musical styles in recent issues of periodicals such as *Ethnomusicology, African Music,* and *Journal of the International Folk Music Council,* and classify them according to their approach; also, make a critical analysis of such a description.

(b) Make individual analyses of songs and pieces in some standard collections which do not contain these already. The following are possibilities: Cecil Sharp, *English Folk Songs from the Southern Appalachians* (1932; reprint 1952); Marius Schneider, "Primitive Music" in *New Oxford History of Music,* vol. 1 (1957); Harriet Pawlowska, *Merrily We Sing, 105 Polish Folksongs* (1961); Rose Brandel, *The Music of Central Africa* (1962). Use the methods given in Chapter 5.

(c) Listen to recordings of music from various cultures and classify them according to the cantometrics system of Alan Lomax (see Lomax, "Song Structure and Social Structure," *Ethnology* 1:425–51, 1962, for details of the method).

(d) Convert the tempo markings of some short classical, popular, or folk music pieces to the Kolinski method of expressing tempo.

(e) Take a small collection of folk music (for example, all of the tunes for one song in Sharp's *English Folk Songs from the Southern Appalachians,* or a similar folk song collection) and make counts of the intervals, note values, and other features; prepare a brief description of the style of these few tunes as an exercise preparatory to making descriptions of larger and more valid samplings.

(f) Read a description of a musical style, then go through the transcriptions on which it is based and try to find exceptions to the author's statements.

Chapter 7

(a) Visit one (or more) museums of musical instruments, or which contain instrument collections. Try to classify some of the instruments according to the Sachs-Hornbostel classification. (Take along a copy of *Galpin Society Journal* 14, 1961, which contains the classification system.)

(b) Without consulting published sources, make as complete as possible a description of a relatively simple instrument which you have available—guitar, violin, recorder, etc. Pretend that you are describing an instrument not known before. Include a description of the technique used in playing.

(c) Take a series of photographs of an instrument which could be used to show someone who has never seen it before just what it is like.

Chapters 8 and 9

(a) Using standard library techniques (card catalog, periodical indexes, etc.), go through the ethnographic literature of a tribe and note the references to music and musical activities. Make a list of these and try to write a picture of the musical culture of that tribe.

(b) Ask a person from another culture who is visiting your community or someone with a village background to describe his native musical culture.

(c) Go through the most important items in ethnomusicological literature mentioned in Chapter 8 and make a list of musical maps; write a critique of the methods used in compiling the information and in presenting it on a map.

(d) On the basis of some standard books on the history of Western music, try to find out what approaches to musical change are usually taken, and what theories are used to explain musical change.

(e) Make a study of the relationship between the words and music of one folk song, using the methods in Chapter 9 and a standard collection of transcriptions made from field recordings.

(f) As you see motion pictures (commercial and educational), make a list of the examples of non-Western and folk dancing which are shown. Criticize them from the viewpoint of their usefulness for research.

(g) Try to find and list traditional and published classifications of music in your own cultural environment.

INDEX

Abraham, Otto, 17, 30, 106, 108, 109, 192
Acculturation, 4-5, 169, 172-173, 174, 180, 233-34. *See also* Change in music; Cultural context of music; Diffusion
Adler, Guido, 14, 15
Aerophones, 213
Aesthetics, 73, 231, 274
Africa: music of, 48, 183, 232, 240; Central, 193; instruments of, 209; polyphony in, 250; musical areas of, 254, 257; tone languages of, 290-91. *See also* names of tribes; Negroes
Algonquian Indians, 233
American Indian music: discussed, 13, 240, 248, 253, 271-72; bibliography of, 51; modes in, 185; tempo in, 189-90; areas in, 258-60. *See also* names of tribes and areas; South American Indians
American Indians: as anthropologists, 70; instruments of, 219; values of, 273-74. *See also* South American Indians.
American Museum of Natural History, New York, 211
Amiot, Joseph Marie (Pere), 13
Analysis of music: problems of, 98; methodology for, 131-32. *See also* Mechanical aids in analysis
Anthropology: scope of, 1-2; need for musical information in, 3-4; contribution to ethnomusicology of, 15, 20-21, 23-24; American approach to, 20; methods of, used in ethnomusicology, 225. *See also* Ethnomusicology
Antiphonal singing, 258
Apache Indians, 171, 234, 237
Apel, Willi, 146
Arapaho Indians, 156, 257, 287, 291
Archeology: in research on instruments, 207

Archive of Folk Song, Library of Congress, 54, 72, 95
Archives: of recordings, 17-19, 54-55; with specialized holdings, 96
Archives of Folk and Primitive Music, Indiana University, 18, 54, 96
Archiving, 92-95
Areas, music: discussed, 176-77, 243-53; in ethnomusicological literature, 253-55; identification of, 255-58; and other kinds of distribution, 258-61; as independent units, 261-63. *See also* Culture areas; Natural areas
Art music, European. *See* Western civilization
Arts, interrelationship of, 32-33
Asia, Southeastern, 257
Australia: aboriginal music of, 272-73
Authenticity, 22-23, 180-84
Automatic transcription, 101, 120-26, 128
Bake, Arnold, 168
Bamboo, 217
Bar lines: in transcription, 117
Barbeau, Marius, 227
Baroque music, 270
Bartók, Béla, 16-17, 40, 42, 43, 48, 56, 105, 106, 172-73, 179, 193, 242, 291
Bascom, William, 56
Bashi, 212, 216
Batteries, 90
Beats, 149
Bella Coola Indians, 14, 37, 101
Berlin school, 37
Bibliographies: ethnomusicological, 50-54; current, 52
Bi-musicality, 10-11, 21-22, 64-65
Biographical data in field work, 67
Blasquintentheorie, 31
Boas, Franz, 15, 19, 20, 70
Book reviews, 47-48
Borrowing in composition, 239-40